**FOR ANYONE—FROM CONSUMERS AND STUDENTS
TO PROFESSIONALS AND BUSINESS PEOPLE**

IF YOU WANT TO RESEARCH . . .

Quick, reliable consumer product information
Latest treatment choices for cancer patients
Stock market analysis
Career guidance
Family background or genealogy
A high school term paper
A doctoral dissertation

STATE-OF-THE-ART FACT-FINDING BRINGS YOU

Tips, tricks, shortcuts,
and step-by-step guidance for
• Getting organized
• Researching *anything* you need to know
• Compiling great results

**IT'S AN INDISPENSABLE GUIDE FOR EVERYONE WHO
NEEDS TO KNOW!**

STATE-OF-THE-ART FACT-FINDING

NEW WAYS TO FIND THE INFORMATION YOU NEED, NOW

THE MOST INNOVATIVE, COMPREHENSIVE GUIDE TO HIGH TECH, OUT-OF-THE-ORDINARY, AND TRIED-AND-TRUE SOURCES FOR–

❑ BUSINESS ❑ REAL ESTATE ❑ EDUCATION ❑ MEDICINE ❑ CONSUMER PRODUCTS ❑ LAW ❑ SCIENCE RESEARCH PAPERS AND THESES... AND MORE

TRUDI JACOBSON, M.L.S., & GARY McCLAIN, PH.D.

Produced by The Philip Lief Group, Inc.

A DELL TRADE PAPERBACK

A DELL TRADE PAPERBACK

Published by
Dell Publishing
a division of
Bantam Doubleday Dell Publishing Group, Inc.
1540 Broadway
New York, New York 10036

Published by arrangement with The Philip Lief Group, Inc.
6 West 20th Street
New York, NY 10011

ISBN: 0-440-50499-6

Printed in the United States of America

Published simultaneously in Canada

August 1993

10 9 8 7 6 5 4 3 2 1

BVG

Contents

1. Harnessing the Information Explosion   1

2. Preparing Your Research: Efficient Planning   10

3. The State-of-the-Art Library   27

4. When Print Resources Still Say It Best   52

5. Making the Government Work for You   79

6. Searching Off the Beaten Track   105

7. Unlocking Business Secrets   125

8. Dial an Expert   161

9. Going International   179

10. Information Brokers and Services   214

11. What You'll Need to Set Up at Home   229

12. Information from a Compact Disc   256

13. Boot It Up: Finding Purchasable Information Software   281

14. Going Online: Using Online Databases and Information Services   302

15. When the Information Keeps Hiding   339

16. Organizing Results   346

17. Time-Saving Tips and Advice   366

Appendix: Resources for State-of-the-Art Fact-Finding   375

About the Authors   391

STATE-OF-THE-ART
FACT-FINDING

1

Harnessing the Information Explosion

Think about how often you need some kind of information—facts, figures, advice, answers—during an average day. Business people look for economic statistics, market trends, or information about other companies. Students search out that last little detail, such as an ancient philosopher's birthdate, to flesh out a research paper. Writers and reporters gather quotations to add flavor and credibility to an article.

And in the evening, you may be sitting around with friends and one of those little questions that begs for an answer comes along. A question like "Where did 'tie a yellow ribbon' come from?" Before you know it, you're digging for more information on your own time.

We are surrounded by information, even drowning in it. Yet while more books and magazines are being printed than ever before, a whole world of information exists beyond the shelves of your library. Archives and specialized libraries. Organizations and associations with their own experts. Museums and bookstores. Information brokers. And the computer is opening up a whole new realm of information through CD-ROM and online services. The possibilities are so numerous that it's easy to become intimidated and assume that state-of-the-art information resources, like online databases, are expensive, difficult to use, or restricted to "professional" researchers.

If you've ever felt that way, *State-of-the-Art Fact-Finding* is your book. It is written for *anyone* who wants to harness the information explosion—to know more about myriad information sources that exist and how to use them with confidence.

What's Out There

If your idea of conducting research is to thumb through the card catalog and search the stacks at your local public library, you are missing out on the potential of the Information Age. In the first place, many library card catalogs are now computer-based, and you might be surprised to discover that the process of locating the right books begins with the keyboard of a computer. Instead of using cards, you can walk up to a computer terminal and, with a few keystrokes, go "online" to quickly search under the subject headings, authors, and titles that you type on the keyboard. Secondly, more and more information is *not* found between the covers of a book. Here are some of the other options to consider:

Archives

An archive may be sponsored by a university; local, state, or federal government; or an association. They can contain anything from documents pertaining to a specific period of history, like the Civil War, to photographs taken by well-known photographers. Examples include the Arthur Schoenberg Institute Archives at the University of Southern California, or the Rodgers and Hammerstein Archives of Recorded Sound at the New York Public Library. Archives are described in Chapters 4 and 6.

Professional and Trade Associations

As professions become more specialized, so do the associations that professionals join. Trade associations serve not only their members, but the inquiring public as well. They offer pamphlets and other publications, as well as information on electronic media. Some also offer consultation services. Read more about professional and trade associations in Chapters 6, 7, and 8.

Special Interest Organizations and Associations

People with similar interests, from stamp collecting to history to politics, form organizations and associations to exchange information and work on projects of mutual interest. These groups publish information, hold national and regional conferences, and are vehicles for locating other people with specific expertise. Special-interest groups are discussed in Chapters 6 and 8.

Information Brokers

With the plethora of available sources of information and ways to access it, a new profession has emerged: information brokers. These individuals are professional information gatherers who, for a fee, will conduct research for their clients. Many information-gathering experts work independently, assisted by their home computers. Information brokers and their services are described in Chapter 10.

CD-ROM

More and more information is being offered on CD-ROM. CD-ROM stands for Compact Disc—Read-Only Memory. A CD-ROM disc can hold large amounts of data and, when "played" on a special machine, this information can be viewed on the screen of a personal computer. Index publishers were among the first to make use of this medium, offering citations to, and sometimes abstracts of, articles on CD-ROM, as an alternative to printed indexes. CD-ROM is described throughout this book, but particularly in Chapters 11 and 13.

Online Databases

A wide variety of online databases can be accessed through the use of a personal computer and modem. Some offer general, consumer-oriented information and services, such as assistance in planning a trip, while others offer access to highly specialized databases, like legal, business, and scientific information. Online databases are discussed in Chapters 11 and 14.

Software

Information is also being offered on diskette. For example, maps, almanacs and thesauri all exist in this form. Generally, periodic updates are also available. Purchasable information software is the focus of Chapter 13.

Your Library Is Growing with You

In spite of the growth of available sources of information outside of the library, in most cases it is still the place to begin your research. As you'll read more about it in Chapter 3, many libraries have taken the information age by storm, supplementing books and microfilm with CD-ROM and computers with access to online databases. Additionally, libraries are connecting to networks of libraries, so that if your library doesn't have the resource you need, chances are you can be placed in touch with one that does. The person to ask is your librarian.

Examples of
State-of-the-Art Fact-Finding

For all the questions that you can answer by going to a library or bookstore and finding a book, there are even more that are not answered quite as easily. Expressions of speech, based on old customs or isolated historical events, for example, or current events that are unfolding at a rapid rate, are more difficult to research. Here are some examples:

"Will It Play in Peoria?"

You're involved in a conversation with a friend concerning a new product you heard is about to be placed on the market. You conclude: "It will never play in Peoria." "Cliché," your friend says. And then you wonder, "Where *did* that term come from?"

You might begin by checking through a few quotation books, most likely without luck. You also call another friend, who tells you he heard it was used during the Nixon presidency. So you consult the indexes and scan the pages of a couple of books written about the Nixon administration. The phrase is alluded to in relation to Nixon, but that nagging doubt remains: "What if it originated before that?" The word "play" makes you think of theater, so the next step is to check through a few theatrical history books, beginning with the vaudeville era. Still nothing.

But wait. Peoria. You call the Peoria Public Library and ask to be connected with a reference librarian. She just happens to have compiled a file that charts the use of that phrase.

"Tie a Yellow Ribbon"

During Operation: Desert Storm, the yellow ribbon became associated with the return of the troops. Have you ever thought about how a yellow ribbon became a homecoming symbol? Did it originate with the song, or has it been around longer than that?

You might check the quotation books first, just in case somewhere through the years a famous person said it. And because it was used in a song, you might also consult a few music books. Sometimes songs are accompanied by a brief history. Since yellow ribbons are associated with solidarity with the military effort and thus with soldiers returning from combat, you might also try a military history book, beginning with the one on Civil War.

When none of these resources yields an answer, you try old newspaper articles. Your library has a CD-ROM index of newspaper articles and, after looking up "yellow ribbon," you discover that numerous feature articles have been written about this custom. One of them was in your local newspaper, which is on microfilm.

"The New Germany"

Without fail, just when you think the world is holding still, it shifts again. The fall of the Berlin Wall, and the New Germany, is a prime example. Suppose that you are a businessperson interested in potential new business opportunities resulting from the unification of East and West Germany.

You might start with standard business directories that could at least provide you with the names and addresses of import/export organizations and chambers of commerce to contact. Recent magazine and newspaper articles, many of which may be indexed on CD-ROM, would also be helpful.

Finally, international information companies often maintain their own online databases, often accessible through online database vendors. Your local library might subscribe to the database you need to assist you in identifying this information.

Information is everywhere. While books and other publications are often the first, and certainly the easiest, place to look, they should by no means be the ending point. *State-of-the-Art Fact-Finding* is organized to help you zero in on the information you need, from the beginning of your search to the final informative answer.

How This Book Is Organized

State-of-the-Art Fact-Finding covers four main areas:

Knowing How to Start

The key to research is asking the right questions. A plan for conducting state-of-the-art research is described, beginning with formulating the questions, and choosing, and then using, the resource options.

State-of-the-Art Research Strategies and Resources

State-of-the-art resources, including information from government resources, experts, information brokers, business, and international information, are all explored.

State-of-the-Art Resources for Your PC

Guidelines for setting up your own PC-based system, where to locate computer-based resources, and how to use them, are all covered in this section.

Putting It All Together

This section details how to fill in any last minute gaps, and organize the results.

"Tricks Librarians Use"

Librarians are asked hundreds of questions daily, and they learn to depend on their own references along the way. They are described under the heading "Tricks Librarians Use," included in each chapter of the book.

Also interspersed throughout the book are boxes that provide definitions, hints, and tips that will be useful as you conduct your fact-finding.

State-of-the-Art Fact-Finding is filled with specific resources that you can pursue for your own research. These resources are described in individual chapters. For example, business information resources are provided throughout Chapter 7, "Unlocking Business Secrets," while international resources are included in Chapter 9, "Going International."

Ripe for the Harvest

The world is full of information, and most of it is at your bid and call, if not at your fingertips. *State-of-the-Art Fact-Finding* is written to be your guide as you explore what's out there and how you find it. Each chapter is filled with advice and guidelines, tips on where to start, and resources to use as you get more involved in your search.

Remember that research is a gradual process. You start with a question, or maybe a list of questions, and you refine your search as you get closer to your answer. Some promising routes turn out to be blind alleys, leading nowhere, while others can yield surprises. Still others suggest more questions to explore.

Be patient as you conduct your fact-finding—the answers exist, you just have to follow the chain of resources until you find the link you need. Along the way, it will be an exciting, and always mind-expanding, process.

Be adventuresome. Don't be afraid to sit down in front of a computer terminal. Connect to a telephone line for an online database. Pop in a compact disc. Call the public information department of an obscure academic society. Drive to an old bookstore in a nearby town.

And above all, don't be afraid to walk up to your librarian and ask where to start. After reading *State-of-the-Art Fact-Finding*, the two of you will have a lot in common.

2

Preparing
Your Research:
Efficient Planning

An old cliché goes something like this: "If you don't know where you're going, you'll never get there." As in life, this is also true in fact-finding. If you don't have a plan, beginning with specific questions to answer, you'll either end up wallowing in a lot of information, much of it extraneous to your needs, or with nothing but wasted time. Chapter 2 provides you with a formula for planning your research, and getting yourself organized before you begin your work.

Why Plan Ahead?

Politicians often conduct fact-finding missions to ask questions, compile facts, and analyze the results. Based on the information they uncover and their analysis of it, they develop their legislative positions on major issues.

The process of conducting research is much the same, regardless of whether you're trying to decide what kind of refrigerator to buy, settling a bet with friends over a piece of trivia, or writing a historical romance novel. You have a gap to fill—a question to answer—and the information you need is out there. Somewhere.

To get to it quickly, in the shortest time possible, you need a plan, even a road map, so that you focus in on your destination, and plan for the most expedient route.

When you effectively plan you save on two important resources:

1. Time

You can spend hours, weeks, and even years going through volumes of materials. This can be a fascinating, educational, and even fun experience. If you have lots of time, the *best* route may be *no* route. Who cares if you don't find what you're looking for? You'll have so much fun that, after a while, you'll forget what you needed anyway.

Most of us, however, need to get to the meat of the information as soon as possible. A carefully drawn-out plan is the best start. And after the work is done, you can still go back and browse.

2. Money

Time is money—*your* time and *your* money. Hours spent at libraries. Taking up someone else's time as they try to help you figure out what you want. Trips to bookstores to buy the wrong book or magazine. Long-distance phone calls. Computer time, which may include connect time to an online database of information. The costs can add up as you accumulate one online connect fee after another, while still coming up factless.

Also consider that information resources cost money to operate. Part of it may be your money in a different sense—your tax dollars—and advance preparation can save your (and everybody's) hard-earned income.

So you're convinced? We've been talking about the importance of a plan. Now, let's get down to the specifics: What it is. How it works. How you can make it work to your advantage.

One Plan Fits All

Our plan for state-of-the-art fact-finding is contained in three parts, beginning with formulating exactly what is being sought, to listing the optional resources, to actually conducting the research. Here's what it looks like:

1. Formulate the question.
2. Line up the resources.
3. Go for the facts!

Let's take a closer look at how each of these steps works.

Step 1: Formulate the Question

Remember that cliché "If you don't know where you're going . . ." Each time you go on a fact-finding mission, you are seeking an answer to a question. The question may be singular, such as finding a specific date: When was George Washington born? When did Company X merge with Company Y? Or the question may be more complex and even require a series of questions, such as: What were the stages in the development of the polio vaccine?

Coming up with this question may take some focusing on what you really want. Often, when seeking information, it is human nature to be a little bit lazy, and rather than asking specific questions, to simply try to "find out about something." Sound familiar? Librarians often tell stories about people who come up to them and express their research needs with similar terms: "I want to know about the Vietnam War," or "I want to find out about Paris." Know *what*? Find out *what*?

Exploring a topic is fine as a leisure-time activity. Exploring *for* a topic, for a term paper, or a business opportunity, can lead to its own rewards. But state-of-the-art fact-finders take time to do their homework, to ask *themselves* questions and get down to the specifics of what facts are really needed. Then the search begins with a goal.

There's just too much information out there not to take time—up front—to plan the search strategy.

What's the best way to come up with your fact-finding questions? Start at the end. In other words, what kind of information do you want to know? A date? A chronology of events? A description of a place or person? A solution to a problem? A product recommendation? In other words, in broad terms, what do you hope to have when you are finished?

Once you've taken the time to decide what you are looking for, you will have a broad concept of your question. Then, you can start breaking it into the pieces—the component questions that you will need to answer to get you to your final destination.

Think of it this way: Back to front, to give you the questions, and then front to back, to get to the answer. Here's an example to think about as we go into some more depth on formulating your research question.

"What Are the Next Blockbusters?"

Let's suppose you want to do some research on movies. Maybe you're looking for an investment opportunity, or a career, or a term paper topic, or you simply want to solve a bet. You could walk into a public library and tell the librarian that you want to know more about movies. Most likely, you'll be pointed in the direction of a shelf of books and, possibly, videotapes.

Now let's assume that you've narrowed your interest to movies made during the 1980s. You want to find out what kinds of movies were produced during that time and how these movies were influenced by the events, and the social and political influences, of the decade. And you want to know which movies were successful, so that you can predict what films will be successful in the 90s.

Before you can take your place among the movie moguls of the future, you need to support yourself with the facts.

Back to Front

In our movie example, the basic goal is clear: to predict the success of movies in the 90s. Based on the concept of working from back to front, the research questions can be formulated by reducing this goal to a series of questions that have to be answered. These questions include:

1. What movies were most successful during the 1980s?
2. How is success of a movie defined—critical acclaim or gross revenues? Do the two ever cross? And when they do, is the movie even more successful?
3. What were the major international events of the 1980s?
4. What was the political climate like? The economy? Social conditions?
5. Who were the major moviegoers, based on age group and economic status?

6. What celebrities were the trendsetters during the 1980s? Did these celebrities appear, or were they imitated, in movies?
7. How did the movies of the 1980s compare to the movies of the previous decades?
8. What did the major social commentators of the 1980s say about the movies?
9. What are the trend-spotters predicting for the 1990s? For the early 21st century?

Achieving the goal of predicting movie success is based on answering a series of questions, as outlined above.

If this seems like a lot of questions, you can list the questions as statements, or as sentences to complete, such as "The most successful movies during the 1980s were _____." You can fill in the blanks as you continue your work.

The list of questions can get long. If you are researching a multifaceted topic, your list of questions can run on for pages. But each of these questions is a small stepping stone toward your goal: you answer each one in turn as you gain the information you need.

Getting Specific

The bottom line of formulating your questions before you begin the actual process of gathering information is that it forces you to get specific. You take the time to really think about what you want to know and why.

People often report that this is anxiety producing. They would rather look around, and then figure out what they want based on what is available. This method isn't recommended because you can waste a lot of time trying to come up with the questions before you can get serious about the answers. Again, it all comes down to having a healthy respect for the value of your time, and that of others.

This doesn't preclude doing an initial search, and deciding that you are interested in a different aspect of what you wanted. In fact, as you'll find in Step 2: Lining Up the Resources, this often happens.

Step 2: Lining Up the Resources

At this point, you may be asking, "How many preliminaries do I have to go through before I can get started?" The answer depends on how much you want to know, and on the complexity of the topic. Once you know what you're looking for, you can simply dive in. Or, like many people, you will hand the list of questions to a librarian and hope that she or he is willing to point you in the right direction.

In Step 2, go through your list of research questions and, one by one, ask two more questions:

1. Who would be interested in this information?
2. Where would it be kept?

Lining up the resources is another one of those tasks that saves time in the long run by adding time at the beginning of the search. Once you have formulated your research questions, taking a little more time to plan what resources to use will make your search even more targeted. It's all about brainstorming, thinking through the questions, and jotting down answers to the Who and Where questions. Sit back, relax, and let your mind wander from idea to idea. Jot each one of them down. The appropriate resources for some questions will be more apparent than will those for others. You may even find yourself coming up with additional, related questions that you want to answer.

Remember that state-of-the-art information resources may, or may not, involve library books. Information can be obtained from an online database, available on CD-ROM, on microfilm, by talking to an expert . . . the possibilities are endless.

The Who may be an author, or a reference book, a magazine, an expert, or an organization. The key question is what kind of individuals would be interested in this information, and where would they in turn make this information available to others. The Where may be as simple as making a trip to a library or bookstore, or it may require a few extra steps, like making a few phone calls, using a CD-ROM index, or dialing into an online database.

What's important is that you take the time to really think about what you need, and where you might find it. You may come up with a few options for each, and that's all for the better.

"Who Cares About Movies?"

To illustrate how you might use Step 2 in planning your research, let's start with Question 1: What were the most successful movies during the 1980s?

Who would be interested in recording this information? The possibilities include the following:

1. The subject may have been discussed in an issue of a movie magazine, published, perhaps, at the end of 1989.
2. It might be included in a reference book on the movie industry, or a book that chronicles the 1980s.
3. A film archive might keep these records.
4. An organization of professionals in the film industry, or a group of movie buffs, might keep track of the success of movies.
5. A graduate school of film might maintain a special research library.

Now that you have a list of potential Whos, ask: Where would these individuals keep the information? Go through your list of sources, and answer this question for each. Based on our movie example, you might come up with the following:

1. Movie magazines may be available in your local library, or through the magazine publisher.
2. Reference books will be available in the library, or through bookstores.
3. A film archive may need to be contacted directly. You will first need to obtain a list of film archives, most likely through a directory of special libraries. You would then contact the archive for either a publications list, or talk directly with a representative.
4. Professional organizations will be listed in directories of organizations. This kind of information may also be available online, through a service or a bulletin board.

Go through each of your research questions and formulate a possible list of information resources for each one. Use the same numbering system as you did for your list of questions. For ease of reference, build a list that looks something like this:

Question	Source	Where
1. Successful 1980s movies?	Movie mag	*Reader's Guide to Periodical Literature*, in the library
	Reference books (even an almanac)	Library catalog

Question	Source	Where
	Film archive or research library	Directory of special libraries
	Professional organizations	Directory of organizations
	Movie reviews	*Reader's Guide to Periodical Literature*, in the library.
2. Define success?	Business books	*Subject Guide to Books in Print*, library catalog
	articles	*Reader's Guide, Business Periodicals Index*
3. Major events?	News digest, like *Facts on File*	Library catalog
	Almanacs and other reference books	Library catalog
4. Political, economic climate?	Local and national newspapers and magazines	Newspaper indexes, *Reader's Guide*
5. Moviegoers?	Statistics in movie and business magazines	*Business Periodicals Index, Film Literature Index*

Question	Source	Where
	Professional organizations	Directory of organizations
	reference books	library catalog
6. Trendsetters?	Newspaper, magazine articles	Indexes, print, or CD-ROM
7. Previous decade?	Movie magazines	*Reader's Guide, Film Literature Index*
	Reference books	Library catalog
	Books on the history of movies	Library catalog
8. Major critics?	Newspaper and magazine articles	Indexes
9. 1990s predictions	Books	Library catalog, *Subject Guide to Books in Print*
	Experts in organizations	Directory of organizations

Some questions will be easier to find answers to than others. For example, trend-spotters generally write books, and a librarian or bookstore employee can probably refer you to one of these volumes. Finding the major international events might take a bit more work, beginning with a CD-ROM index, and moving on to newspapers and magazine articles. You might also use CD-ROM to locate citations to articles that movie critics have written.

Don't forget that when you list resources, you are listing potential sources—places to start. You'll encounter some instant successes, some blind alleys, and more likely, you'll get referrals for where to continue. The key is to think through the process beforehand, and to streamline your fact-finding as much as possible.

Remember to Be Specific

Just as you need to have specific questions, you also need to be as specific as possible about potential sources of information. If it's a book, where will you find it? If it's an organization, which one, or at least, who might belong to it? After you have completed your list of Who and Where for each question, go over the list a few more times, checking to see if you can add anything else or narrow down the Wheres just a bit more.

You won't always know where to find some of the information you need. For example, you may not know that an organization offers an online database, or that a CD-ROM index exists for your topic. Your librarian will have access to directories that can help you take your fact-finding to the next step.

Consider Multiple Perspectives

Always keep in mind that different authors, experts, and data collectors have a different perspective on the information they are collecting. For example, the Republicans might have a much different view on the economic issues of the 1980s than would the Democrats. Thus, two different sources might give you two very different viewpoints. As you list potential resources, you may want to look for multiple perspectives, even if one is purported to be "right."

This is also true of indexes. A CD-ROM database of magazine articles citations may only include articles from magazines offered by one specific publisher. Ziff-Davis, for example, offers a CD-ROM disc, as well as an online database, with abstracts of articles from its own publications, including *PC Magazine* and *PC Week*. While these publications offer comprehensive coverage of the industry, you might also want to peruse other indexes for references to magazines from other publishers. Indexes (CD-ROM or printed) may also have a slant toward popular magazines versus scholarly journals. And an index may have a political slant, as with *The Left Index*.

Make it a regular practice to list multiple sources for the same information, just to insure that you are getting a balanced perspective.

Step 3: Go for the Facts

If you have carefully followed Steps 1 and 2 in the research plan, you have two important elements: a list of questions, and a strategy for finding answers. Now it's time to get started.

Attack your list by going through each question, one by one, and begin to work the resources you chose to pursue. You may want to start with the first question, if the questions are in some type of order. Begin with the easiest route for each question. If you think the easiest route is a book, start there. Then move on if that doesn't pan out.

You'll be redefining your search as you go along. Remember, your plan is flexible. As you get into your topic, you may need to further define or even narrow it. If your interests change, or you stumble upon an area that is even more intriguing, you may want to shift directions, if you have that luxury.

During your search, remember to use experts, like librarians, to guide you toward appropriate sources.

"And the Blockbusters Will Be . . ."

The envelope, please! Predicting movie success is about as difficult as predicting anything else that involves human nature. Here are some highlights of the search for movie blockbuster prediction.

The state-of-the-art fact-finder was able to consolidate much of the work needed to gain insight into movie predictions for the 90s. While tackling one question at a time, each resource was gleaned for whatever it could offer in answering multiple questions. For example, a few of the questions on the list involved the use of the *Reader's Guide to Periodical Literature*. Having thought through this ahead of time, the fact-finder located potential citations for all of them. The *Film Literature Index* was used in the same way.

An expert also shed light on numerous aspects of the topic. In a directory of organizations, the fact-finder located the name of a small society of film buffs in a nearby town. Through a few phone calls, she found the name of an individual with an extensive collection of movie memorabilia, who not only answered questions about movie history, but also sent copies of clips from magazines and newspapers, and suggested other references. This individual also belongs to a discussion group that communicates through an online service. After mentioning the fact-finder's request through the group's bulletin board, the fact-finder was barraged with suggestions for potential references, as well as some of the members' own theories about future blockbusters. This saved time by allowing the fact-finder to avoid some of the searching, and also added some color to the research.

By the way, the research was inconclusive: there's no accounting for taste. But at least in the case of movies, there is solid evidence, and a historical basis, for this conclusion.

Make the Domino Effect Work for You

Don't give up. A resource, even if it doesn't pan out, can lead you to the next one. Books have bibliographies listing other books to investigate. Magazine articles often include names of organizations. CD-ROM indexes list various articles in numerous publications. One personal contact can lead to another.

The trick is to keep moving from one resource to the next until you find what you need. Make the domino effect work in your favor.

Don't Forget . . .

Here is a list of potential resources to include in Step 2 of your research plan.

Media director of an association
Used bookstore
CD-ROM
University, public, or special library
Online database
Directories, of publications and organizations
Magazines and newspapers
Reference books

Moving Targets, or What To Do When the Situation Is in Flux . . .

Sometimes your research topic changes frequently—weekly, daily, or hourly. To stay on top of the changes, you'll need to take a few extra steps to keep your facts as current as possible.

Here's an example. As East and West Germany become one unified nation, business people are discovering multitudes of business opportunities in the New Germany. However, as the governments of these two nations become one, policies in areas such as business development are changing.

Standard business directories and reference books with an international focus will provide a general orientation to trade policies and procedures, as well as the names of organizations, such as chambers of commerce, who are involved in business issues. These organizations can in turn be contacted to keep abreast of the latest published information, and to obtain the names of experts who may be contacted for additional guidance. Magazine and newspaper articles should also be consulted often, to stay on top of major developments. An import/export database and bulletin board, through an online database service, will provide another avenue for up-to-date information.

Tricks Librarians Use

Terminology. When consulting any reference source, be it an index, abstract, reference book, online catalog, etc., make sure you and your resource are speaking the same language. Usually you can look in a table of contents or subject index to find the names of headings before you begin your search. But sometimes, you will need to be more creative, coming up with your own synonyms when the word you use doesn't pan out.

For example, if you are searching for information about "films" or "movies," and coming up empty-handed, it may be because your resource groups this information under the heading "Motion Pictures." Always be ready to try an alternative before you give up. Keeping a thesaurus handy may save the day.

Tricks Librarians Use

Keep records. When conducting research, there is nothing more frustrating than having a vague déjà vu experience as you spend hours going through CD-ROM index or rolls of microfilm, only to find what you need and then to realize you found it once before—and it wasn't the correct resource then, either. Accurate recordkeeping will prevent this occurrence. You may want to use a notecard for each resource that you use, and then, with a red pen, subsequently record when you looked into a resource, and even make notations about what you did or didn't find, and why. By the time you finish, you will have built a file that you can add to as you complete other research projects. This can save hours of time and frustration. And if you're really going state of the art, you might keep all of this information in a database, in your PC at home.

3

The State-of-the-Art Library

Libraries are much more than big buildings filled with dusty old books. Many state-of-the-art information resources are available through your local library. In this chapter, we'll be looking at what your local library can offer you, and how to make the most of these resources.

The New Library

If you haven't stepped foot in your library in a few years, you might be shocked, amazed, or even confused. Libraries have not ignored the Information Age. As new methods of storing and retrieving information proliferated during the 1980s, they became easier to use and, gradually, also less expensive. And as this occurred, libraries became increasingly nontraditional. If your local public or college library hasn't changed all that much, be patient. Most likely, by the end of the century, it will change as library users begin to demand more state-of-the-art resources, and costs continue to decline.

The New Librarian

Librarians have been on the forefront of information technology. They have been in advisory roles to companies developing information storage and retrieval products, advocating for standards in how the information is organized, as well as helping to ensure that the information is easy for users to access. They have also lobbied within their own libraries for increased use of online and CD-ROM information. Most library schools teach the use of computer-based resources, and many even offer a specialization in this area. In fact, many of the library schools, where librarians receive graduate education, are now being referred to as schools of information science.

Librarians can do much more than merely suggest a reference book, or provide a few hints on related subjects to look up in the card catalog. Librarians are trained to be problem-solvers, even consultants. They can help you in honing down your research questions so that you have a manageable amount of information to gather. They can suggest areas that might be most fruitful, within your interest area. They can suggest specific directories, organizations, and collections for you to consider. Librarians can also direct you to various nontraditional resources, such as those that are computer-based and available in the collections at their library, as well as advise you on how to obtain resources from other libraries.

Quick Definition: CD-ROM

CD-ROM stands for Compact Disc—Read Only Memory, with *read only* referring to the ability to "read" data from the disc, but not "write" on the disc. With CD-ROMs, information is contained directly on the disc, and it is accessed with the use of a microcomputer and CD-ROM player. One compact disc has enough storage space for the equivalent of 275,000 double-spaced typed pages. CD-ROM is commonly used for storing citations to newspaper, magazine and journal articles (similar to *Reader's Guide to Periodical Literature*), although some include full-text, as a directory of encyclopedia would.

Online Catalogs

One of the first things you will notice in many libraries is that they have become increasingly automated. The card catalogs have been supplemented or even replaced by online catalogs. You might be directed to a row of computer terminals, instead of the card catalog, and instructed to follow simple directions on the computer screen, for looking up authors, titles, and subjects. At first, this might seem to be a great leap from thumbing through the old reliable card catalog. After flipping through the library's holdings—from A to Z—without moving from one spot, you'll wonder how you ever did it before.

Here's an example of a selection screen from an online catalog, indicating the type of search that the library user can perform. Keep in mind that not all online catalogs offer the same choices.

Online Catalog Options

What type of search do you want to do?

1. TIL   Title, journal title, series title, etc.
2. AUT   Author, illustrator, editor, organization, etc.
3. A–T   Combination of author and title.
4. SUB   Subject heading assigned by library.
5. NUM   Call number, ISBN, ISSN, etc.
6. KEY   One word taken from a title, author, or subject.
7. BOL   Boolean search on title, author and subject.
8. PAT   Patron information: your fines, loans, holds, etc.
9. RES   Find out about items on reserve.

Enter number or code: Then press SEND

This selection screen is the "keys to the kingdom" in the state-of-the-art library, allowing you to search high and low through the library's catalog, without having to move from the keyboard. Think of the wear and tear on your back that you're spared by not having to bend and reach from one drawer in the card catalog to another, not to mention the time you'll save.

For example, you can search for specific titles or authors, or if you know both the author and title, you can search even faster. You can also search by subject, or with other combinations such as keywords or Boolean logic. When you use Boolean logic, you combine search topics by using connecting words like "and" and "or." For example, using "movie and motion picture" in the same search would yield listings that meet both criteria.

Once you key in your search criteria, you are presented with the listings that meet your criteria, just as if you located this group of cards in the catalog. Thumbing through

Figure 3-1

```
080 MAIN LIBRARY    —GEAC LIBRARY SYSTEM — ALL *SUBJECT SEARCH

                                    matches      188 citations
Ref# Author                    Title                              Date
    13 Bal zs, Bla, 1884–1949.> cinma : nature et volution d'un>   1979
    14 Bazin, Andr, 1918–       What is cinema?                    1967
    15 Bazin, Andr, 1918–1958.  Qu'est-ce que le cinma?            1958
    16 Bellone, Julius,         Renaissance of the film.           1970
    17 Bennett, Tony.           Popular fiction : technology, ideol>  1990
    18 Beno

t-Lvy, Jean Albert>        art of the motion picture          1946
    19 Bertrand, Daniel, 1901–    motion picture industry.          1936
    20 Bettetini, Gianfranco.    language and technique of the film  1973
    21 Bloem, Walter Julius, 1898>  soul of the moving picture,      1924
    22 Bluestone, George.        Novels into film.                  1957
    23 Blumenberg, Hans C.       Film positiv; Regisseure, Stars und>  1968
    24 Blumenberg, Richard M.    Critical focus : an introduction to>  1975

Type a number to see associated information -OR-
    IND - see list of headings        FOR  - move forward in this list
    BAC - move backward in this list   REF  - see related headings
    CAT - begin a new search           CMD - see additional commands
Enter number or code: FOR                     Then press SEND
```

the choices is a matter of using the forward (FOR) and backward (BAC) keys on the keyboard. Figure 3–1 is an example from the online catalog at the State University of New York of what might be displayed if you entered the subject "Motion Pictures."

From here, you could choose to view a brief or full description of any of the entries on the list. Figure 3–2 shows the full description is the same information that you would view on a catalog card:

Figure 3-2

```
080 MAIN LIBRARY   — GEAC LIBRARY SYSTEM — ALL *SUBJECT SEARCH
TITLE: Popular fiction : technology, ideology, production, reading / edited by
       Tony Bennett.
IMPRINT: London ; New York : Routledge, 1990.
PHYSICAL FEATURES: xix, 486 p. : ill. ; 22 cm.
```

Figure 3-2 *continued*

SERIES: Popular fiction series
NOTES: Includes index. * Bibliography: p. [461]—474.
OTHER AUTHORS, ETC: Bennett, Tony.
SUBJECTS: Mass media. * Popular culture. * English fiction -- History and
    criticism. * Popular literature -- History and criticism. * Motion pictures.
    * Television broadcasting.
CALL NUMBER: P 91   P63   1990
LC CARD: 88014865
ISBN: 0415025176 * 0415025184 (pbk.)

BRF - see locations and call numbers	CIT - return to your citation list
IND - see list of headings	FOR - see next citation in list
BAC - see previous citation	REF - see related headings
CAT - begin a new search	CMD - see additional commands
Enter code	Then press SEND

And you might find that the online catalog, or even the
traditional card catalog, leads you to much more than books.
Some libraries, though not large numbers of them, offer
access to tape-loaded databases through their online catalogs. These are databases that might otherwise be found in
CD-ROM form, like Business Periodicals Index or Social
Sciences Index. The information is the same, but the way
to access it differs in that you can do it all from one keyboard.

While libraries are still storehouses for large numbers of
books, they are supplementing their book collections with
other kinds of resources.

CD-ROM

Compact discs have taken the music industry by storm,
offering sound so clear that the performer may as well be
in the same room. Compact disc technology is also being
used increasingly in the computer industry. The discs hold
much more information than standard diskettes and, because of their design, also provide a basis for quick retrieval.
CD-ROM discs are to be "read only," and cannot be used
for recording information. They are "played" on a CD-ROM

drive that the computer accesses just like a hard-disk drive or a floppy-disk drive.

The use of CD-ROM technology in libraries is expanding, because it provides library users with the following benefits:

Ease of use   You don't have to consult annual volumes of printed indexes. Instead you can check multiple years of the same volume at once (the number of years depends on the product you are using). This saves time.

Power   With a printed index you are limited to searching by subject, or by author. When searching with CD-ROM, you have many more access points, allowing you to search by particular journal, language, keywords in the title of the article, and with Boolean logic you can search with combinations of criteria. Again depending on the product you are using, your searching becomes that much more flexible.

Hardcopy   In most libraries, you can print citations, rather than copying by hand. And if you are using CD-ROM, in the library or at home, you can download information onto a hard or floppy disc, modify it with your word processing program, and print your results (this will be described in more depth in Chapter 13).

Flexibility   On the horizon are CD-ROM discs that can be modified so each item in a CD-ROM-based index will be annotated to indicate whether or not the item is available in your library. This way, you'll know at once whether the item is immediately available to you.

Many reference materials are now computer based. For example, *Grolier's Encyclopedia*, a resource that students and researchers have been depending on for decades, is now available in a CD-ROM version. And the materials stored on microfilm and microfiche are still there, but you might also be directed to a CD-ROM disc to locate newer journal articles, or for abstracts of articles from a variety of magazines and journals. Many of these references are described in Chapter 13.

CD-ROM is gradually becoming less expensive to purchase or lease. Larger libraries are rapidly adding to their CD-ROM collections, and smaller libraries are also expanding into the CD-ROM format. The vast majority of libraries do not charge the user for the use of CD-ROM materials. Keep in mind that most CD-ROM offerings are also available in printed form, so that even if your library does not have extensive CD-ROM offerings, you will not necessarily be limited in your access to the actual information. In fact, the materials being committed to CD-ROM, such as indexes to journals, are references that have been available in printed form for decades.

Online Databases

You might also want to go online to search for information related to a specialized topic. Online databases, increasingly available in libraries, provide you with timely information on your topic. Additionally, many online services offer bulletin boards, which can be a vehicle for broadening your search, by offering the opportunity to post a note to users with similar interests. Though libraries vary greatly in terms of the online services they subscribe to and how available online searches are to users, in some situations going online can be the best way to get to the information you need. Here are some of the distinctive benefits of online databases:

Timeliness   While some online databases are only up-dated quarterly, others are updated monthly or even *daily*.

Uniqueness   Library users can access information through an online database that is not available else-where. For example, business and financial news services, often offered both online and as a wire service, cover timely news that would only be available in a newspaper arti-cle, published at a later time, if at all.

Ease-of-Use   Many online database services combine ease of searching with large back files, so it's like using a CD-ROM that provides information for a greater number of years.

While online databases include specialized services like Westlaw, which serve the legal industry, and Lexis/Nexis, most online services are available, and are even focused at, the home market. A few, however, are available only to libraries. The most notable of these is FirstSearch.

FirstSearch

FirstSearch, a service of Online Computer Library Center (OCLC), a nonprofit organization, is an online reference service, available within libraries. A variety of databases are available through FirstSearch, the major one being WorldCat, which is the world's largest bibliographic and holdings database. The WorldCat database holds records of literally millions of books, and gives library users access not only to information on these books, but also indicates which libraries hold them. Other databases available through FirstSearch include ERIC (Education Resources Information Center), the Government Printing Office Monthly Catalog, Consumers Index, PsycINFO, and BIOSIS/FS, a subset from the Biological Abstracts portion of the BIOSIS database. Other databases will be added.

The WorldCat database of FirstSearch is especially useful for locating books that you can't find in your own library and that are out of print (and therefore not listed in *Books in Print*). You can check the title in WorldCat, and obtain the author, publisher, and publication date, as well as the names of libraries who do own it. You can also use WorldCat to find out the titles of all of the books written by a specific author, regardless of whether the books are in print or not. If your library does not offer WorldCat through FirstSearch, your librarian may well be able to access the same information for you.

Watch the Clock

Through an online database, you can get up-to-the-second information on your topic. But there is a downside. Online services can be expensive, and while libraries may or may not charge their users for this service, they are more likely to charge for online searching then for the use of CD-ROMs. Some services, like FirstSearch, charge for each search query. Most services, however, charge for the time that you are actually connected with the service, and, possibly, long distance charges. The cost may be $80–120 per hour for using the service, and the library may include additional overhead costs, for example, to cover the librarian's time. You will want to be aware of potential charges before you actually use the library's online service.

Among libraries, there are two general models for the

use of online database services. In one, the user makes an appointment with a librarian who actually does the searching. Because the librarian is trained to use the service, and is proficient in performing online searches, the result can be a very efficient and economical search. In the other model, the library user does his or her own searching, but only after having undergone some form of training. Generally, unsupervised searches are done through lower-priced versions of major database vendors, and the user may be limited in the amount of online time allotted.

To avoid costs, it is helpful to carefully map out what you want to search for, and what terminology is required, before you actually make the connection. With an online service, there is a direct connection between time and money, and the better prepared you are to use the service efficiently, the less money you will spend. Talk with the librarian about how to use the service before you actually go online.

If the library does not charge you directly for using the online service, someone is still paying for it. Library funds are always stretched tightly, and as a result, librarians may be reluctant to offer use of the online services to everyone. You may need to ask to use it, rather than wait for it to be offered. And be prepared to be closely supervised by a librarian while you use it.

Gateways

Many libraries offer computerized access to the holdings of other libraries through gateways. Technically, a gateway is established between two mainframe computers, allowing a user on one computer to access information stored on another.

Libraries use gateways to connect their online catalogs, extending the users' ability to access information far beyond

the limitations of their own collections. For example, libraries in the same city or state often establish gateways so that
users can check to see if cooperating libraries have materials
that are not available in their own library. Actually retrieving the items may involve the use of interlibrary loan, or it
may mean traveling to the other library. On a much larger
scale, major research libraries across the country also connect their online catalogs through gateways.

Gateways between online catalogs can be useful in veri-
fying information about a book, i.e., the publisher or date
of publication. Users can also perform a search, based on a
specific subject, of both their library's own holdings as well
as the other libraries connected to the gateway. And, if
planning to visit another library, gateways make it possible
to search its collection in advance.

An example of a sophisticated gateway system, and possibly the system of the future, is the Gateway to Information
at Ohio State University. It is designed to help library users
define their information needs, as well as find, evaluate, and
select the appropriate library materials. The Gateway to
Information is easy to use, with an invisible interface on the
Gateway work stations (Apple Macintosh computers), using
graphics and simple commands. The Gateway is linked both
to a computer-based library catalog as well as to other computer files, including CD-ROM-based encyclopedia articles
and journal indexes. For example, students can use the
Gateway to identify appropriate dictionaries, subject encyclopedias, book review indexes, biographical sources and
specialized statistical sources. For each resource, the library user is provided with a brief description and the Ohio
State University locations where the materials may be obtained.

The Gateway to Information goes even further than the
standard online catalog by providing online instruction and

guidance in identifying what materials will be most helpful, and assisting in the evaluation and use of the materials. All of this is initiated through graphical icons and commands.

While storage of printed materials is being streamlined through the use of CD-ROM and online database storage, with access extended and simplified through online catalogs and gateways, libraries are also taking advantage of technological advances in other media.

Interactive Media

More and more libraries, particularly at the university level, are adding interactive media centers. As the title implies, interactive media centers provide opportunities to see and hear information, instead of only reading it. This area provides a central focus for the library's computer-based resources, and is supplemented by videotapes, videodiscs, hypermedia (see below), and various interactive programs.

A State-of-the-Art Library:
SUNY's Interactive Media Center

The library at the State University of New York–Albany has one of the most well-equipped interactive media centers in the country. Students may walk in and view lectures and documentaries on historical figures, such as Malcolm X, or on topics like Native Americans.

SUNY-Albany's Interactive Media Center also offers an extensive hypertext and hypermedia collection. This technology, in the words of Brenda Hazard, the Center's coordinator, is a "nonlinear medium in which related pieces of information can be linked in ways analogous to footnotes." For example, with hypertext, the user can use a mouse to "click" on a word of text and go to related text, so that a word could be defined when needed. With hypermedia, sound and visual information can also be connected to text.

39

Hazard discusses a program for music students as an example of a hypermedia program. In a module on Beethoven, text is presented on a computer screen discussing the composer's life and how he developed his compositions. The student might read a specific passage about how violins were used in Beethoven's compositions. He or she could then use the mouse to point to the phrase, causing the program to move to a section on the violin that includes a visual demonstration of how a violin is played and how it sounds in a Beethoven composition. Upon returning to the text, the student could point to the word *concerto*, and be presented with an audiovisual example of a concerto being performed.

Similarly, art students can read about an artist on the screen, and choose to be presented with examples of the artist's works. Additionally, students can point to specific areas of a painting, and be presented with details for closer observation.

Computer-based training courses are being augmented by interactive video. A videodisc is loaded into a videodisc player, which is connected to the computer. During the process of going through the course, students are presented with short lectures that are "illustrated" by the videodisc. Intermittent quizzes determine the sequence and pace of the course. For example, a course on child abuse for nursing and education students includes visual examples of the indicators of child abuse with scenarios demonstrating how professionals should respond.

According to Hazard, many library users are slow in realizing the benefits of interactive media, because they associate it with entertainment. "Most users are still in the mode of 'anything helpful will be in printed form, or directly out of a computer.' Interactive media seems like too much fun to be a source of information." Currently, most programs are on specialized topics. Available subjects will also need to be expanded for additional use to the general public.

Hazard predicts, however, that as interactive media becomes easier to use, and less expensive, it will also become more widespread. At some point in the near future, you will be able to learn about almost anything through an interactive media program.

Something for Everyone

Libraries are more than a place to grab a few books to complete a term paper, or to drop off the kids on a summer afternoon. They are there to serve the needs of the community—and that includes not only young children and students, but also business people and consumers. The key to finding out what your local library can offer is simply to stop in and ask the person who can lead you to all of its rich resources—the librarian.

A Time to Browse, a Time to Act

Should you browse for a while, should you go straight to the catalogs, or should you talk with a librarian? All three parts of this question can be answered "yes," depending on your overriding purpose.

Browsing in your library, going from shelf to shelf, finding the books or magazines that relate to your topic and conducting your own informal review of the literature can be a fun and relaxing way of beginning your search. It gives you a chance to "see what's out there," at least in print, and to familiarize yourself with it. For example, thinking back to the movie example in Chapter 2, you might go to the shelves where the movie books are located and spend an hour or so thumbing through a few of them. If nothing else, the pictures of old films will get you in the mood to dig deeper.

Generally, however, browsing can quickly become a waste of time, and even a distraction, as you get caught up in interesting, yet irrelevant, details. And while browsing may help you to get a handle on available resources, you should not assume that you are limited to what you see on the shelves. Many of the holdings in a library are not visible to the "naked eye." This applies not only to those that are computerized, but also to resources available through inter-library loan and other linkages. You may stumble upon some of these resources as you browse your way through the catalog, or even by walking around. But the best way to get directly to what you need is to consult with the librarian.

Librarians Are There to Help You

While librarians are qualified, and willing, to help you in your search for information, there are both efficient and inefficient ways to make use of their time. Here are some guidelines to keep in mind as you consult a librarian during your fact-finding.

1. Don't be afraid to approach a librarian.
Librarians have a vast knowledge of resources that they can draw on to help you get to the information you need, and they're usually looking for a new challenge. All you have to do is walk up to one and start the process by asking a question. By the way, many different kinds of professionals and assistants work in libraries. If you have a question about the use of library materials, make sure the person you are asking is a librarian.

2. Don't assume you know more than the librarian.
You may know more about your topic than the librarian, but chances are he or she has helped others in seeking related information. Along the way, your librarian has discovered a few resources that you haven't thought about. Even if you have your resources mapped out, you may want to check them with the librarian, just to make sure you haven't

missed anything. For example, the librarian may be able to point out an online database that you weren't aware of that contains exactly the facts you need.

3. Get down to specifics.

The importance of asking specific questions was discussed in Chapter 2. If you have taken time to plan your fact-finding, you will already have this base covered. Librarians have limited time to spend with each library patron, and they appreciate it when those seeking assistance have a clear picture of what they need. This will save the librarian time in trying to figure out what you need, and it will save you from poring over resources that aren't very helpful. You may even want to show your research plan to the librarian, who can then go over it with you and suggest other resources to consider.

4. Ask what tools are available.

Always be ready to ask about available tools. Again, many of the resources of the library are not obvious, and library patrons are not always risk takers by nature. Make sure you have indicated your desire to know about any resource that might be made available. Don't settle for the quick reference book when a computer-based reference—CD-ROM or online database—might give you the detail you really need.

5. Look for brochures and handouts.

Most librarians have a rack that contains brochures and one- or two-page handouts. Associations and other organizations, including government offices, may offer slick, colorful brochures describing their services and publications. Handouts may have been written and photocopied by the library staff, on topics such as "Using the online catalog" or "Resources available on CD-ROM." Handouts that describe specific holdings in specialized topic areas, such as Business, Social Sciences, or Literature may also be available. These handouts will answer questions that you have about the library's holdings, and provide you with some ideas about other potential references.

Here are some examples of library handouts:

Library Terms Translated

How to Research Federal Agencies

How to Locate Biographical Information

You might be surprised to find that one of these handouts has just what you need, with tips on finding what you're looking for, and even a list of available resources to investigate. Librarians also compile bibliographies on specialized topics, based on commonly requested research questions, as well as their own personal interests.

Here are some common topics for bibliographies:

"Foreign Country Information and Statistics"

"Investment Sources"

"Resources for Historical Research"

Take a few moments to go through the handouts at your library—this may be time well spent, and help you to avoid a lot of your own legwork in "reinventing the wheel" by taking advantage of an expert.

6. Ask about interlibrary loan.

If the resource you need is definitely not available through your library, don't panic. You may still be able to get it through interlibrary loan. Many libraries belong to federations of one kind or another, and can access libraries in bigger cities within the state, nationwide, or even internationally. Also, many states have set up systems such that local public libraries can have access to state libraries and the libraries of state universities. Your librarian is best able to give you instructions on how to initiate an interlibrary loan request. You need to use the interlibrary loan service at the library that serves your area (i.e., your public library or the academic library you are affiliated with).

In addition, a librarian may be able to tell you which libraries in your area have particular books and magazines, so you can go and get them yourself, saving the time involved with using interlibrary loans.

7. Ask about gateways.

In addition to interlibrary loan, your library might also have gateway access to materials in other libraries. Check to see if the gateway is available through the online catalog, or if a separate computer system has been set up. Also ask about potential costs.

8. Ask about training.

Libraries are increasingly offering specialized training on topics such as research methods and the use of computer-based resources. This is a great way to receive some intensive instruction, and will streamline your work in the future.

Start with the Plan

Regardless of how much assistance you expect to receive from a librarian, keep in mind that you will be further ahead if you have done your homework—that is, formulated the questions as well as the potential sources of information. On the other hand you may feel that you have done enough planning to act as your own librarian. You may be correct. However, a quick consultation with a librarian can only enhance your fact-finding. A librarian can point out any potential resources that you missed and give you some hints on where you can find the information fast. But keep in mind that available resources change so quickly that sometimes even librarians have a hard time keeping up.

Don't Limit Yourself

Most of us have grown up learning to associate seeking information with going to the library. Libraries exist to serve the information needs of the people in their communities, and they have expanded to include business and consumer information, available through a wide variety of media, including computer-based. While you won't always find everything you need in the library, in most cases, it's still the place to begin. If you can't find what you need there, you can probably discover where to look next.

Tricks Librarians Use

When you're looking for information under a specific subject heading, and you don't find anything, use alternate headings. Many of the information tools available in libraries are based on Library of Congress Subject Headings. Keep a list handy so that you save valuable time by searching with the correct terminology. For example, conducting a search based on "movies" would result in 0 retrievals when "motion pictures" is the correct term.

However, not all reference tools are based on Library of Congress headings. Ask a librarian if there is a list of official subject headings (usually called a thesaurus) for the tool you are using, be it an online catalog, card catalog, CD-ROM database or online database.

Tricks Librarians Use

Just as with different library collections, librarians all have varied subject strengths. Exploit these collections and this knowledge by asking the librarian you are dealing with if another library collection is stronger in the subject you are researching, and if there is a librarian who is a specialist in your general topic, at the library in which you are working, or in another area library. This is especially true in large public, university, and research libraries.

A Quick Review of Library Terms

Just in case you haven't been in a library in a few years and have forgotten a few of the buzzwords—or are wondering if some of the terminology has changed with the advances in technology, here's a quick review, based on a handout from the University Libraries at the State University of New York at Albany:

Abstract: A brief summary of the contents of a book or magazine article.

Almanac: A yearly publication often containing statistics and data of all kinds and information on the events of the previous year.

Archive: An organized body of papers or records preserved for future reference and research.

Bibliography: A list of published materials, books, and/or articles by one author, or on one subject.

Bound Periodical, Bound volume: Several issues of a magazine or journal placed together, in order of date, between hard covers.

Call Number: A code that combines letters and numbers to describe the subject of the material and to locate it on the shelves.

    Example: LA   = History of Education
                      11   = General Works
                      C545 = Author identification
                      1986 = Year published

Card Catalog: A large card file arranged alphabetically listing a library's books separately by author or title or subject.

Citation: A complete reference to a book or journal article containing all the information necessary to find and identify it. Example for a book:

LA	Cleverly, John F.	*Visions of Childhood:*
11		*Influential Models from*
C545		*Locke to Spock* (title) rev.
1986		ed. (revised edition) New
(call number)		York, N.Y.: (place of
		publication): Teachers
		College Press (publisher),
		c. 1986 (year of
		publication).

Classification: System used to group materials on the library shelves in the same subject. The two major classification systems in use in the United States are Dewey Decimal (begins with numbers) and Library of Congress (begins with letters) which is used here.

Cumulate: To build up by adding new material; indexes to magazines are frequently issued monthly in paper covers and then accumulate at the end of a year into one, combined alphabetically and arranged in a bound volume.

Document: An original or official paper or publication.

End-user Search: Any computer search service that can be used by the user independently. The CD-ROMs are an example of an End-user search.

Holdings: The books, or years of a magazine title, a library owns.

Journal: A magazine, usually published by an institution or a group of scholars. Articles may use a special vocabulary appropriate to a field of study and have footnotes and a bibliography.

Library of Congress Subject Headings: Subject headings established by the Library of Congress.

Magazine: Any publication that comes out frequently on a regular basis and contains several articles. A magazine is usually aimed at a more general audience than a journal and may be for recreational reading.

Microforms: A general term for several kinds of reduced-print photographic formats. The most common are microfilm and microfiche. The former is on a long strip, the latter is on individual sheets of film.

Online Catalog: Computer system with terminals on which library users can check by author, title, or subject to find out what the library owns. Some libraries give their online catalogs special names; the University at Albany refers to their online catalog as GEMINI.

Periodical: Any publication that appears at regular intervals and contains separate articles. It is a general term applied to magazines and journals.

Periodical Index: Alphabetical author or subject list that refers you to articles in periodicals, including newspapers.

Primary Source: Original document, such as a manuscript, typed or handwritten text.

Publication Date: The year the work comes off the press; may be the same as the copyright date, but occasionally the copyright date is earlier. The publication date is usually listed on the back of the title page.

Reference Book: A book in which to look up information. Because many people may need to use these every day, they do not circulate. Dictionaries, encyclopedias, almanacs, directories, and atlases are all usually called reference books.

Stacks: Library shelves.

Subject Catalog: The card catalog is divided into two main parts, the cards for authors' names and titles are in one section and the cards by subjects are filed alphabetically in another section.

The Dewey Decimal System vs. the Library of Congress

The Dewey Decimal System and the Library of Congress differ greatly in their approach to classifying information. Below are the major categories for both systems.

Dewey Decimal System

000–099 General Works
100–199 Philosophy, Psychology, Ethics
200–299 Religion and Mythology

300–399 Social Sciences
400–499 Philology
500–599 Science
600–699 Technology
700–799 Fine Arts
800–899 Literature
900–999 History, Geography, Biography, Travel

Library of Congress

A   General Works
B–BJ   Philosophy
BF   Psychology
BL–BX   Religion
C–D   History (General and Old World)
E–F   History (America)
G   Geography—Recreation—Anthropology
H   Social Sciences (including Business)
I   Political Science
K   Law
L   Education
M   Music
N   Fine Arts
P   Language and Literature
Q   Science
R   Medicine
S   Agriculture
T   Technology
U–V   Military Science—Naval Science
Z   Bibliography—Library Science

4

When Print Resources Still Say It Best

Print resources are everywhere, in the form of books—new and old—magazines, newspapers, journals, and newsletters. Some are easy to find, others require varying amounts of digging. In this chapter, alternatives among printed materials are described—what they can offer and where you can find them.

Printed Materials Are not Going Away

Even with the proliferation of high technology and resources like CD-ROM, printed materials are not going away. Books are still the first place most of us look when searching for information, and there are a lot of reasons why that's a good idea. In the first place, printed materials are easily accessible. In fact, they're everywhere. It's easy to walk into a bookstore and pick up a book, or grab a magazine or newspaper at almost any kind of store. Going to a library might require a little more work.

With expanding computer literacy, and lower prices on equipment, it is much less uncommon to use computer-based materials for research. Still it is not yet commonplace to carry around a CD-ROM player, at least not for information purposes. While you might use a portable PC on a long trip, it's easier to pick up a book and thumb through it on a bus or train ride. And using a modem to access an online database is still not an everyday occurrence for the average person.

Printed materials are the "decades old" media of choice, not only because of convenience, but because of the types of information they include. Material that is at all dated, such as that found in scholarly journals, is likely to be more easily accessible in printed form, though online storage became more widespread in the 1970s and CD-ROM storage entered the picture in the 1980s. This is not to imply that older citations are not available electronically, because in some cases, they are. Still, whatever you can find through a computer-based medium is almost always available in print as well.

The information found in books is generally much more in-depth and, depending on what you are looking for, also more conceptual than computer-based information. Ideas and concepts are more easily developed in a book, with illustrations.

Additionally, what you gain through databases, either online or CD-ROM, is *citations* to sources. In many cases, the actual text of the articles and books will be found in print only. While full-text databases are a growing trend, with entire articles, rather than summaries, many databases are still bibliographic.

Start with a Specific Focus

Library catalogs—whether online or organized by cards—generally break down large subjects into the types of references available. This makes it easier to target the exact kind of information you are seeking. For example, references for Motion Pictures will be arranged under subheadings in the card catalog. Here's a sample online catalog of the library at the State University of New York–Albany:

Figure 4-1

```
080 MAIN LIBRARY   — GEAC LIBRARY SYSTEM — ALL *SUBJECT SEARCH
```

	No. of citations in entire catalog
1 Motion pictures and theater -- Germany.	1
2 Motion pictures and youth	1
3 Motion pictures and youth -- United States.	1
4 Motion pictures -- Appreciation	7
5 Motion pictures -- Asia -- History.	1
6 Motion pictures -- Australia -- History.	2
7 Motion pictures, Australian -- History	1
8 Motion pictures -- Awards	1
9 Motion pictures -- Awards -- Dictionaries.	1
10 Motion pictures -- Belgium.	1
11 Motion pictures -- Belgium -- History.	1
12 Motion pictures -- Bibliography.	20
13 Motion pictures -- Biography	13

```
Type a number to see more information -OR-
    FOR - move forward in this list        BAC - move backward in this list
    CAT - begin a new search               CMD - see additional commands

Enter number or code: FOR                          Then press SEND
```

(several screens were skipped)

```
080 MAIN LIBRARY   — GEAC LIBRARY SYSTEM — ALL *SUBJECT SEARCH
```

	No. of citations in entire catalog
1 Motion pictures -- Directories.	4
2 Motion pictures -- Distribution	2
3 Motion pictures -- Distribution -- Data processing.	1
4 Motion-pictures, Documentary Known as: Documentary films	49
5 Motion pictures, Documentary -- France -- Nice.	1

Figure 4-1 *continued*

6 Motion pictures -- Editing.	3
7 Motion pictures -- Editing -- Biography.	1
8 Motion pictures -- England -- History.	1
9 Motion pictures -- Europe, Eastern.	1
10 Motion pictures -- Europe, Eastern -- Congresses.	2
11 Motion pictures -- Europe, Eastern -- History and	
criticism >	1
12 Motion pictures -- Europe -- History.	2

Type a number to see more information -OR-
    FOR - move forward in this list   BAC - move backward in this list
    CAT - begin a new search   CMD - see additional commands

Also keep in mind that smaller subject areas, like *Gone with the Wind*, will not be subdivided:

Figure 4-2

080 MAIN LIBRARY   — GEAC LIBRARY SYSTEM — ALL *SUBJECT SEARCH

Your Subject: GONE WITH THE WIND   matches   2 citations
      matches: Gone with the wind (Motion picture)

Ref# Author	Title	Date
1 Bridges, Herb, 1928—	filming of Gone with the wind /	1984
2 Myrick, Susan.	White columns in Hollywood : report>	1982

Type a number to see associated information -OR-
    IND - see list of headings   CAT - begin a new search
    CMD - see additional commands

Enter number or code: Then press SEND

If you have done your homework ahead of time, and have a basic idea of the kinds of references you need, going to the correct subheading can save you time.

Reference Books and Almanacs

There are times when you need to spend hours with a book on a specific topic to obtain the information that you need. For example, if you are writing a paper on the Civil War, you will most likely need to accumulate fact after fact, as well as commentary and opinions, to get a clear picture of the war and its impact. However, there are also times when you simply need a few dates, such as when the Civil War began and when it ended. Sometimes all you really need to do is to look up dates. In situations like this, don't forget about books that simply contain large numbers of facts, like reference books and almanacs.

One way to locate reference books, in addition to the online or card catalog, is:

Guide to Reference Books, edited by Eugene Sheehy, and published by American Library Association. It is an excellent source for identifying indexes, handbooks, encyclopedias, glossaries, dictionaries, yearbooks, and other reference sources for a wide range of subjects.

Reference books and almanacs vary greatly from one to the next. Some are comprehensive, with page after page of specific details. Others are oriented toward certain topics, like history, or markets, or consumers. Here are some examples of major reference books and almanacs:

Statistical Handbook on Women in America, by Cynthia Tauber, and published by Oryx Press, is a statistical handbook that illustrates in detail the changes in American women among different generations. The handbook reports their numbers, characteristics, socioeconomic conditions, employment and education status, health aspects, and the possibilities for the future.

The Negro Almanac: A Reference Work on the African American, published by Gale Research, presents in great detail nearly five hundred years of history through a combination of historical narrative, biographical sketches, and statistical tables and graphs.

Current Biography Yearbook, published annually by H. W. Wilson, contains an average of 300 international biographies.

American Men and Women of Science, published periodically by R. R. Bowker, contains biographical sketches of living American scientists, arranged alphabetically, who have made significant contributions to their fields.

And one of the most useful almanacs:

The World Almanac and Book of Facts, published and updated annually by Pharos Books, contains facts and figures on an extensive variety of topics.

Going back to the example from Chapter 2 of searching for information about movies, you would find a surprising amount of information about that topic in *The World Almanac and Book of Facts*. Under the heading of "Movie," in the index, are topics that include "Academy Awards," "National Film Registry," "Top 50 Films, all time," and others.

Directories

Hundreds and thousands of directories are available in print, many of which are updated annually. In terms of content and approach, directories may overlap with other types of reference books. Generally, however, directories should be considered guides to other resources, including organizations and publications.

Many directories are highly specialized, and include membership directories from business, social and cultural organizations; newsletters and other publications; almanacs and other reference books; CD-ROM and computer-based information directories; and many other information sources that you probably have never thought about.

To gain a clearer picture of what kinds of directories are

available, you should also consult *Directories in Print*, an annotated guide to over 14,000 directories from around the world, published by Gale Research Inc. (Detroit) and updated annually.

Many libraries will have *Directories in Print* available in the Reference Department.

You will also find available directories included in the online or card catalog, under the specific topic you are researching. For example, directories of film organizations or the *International Motion Picture Almanac* (Quigley Publishing Co.) would be included in the online or card catalog under "Motion Pictures. Other specialized directories include:

> *The Career Guide: Dun's Employment Opportunities Directory*, published by Dun's Marketing Services, with employer listings presented alphabetically, geographically, and by industry classification. Each firm listing includes company name and address, title, and telephone number of the person to be contacted for employment information, a description of the company's history and lines of business, and other information.

Encyclopedias and Dictionaries

Most of us grew up in a household with a set of encyclopedias, which were dusted off from time to time and used in gathering the facts for reports and term papers. Depending on how often they were updated and replaced, and in most families the set of encyclopedias is a one-time purchase, the information in the volumes may not have been very current. By the time you reached high school, you probably didn't bother to read them anymore.

While an encyclopedia can be a generic multivolume set covering every topic imaginable from A to Z, encyclopedias can also be very specific in nature. For example, encyclopedias are published in such diverse fields as material science, infant psychiatry, and Mexican American history. These specialized encyclopedias offer detailed and, depending on the publication date, current information.

So, a good place to start your research is:

The Master Index to Subject Encyclopedias
Published by Oryx Press, *The Master Index to Subject Encyclopedias* is a comprehensive list of topics and keywords, in alphabetical order, with specialized encyclopedias listed where these topics can be researched more fully.

Examples of specialized encyclopedias include:

McGraw-Hill Encyclopedia of World Biography. Contains biographies representing prominent and near-prominent persons in all fields past and present. Each biography is followed by an annotated reading list of further readings on the subject.

Encyclopedia of World Art, also published by McGraw-Hill. Written by specialists from various parts of the world, this reference covers artists, genres, periods, and movements, and each includes an extensive bibliography.

Benet's Reader's Encyclopedia, edited by William Benet and published by Harper & Row (1987). A comprehensive one-volume work with brief articles on famous people of all fields and periods, it includes works of art, literature, and music, and literary schools and movements.

Encyclopedia of Philosophy, published by Macmillan & The Free Press (1972). This has complete coverage of the field of philosophy, including signed articles by experts, and bibliographies.

The Encyclopedia of Education, published by Macmillan (1969). A multivolume encyclopedia of education that contains over 1,000 detailed, signed articles with bibliographies.

International Encyclopedia of the Social Sciences, published by Macmillan (1968). A comprehensive and scholarly encyclopedia of the whole field of the social sciences. Topics include political science, economics, law, anthropology, sociology, penology, biology, geography, medicine, art, and others.

Encyclopedia of Psychology, published by John Wiley & Sons (1984). Contains 1500 subject entries and 650 biographical entries.

Grzimek's Animal Life Encyclopedia, published by Van Nostrand Reinhold (1972–76). Describes the appearance, behavior, and habitat of animals. It includes volumes on "lower animals," insects, mollusks and echinoderms, fish (including amphibians), reptiles, birds, and mammals.

McGraw-Hill Encyclopedia of Science and Technology, published by McGraw-Hill (1982). A comprehensive encyclopedia offering authoritative articles on all fields of science and technology. Bibliographies follow the articles.

To find what specialized encyclopedias are available in your library, check with the reference librarian or look for a list in the Reference Department.

A dictionary can also be much more than a place to look up the definition of a word. Multivolume sets, with the word "dictionary" in the title, are actually encyclopedias. Titles include:

Dictionary of American History describes terms such as "Astoria" and "Astor Place Riot," "Pacifism," "Filibustering," and "Campaign Songs," through detailed historical information.

Dictionary of Literary Biography is an enormous set of reference books that includes lengthy entries tracing the development of hundreds of authors' works.

Dictionary of American Biography, published under the auspices of the American Council of Learned Societies, summarizes the likes of noteworthy persons of all periods who lived in the United States. It does not include living persons.

New Grove Dictionary of Music and Musicians, published by Grove's Dictionaries of Music, is the standard music encyclopedia in English covering the field from 1450. It includes articles on composers, musicians, works, instruments, musical terms, and periods.

Who's Who in America: A Biographical Dictionary of Notable Living Men and Women, issued biannually by Marquis, is considered the standard source for contemporary American biography.

As with encyclopedias, dictionaries are also included in the Reference Department.

Finding Books

Books are everywhere, but if you are interested in a specific topic, or a specific title, you may have to do some more focused searching. Most libraries (and bookstores) will have reference publications that will help you find out what books are actually available. These publications include:

Books in Print, published by R. R. Bowker, is an annual, comprehensive listing of the full range of English-language books currently distributed or published during a given year. The most current issue features over 135,000 new titles, arranged by title and/or author. Supplemental publications include *Subject Guide to Books in Print*, with access by subject to all nonfiction books included in *Books in Print; Forthcoming Books*, listing soon-to-be-published books; as well as midyear supplements. An additional supplement, *Out of Print—Out of Stock Indefinitely*, lists books that have gone out of print. *Books in Print* is also available on CD-ROM, microfiche, and online.

Indexes and Bibliographies

Numerous specialized indexes and bibliographies function basically as guides to information. The terms *index* and *bibliography* are often used interchangeably, though bibliographies tend to be focused on a specific subject area. You can save steps in your research by locating a bibliography specific to your topic—it's like hiring someone else to come up with a list of resources for you.

General indexes and bibliographies include:

Bibliographic Index: An index to bibliographies that have been published separately, or that are parts of books, pamphlets, or periodicals. Bibliographies must contain fifty or more citations to be included.

Biography Index: A quarterly index of biographical materials appearing in magazines and books.

Biography and Genealogy Master Index, 1981– : Published by Gale Research, with the base volume released in 1981 and annual updates thereafter, it enables the user to determine which editions of which publications to consult for biographical information. The *Index* provides access to biographical dictionaries and *Who's Who*, subject encyclopedias, literary criticism, and specific indexes. The full-set indexes over eight million biographical sketches.

Dissertation Abstracts International: An index to dissertations from 550 international institutions of higher learning, organized by keyword and author.

Essay and General Literature Index: Published annually, it indexes the contents of collections of essays in all subject areas.

Author Biographies Master Index: A guide to entries in biographical dictionaries. Authors, poets, journalists, and other literary figures are indexed in one alphabetical sequence. In the sources covered, the *Index* lists every place a specific figure appears.

Personal Name Index to the New York Times *Index, 1851–1974*: Indexes all individuals mentioned in the *New York Times* for that time period.

Humanities Index: Published quarterly, indexes English language periodicals.

Art Index, published quarterly, indexes a selective list of U.S. and foreign fine arts periodicals.

Modern Language Association, Bibliography: An annual index to material from books and periodicals dealing with all aspects of English and American literature, as well as European, Asian, African, and Latin American literatures. This publication is also available as a database.

Religion Index One: Published semiannually, with indexed articles from U.S. and foreign religious periodicals. It is also available as a database.

Current Index to Journals in Education: Published monthly, indexes articles from major education and education-related journals, and is also available as a database.

You might also check for bibliographies on specialized topics (such as those you might find in *Bibliographic Index*). Specialized bibliographies might pinpoint the exact references you need. Examples of specialized bibliographies include:

A Bibliography of American Naval History, compiled by Paolo Coletta, and published by Naval Institute Press. It is arranged by time period, beginning with the years before the American Revolution.

A Bibliography of Theatre Technology, by John Howard, Jr., and published by Greenwood Press, with references listed under topics such as acoustics and sound, lighting, and properties.

Women in American History: A Bibliography: a compilation of abstracts of articles from approximately 550 periodicals, arranged by general subject areas with author and detailed subject indexes (published by ABC-Clio).

Also check with your library for bibliographies specific to that library. Often, the library reference staff will compile bibliographies for subject areas, like psychology or technology, listing available resources under specific subheadings.

Finding Difficult-to-locate Books

Books often go out of print rapidly. In the first place, information constantly changes, and books must be updated to keep current. A book that discusses technological advances or current events, for example, is outdated before it even gets off the press. Tastes change rapidly as well, and books that are developed to meet the needs of a specific market are also quickly outdated. Books on disco dancing, for example, peaked at the end of the 1970s, and faded with the decline of disco. On the other hand, books on hobbies such as stamp collecting, constantly appear, only to be pushed out of the way by new and more popular titles.

The reasons for the short lives of books are also economic. Thousands of books are published each year, and the shelf space in bookstores is limited. Books are made available for a short period of time, and depending on turnover, are removed to make room for others. Accounting and taxation also contribute to this practice, as stock can be depreciated quickly. Also, publishers cannot afford to keep many books in print.

Specialized Bookstores

While books turn over quickly in general bookstores, they stay on the shelves longer in bookstores that are more specialized. A computer book that seems to have disappeared may be available in a bookstore that specializes in the technology market. A book on the people and culture of a foreign country might still be available in a travel bookstore. Look for these types of bookstores in the Yellow Pages under the heading of "Bookdealers," as well as under the specific topic that you need, such as "Travel" or "Computers."

Used or Rare Bookstores

Once a book is out of print, that does not mean that it is no longer available. Used and rare bookstores carry books long after they cease to be available in new bookstores. Often located in an overcrowded storefront, bookstores carrying used or rare books can be an adventure in themselves; full of old dusty novels and books on any topic you can imagine, the volumes are frequently shelved in creative ways. The owner is the best person to ask about what is in stock, and where to go if you strike out. Many of these bookstores will conduct a nationwide search for a specific title, free of charge, and then give you the option of actually purchasing the book once it is found.

Mail Order Services

Large bookstore chains publish catalogs, often accompanied by an 800 number, from which you can order books that you haven't seen in your local bookstore, or don't have time to pursue. Mail order services that specialize in locating out-of-print or difficult to find books also exist. Some of these services include:

> Book Call, a mail order service that stocks books and, when not in stock, orders them. The toll free number is (800) 255-2665. Within Connecticut and worldwide, the number is (203) 966-5470.

> A similar service is Bookworld, at (800) 444-2524. Within Florida and worldwide, the number is (813) 758-8094.

Newspapers and Periodicals

Ideally, given the convenience and accessibility, it would be nice to simply walk into a library or local bookstore and pick up the books and other publications that you need. Given the breadth of your public library, or the depth of your pockets, this will often be the case. However, the facts that you need will often be more elusive, particularly if you seek specialized or up-to-the-minute information. Newspapers and periodicals (magazines and journals) will then be your resource of choice.

Though searching for a journal article may at first glance seem inconvenient, information in this form is both focused and reliable. Some articles may be primary resources, first-hand accounts written by the experts, or they may be interpretations of primary sources. This is also true of books. Because journal articles are focused on a narrow topic, you can get the facts without having to glean them by searching through a much longer work. And in many cases, periodicals may be the only source of what you need. For example, finding historical information may require sifting through old newspaper articles. New scientific discoveries may involve the use of journals or newsletters. Locating business information, such as the past performance of a specific company, may require that you pore over old annual reports or articles.

Locating Newspaper Articles

Local public libraries are often limited in the numbers of newspapers they have available, and may only subscribe to the local newspaper, the newspaper from the nearest large city, as well as the *New York Times* and the *Washington Post*. Depending on the library's resources, these may all be available on microfilm or microfiche, and go back many years. In most cases, the most recent issues are displayed on racks. Depending on library policy, back issues will probably only be available on microfilm.

Most newspapers are not indexed, and those that are available are not standardized. For example, the vast majority of local newspapers do not take the time to maintain a detailed index of the contents of each issue. In these cases, you will need to have some specific dates in mind, and then look up those issues and page through them until you find what you need. You may also want to call the newspaper involved, especially if it is local. Many have a library, or "morgue," and might be willing to help you.

Some of the larger newspapers are indexed, allowing you to look up a specific subject and be provided with references to dates, titles of articles, page numbers, and even abstracts of the article. Major newspaper indexes include:

Chicago Tribune Index
Christian-Science Monitor Index
Los Angeles Times Index
New Orleans Times-Picayune Index
New York Times Index
Times (London) *Index*
Wall Street Journal Index
Washington Post Index

Depending on the specific index you use, the amount and kind of information will vary greatly. The *New York Times Index* is one of the best organized and includes not only date, page, and column number, but an abstract of each article. Others, like the index for the *Washington Post*, include a brief identification of the article content.

High Tech Newspaper Indexes
Don't forget to look for a high tech option that might stream-line your search for newspaper articles. *VU/TEXT* is an online index to newspapers that includes articles in full-text. With *VU/TEXT*, you not only locate the articles you need, but you can read them without having to refer to another source. *VU/TEXT* indexes the newspaper from most major cities in the U.S. *Dialog* is also adding more and more news-papers to its "Papers" file. A good CD-ROM resource is *Newspaper Abstracts*, which covers a number of major newspapers. *Newspaper Abstracts* also provides abstracts of articles.

Figure 4–3

MOTION PICTURES—Cont

rendering of panther; lawsuit, filed in January by MGM-**Pathe Communications**, contends that group's use of Pink **Panther name** conflicts with image of its movies; group's **lawyer accuses** plaintiff of homophobia and says her clients **have no intention** of backing down (M), My 27,I,21:2

Black actresses must still wait for starring roles in movies or television; Randall and Juliet was to star Richard Dreyfuss and Sheryl Lee Ralph, but Dreyfuss dropped out because of creative clashes with film's director Coline Serreau; since then, movie has been languishing in development heap because of trouble casting an actor to play opposite Ms Ralph; photos (M), My 29,C,11:1

Article on Federal Trade Commission and state lawmakers expressing growing interest in practice of buying exposure for products and services in motion pictures; examples of 'product placement' noted; issues involving advertising, artistic license and freedom of speech concerning 'product placement' discussed (M), My 31,D,1:1

Caryn James article on images of elderly in recent films; photos (M), Je 2,II,15:1

Vincent Canby article on emergence of two powerful new sources of film financing in France that could change shape of film production in France, Europe and Hollywood; photos (M), Je 9,II,15:1

To protest unauthorized copying of films onto videocassettes in Soviet Union, major United States film studios have agreed not to license any more films for showings there; studios have also agreed, with the exception of several movies already promised, they will not provide films for Moscow Film Festival in July; Jack Valenti, chairman and chief executive of Motion Picture Export Association of America, comments (M), Je 12,C,13:1

Hollywood is facing unusually competitive summer with mounting anxiety; number of films scheduled for release is up sharply but chances of a blockbuster seem to be growing slimmer; with film Hudson Hawk a huge failure, industry's summer may hinge on action-adventure films like Robin Hood: Prince of Thieves and Terminator 2: Judgment Day; Hollywood's eight studios are scheduled to release 51 movies, compared to 37 last summer and independent distributors are scheduled to release additional 22 films; photos (M), Je 13,C,13:3

Correction of June 13 article on films scheduled for release this summer, Je 15,I,3:2

Merchant Ivory Productions' foray into new Soviet film market with its deal with Paritet, Moscow-based company, detailed; case sheds light on differences in moviegoing customs in US and USSR and potential for difficulties that film companies may have in USSR; American Arbitration Assn recently fined Merchant Ivory Productions 2.3 million rubles; photos (M), Je 16,III,7:1

Article on film makers Greta Schiller and Andrea Weiss, who have made films about homosexuals; photos (M), Je 16,XII-LI,13:1

Motion picture industry tries new tactics to promote movie-going; attendance has been stagnant for more than decade; Paramount Pictures this summer offers movie patrons 'scratch and win' cards offering chance to win prizes; at American Multi-Cinemas, nation's second-largest theater chain, customers can join 'frequent movie-goer program' that promises free tickets and refreshments (M), Je 22,I,11:4

Locating Periodical Articles

In a library's catalog, you will find specific periodicals listed by title. For example, if you want to know if your library subscribes to *Psychology Today* or *Newsweek*, you can look up the title of the magazine. The listing will usually include the years that are available.

However, indexes to specific articles in a periodical are *not* listed in the catalogs. To locate a specific article on a subject, you will need to use an index. Most libraries maintain a subscription to the most commonly used index to periodicals, *Reader's Guide to Periodical Literature*. The *Reader's Guide* lists articles by subject and author. Under the heading is listed the author, the title of the article, the title of the periodical, the volume number, the pages on which the article is located, and the date of publication. Many other specialized indexes also exist, as discussed earlier in this chapter. Check your library to see which ones they own.

Abstracting services, more specialized in nature than indexes, provide the same information as an index, but with a brief synopsis of the article. *Psychological Abstracts* and *Sociological Abstracts* are examples of abstracting services.

Both indexes and abstracts are most commonly available in bound volumes, generally one volume per year. Some supplements are published monthly, some quarterly, but most all indexes and abstracts accumulate to one volume per year. When using an index or abstracting service, approach it as you would a card catalog. Look up the subject or the author and, under that heading, browse through the lists of articles for the ones that will be most relevant to your search. Pay attention to the cross references and any additional subject headings that are included in the index. Keep in mind that, because these volumes are organized by year, you may want to look up the same subject in volumes that go back a few years, depending on the timeliness of your topic.

On page 72 is an example of what you would find by looking under "Motion Picture" in the *Reader's Guide to Periodical Literature*.

Notice the many, more specific options under this broad category. Again, this is testimony to the importance of being as specific as possible in your searching.

Most indexes and abstracts do not list complete journal or magazine titles within each citation; instead they are abbreviated, with the complete titles listed at the front of the volume. When you do find articles, pay close attention to abbreviations.

Publications are also available to help you find what magazines and newspapers are available. These include:

Ulrich's International Periodicals Directory
The most current edition of *Ulrich's* contains information on more than 116,000 serials (magazines and journals) currently published throughout the world, arranged under 668 subject headings. *Ulrich's* is updated annually. Also available is *Ulrich's Update*, available online; *Ulrich's Plus*, on CD-ROM; and *Ulrich's Microfiche*.

Gale Directory of Publications and Broadcast Media is published annually by Gale Research, and covers newspapers, magazines, journals, and other periodicals, as well as radio, television, and cable TV, in the U.S., Puerto Rico, and Canada.

Benn's Media Directory
Benn's is published in the United Kingdom, and includes both a U.K. and an international volume.

Media directories are generally arranged by broad subject headings. However, if you know the title of the publication,

Figure 4–4

MOTION PICTURE CRITICS AND CRITICISM — cont.
  Professional ethics
  He lost it at the movies [critic M. Medved's ties with
    motion picture studios] R. Corliss. por *Time* 139:64
    Mr 23 '92
MOTION PICTURE DIRECTORS
  See also
  Almodóvar, Pedro
  Altman, Robert, 1925-
  Black motion picture directors
  Boyd, Daniel
  Capra, Frank, 1897-
  Cronenberg, David
  Glimcher, Arne
  Kurosawa, Akira, 1910-
  Leigh, Mike, 1943-
  Preminger, Otto, 1906-1986
  Ray, Nicholas, 1911-1979
  Scorsese, Martin
  Sirk, Douglas, 1900-1987
  Stone, Oliver
  Suzuki, Seijun
  Welles, Orson, 1915-1985
  Wiseman, Frederick
  Women motion picture directors
  Zhang Yimou
  Dictating taste [comparing motion picture directors with
    dictators] R. Rosenbaum. il *Mademoiselle* 98:82+ Mr
    '92
MOTION PICTURE EDITING *See* Motion pictures—
  Editing
MOTION PICTURE FESTIVALS
  Getaway scenes. R. Seidenberg. il *American Film* 17:16
    Ja/F '92
      Utah
  Up where the air is clear [Sundance Film Festival] D.
    Ansen. il *Newsweek* 119:64 F 10 '92
MOTION PICTURE FILMS
      Conservation and restoration
  See Motion pictures—Conservation and restoration
MOTION PICTURE INDUSTRY
  See also
  Carolco Pictures Inc.
  Fox Inc.
  Merchant Ivory Productions
  MGM/UA Communications Co.
  Motion picture production and direction
  Motion picture theaters
  Paramount Pictures Corp.
  Pathe Communications Corp.
  Republic Pictures Corporation
  Twentieth Century-Fox Film Corp.
  Walt Disney Company
      Employees
  Too old for Hollywood. M. Zeitlin. il *The Progressive*
    56:33-4 Ja '92
      Ethical aspects
  He lost it at the movies [critic M. Medved's ties with
    motion picture studios] R. Corliss. por *Time* 139:64
    Mr 23 '92
      Finance
  Binge and purge at the B.O. R. Corliss. il *Time* 139:59
    Ja 20 '92
  Lee's 'Malcolm X' film exceeds $27 mil. budget. *Jet*
    81:60 Mr 2 '92
  'Maybe the recession was a wake-up call'. R. Grover.
    il *Business Week* p92 Ja 13 '92
  Payback time. J. Kasindorf. il *New York* 25:34-40 Ja
    27 '92
      United States
  See Motion picture industry
MOTION PICTURE INDUSTRY IN LITERATURE
  The book on Hollywood [L. Ross' 1953 book on the
    making of The red badge of courage and J. Salamon's
    book on The bonfire of the vanities] J. Nocera. il
    Gentlemen's Quarterly 2:69-72 F '92
MOTION PICTURE INDUSTRY IN MOTION PIC-
  TURES
  Home movie [R. Altman's The player] J. Kasindorf.
    il por *New York* 25:50-5 Mr 16 '92
MOTION PICTURE MAKEUP *See* Makeup, Theatrical
MOTION PICTURE MUSEUMS
  See also
  Institut Lumière (Lyon, France)
MOTION PICTURE MUSIC *See* Motion pictures—Music
MOTION PICTURE PHOTOGRAPHY
  See also
  Motion pictures—Special effects
  Figueroa in a landscape. A. White. il *Film Comment*
    28:60-3 Ja/F '92

On the set: Luciano Tovoli. R. Tierney. il por *American
    Film* 17:15 Ja/F '92
MOTION PICTURE PREMIERES
  Victory [New York premiere of The Mambo Kings]
    The New Yorker 68:26-7 Mr 2 '92
MOTION PICTURE PRODUCERS
  See also
  Rudin, Scott
MOTION PICTURE PRODUCTION AND DIRECTION
  See also
  Motion picture directors
  Motion pictures—Setting and scenery
  The battle to film Malcolm X. J. C. Simpson. il por
    Time 139:71 Mr 16 '92
  The book on Hollywood [L. Ross' 1953 book on the
    making of The red badge of courage and J. Salamon's
    book on The bonfire of the vanities] J. Nocera. il
    Gentlemen's Quarterly 2:69-72 F '92
  Touch of genius [O. Welles' Touch of evil] C. Heston.
    il *National Review* 44:42-5 F 3 '92
  Two every 15 minutes [casting] W. Schneider. *American
    Film* 17:2 Ja/F '92
  Where great movies come from. J. Culhane. il *Reader's
    Digest* 140:103-8 F '92
MOTION PICTURE REMAKES
  Déjà vu again. J. Hood. il *Reason* 23:46-8 Ja '92
MOTION PICTURE REVIEWS
  1991 ten best & worst. P. Travers. il *Rolling Stone*
    p49 Ja 23 '92
  Wim Wenders's guilty pleasures. W. Wenders. il *Film
    Comment* 28:74-7 Ja/F '92
      Single works
  See also
  Videodiscs—Motion   pictures—Reviews—Single
    works
  Videotapes—Motion   pictures—Reviews—Single
    works
  35 up
    The New Republic 206:26+ F 17 '92. S. Kauffmann
    New York 25:50-1 Ja 27 '92. D. Denby
    People Weekly il 37:17 F 10 '92. L. Rozen
  The Addams family
    America 166:146 F 22 '92. R. A. Blake
    The American Spectator 25:51 F '92. J. Bowman
    Vogue 182:62 Ja '92. J. J. Buck
  Advise and consent
    Film Comment il 28:7-10+ Ja/F '92. D. Thomson
  Alan & Naomi
    People Weekly 37:16 F 24 '92. M. S. Goodman
  Amadeus
    The American Scholar 61:49-66 Wint '92. A. P.
      Brown
  American dream
    The Nation 254:425-7 Mr 30 '92. S. Klawans
    The New Yorker 68:88-90 Mr 23 '92. T. Rafferty
    Time il 139:66 Ap 6 '92. R. Schickel
  American me
    Maclean's 105:51 Mr 23 '92. B. D. Johnson
    The New Republic 206:26-7 Mr 30 '92. S. Kauffmann
    New York il por 25:60 Mr 23 '92. D. Denby
    Newsweek il por 119:66-7 Mr 30 '92. J. Kroll
    Rolling Stone p42 Ap 2 '92. P. Travers
  Article 99
    Jet il 81:59 F 17 '92. S. Flanagan
    People Weekly 37:18 Mr 23 '92. L. Rozen
  Barton Fink
    Film Comment 28:14-15 Ja/F '92. D. Lyons
  Basic instinct
    Jet il 81:61 Ap 6 '92. S. Flanagan
    Maclean's il 105:48-51+ Mr 30 '92. B. D. Johnson
    New York il 25:85-6 Ap 6 '92. D. Denby
    Newsweek il 119:54 Mr 23 '92. D. Ansen
    People Weekly il 37:17 Mr 30 '92. M. S. Goodman
    Time il 139:65 Mr 23 '92. R. Schickel
    Time il 139:64 Ja 27 '92. R. Corliss
  Beauty and the beast
    The American Spectator 25:51-2 F '92. J. Bowman
    The New Republic 206:4 F 3 '92. M. Kinsley
  La belle noiseuse
    Art in America il 80:61+ Ja '92. P. Pearlstein
  Billy Bathgate
    The American Spectator 25:62 Ja '92. J. Bowman
  Black and white
    Film Comment il 28:78-9 Ja/F '92. F. Andreev
  Black robe
    America 166:38-9 Ja 18-25 '92. R. A. Blake
    Commonweal 119:17-18 Ja 17 '92. R. Alleva
    National Review il 44:48-50 F 3 '92. J. Simon
    New York 25:119 F 24 '92. D. Denby
  Blade runner
    Film Comment il 28:17-19 Ja/F '92. M. Wilmington

Reprinted with permission from the publisher, H. W. Wilson Company.

it's quicker to use the title index. What's helpful is an entry for a publication that also includes the names of indexes in which that publication is included, such as the *Reader's Guide*. *Ulrich's* provides this additional information. This way, you'll know which is the best index to use when you want to search for specific articles. The entry will also indicate if back issues are available for purchase, and if the publication is available online.

Finding the actual periodical can be a time-consuming task if you don't take the time to learn your library's system. For example, popular magazines may be stored in one area, while academic journals are stored in another. And within a specific journal, new issues may be stacked on the shelf, those for recent years may be bound, and issues from further back in time may be available on microform. The library may post this information in a centralized area, or you can check with a librarian.

Using Microform

Technically microform fits in the category of printed material. However, that doesn't mean it is available in a document with pages that you can actually turn. Most likely, some materials have been moved to microform—microfiche or microfilm—and locating what you need will require a little more work. For example, newspapers and magazines, both older and more recent, may be available on microfilm. Often magazines that are older than the current month are available only on microfilm. The same is true for newspapers. Scholarly journals may only be available on microfilm or microfiche.

For information on microfiche or microfilm, start at the public library. The online or card catalog will indicate what is available, with a note indicating whether the material is available on microfilm or microfiche. This material is collected and available in one location in the library.

You'll be surprised at what is available on microfilm and microfiche. Not only can you find the back issues of old newspapers and magazines, but also extensive references to other informational sources. Here are a few examples:

Television News Index and Abstracts—A guide to the videotape collection of the network evening news programs (an index without the full text of news shows).

BBC Radio Six P.M. News: Text of the nightly news.

Herstory: This set reproduces "821 newsletters, journals, and newspapers, published by and about women's liberation, civic, professional, religious, and peace groups from the collection of the International Women's History Research Center." Most of the material was published between 1968 and 1974.

College Catalogs on Microfiche: This enables libraries to maintain a complete collection of college catalogs.

National Criminal Justice Reference Service: Microfiche collection of articles, books, government reports, congressional hearings, conference reports, statistical reports, etc., relating to criminal justice.

Your library probably will not have all of these collections. If not, be sure to talk to the librarian about alternative collections, as well as options like interlibrary loan.

Finding It in Print

Let's take a closer look at using printed materials by focusing on a few examples:

The Gettysburg Address

You could gather facts about the Gettysburg Address through a variety of approaches, including:

- A book about the history of the United States.
- A book about the Civil War.
- A book about Abraham Lincoln.
- An article about the Gettysburg Address included in a magazine, found through the *Reader's Guide*.
- Under the heading of "Civil War" (most likely, too broad) or "Gettysburg Address," in a reference book or almanac (for the date it was given), or an encyclopedia (for an overview of the facts). Also consider reference books and encyclopedias written specifically on American history or the Civil War.

Stress

Researching a topic like stress might include a variety of smaller topics, including the causes of stress in individuals, the economic and social effects on society, and how stress has emerged in various times in history. Printed resources that you might consult include:

- Books about stress.
- Articles in scholarly journals, located by referring to *Psychological Abstracts* and *Sociological Abstracts*.
- Articles in the popular media, such as women's magazines, located through the *Reader's Guide*.
- Articles about stress-related crime in newspapers, found by looking through one of the indexes.
- Books and articles about specific periods of history, such as the Vietnam War and earlier wars. Some of these books may be difficult to locate, and may require a visit to a rare bookstore.

Focus on What You Want

The key to getting the most from printed resources is to be directed, yet flexible. Take some time in your research to think about the kinds of resources you might investigate. And then, as you conduct your fact-finding, move from one resource to the next. Don't assume that information in newspapers and other periodicals will be difficult to locate, even when the use of microform is required. It's all a matter of getting comfortable, and that takes practice.

On the following pages is a general guide to help you along the way (courtesy of the library of the State University of New York at Albany).

Figure 4-5

If You Need To Find:	You Need To Use This Type of Reference Source:	The Form Subdivision Used in the Subject Catalog for That Type of Source Is:	For Example:
How many people are killed in automobile accidents each year?	Statistical abstract Almanac Statistical yearbook	—Statistics Example: Alcoholism—Statistics	*Statistical Abstract of the United States World Almanac*
How much oil does the U.S. import from OPEC countries?			
The number of homicides committed each year using handguns.			
A list of sources (books, articles, etc.) on child abuse, acid rain, international terrorism, etc.	Bibliography	—Bibliography Example: Terrorism— Bibliography	*Child Abuse and Neglect: An annotated Bibliography International Terrorism: An Annotated Bibliography and Research Guide*

Figure 4-5 *continued*

If You Need To Find:	You Need To Use This Type of Reference Source:	The Form Subdivision Used in the Subject Catalog for That Type of Source Is:	For Example:
Background or biographical information on jazz and jazz musicians, minicomputers, famous actors, writers, sports personalities, etc.	Encyclopedia General Specialized Biographical reference	—Dictionaries & encyclopedias —Biography Example: Actors—Biography	*The Complete Encyclopedia of Popular Music and Jazz, 1900–1950* *Encyclopedia of Computer Science and Technology* *Current Biography*
Names and addresses, phone numbers, publications, etc. for organizations, agencies or services	Directory General Specialized	—Directories Example: Economies—Directories Ecology—Directories	*Encyclopedia of Associations* *Directory of American Scholars*
Definition of terms in a particular field	Dictionary General Specialized	—Dictionaries Example: Economies— Dictionaries Ecology— Dictionaries	*Dictionary of Business and Economics* *Black's Law Dictionary*
A summary of the current status of year's work in an area	Yearbook	—Yearbooks Example: Political Science— Yearbook	*The Statesman's Yearbook*

Using the Yellow Pages

The Yellow Pages in your local telephone book can be a great reference as to what's available in your own community. However, it's a relatively broad reference, and not particularly user-friendly. Resources are organized broadly. There is a lack of "see" references, and subdivided headings. For example, an art institute might be listed under the general heading of "Organizations," with no headings for "Art" or "Institutes."

Tricks Librarians Use

1. Using the Master Index . . .

When fishing around for a topic within a topic, *The Master Index to Subject Encyclopedias* can be a good place to start. For example, under the subject of "Stress" are subtopics such as "Animals and Stress," "Electromagnetic Field Stress," and "Occupational Stress." These categories can be helpful in focusing a topic that is especially broad.

2. Watch Your Indexes . . .

It's very easy to ask for indexes by abbreviated names and, as a result, completely miss the one you want. For example, don't confuse the *Times Index*, which indexes the London *Times*, with the *New York Times Index*. In libraries, it happens often. As always, the same watchwords: Be specific!

3. Keep Track of Your Indexes . . .

When you use a newspaper index, be sure to jot down the year of the index you are using. The year is often not included in the actual citation and, as a result, you may get to the microfilm desk and not know what year to check. If you have a whole stack of articles to look up, this could result in much lost time.

4. Reference Books . . .

When you're using reference books, first try to find one that is as specific as possible for your topic. For example, if your topic is the Gettysburg Address, use the *Dictionary of American History*, not the *World Book Encyclopedia*.

5

Making the Government Work for You

The Government—federal, state, and local—is obviously the best place to go for information *about* government. But government publications actually cover a wide and diverse range of topics. Chances are, they're a place where you will want to look for information. In Chapter 5, you'll get the facts on what you can expect to find through government and related resources, and how to obtain it.

The World's Largest Publisher

The United States government is often referred to as the world's largest publisher, based not only on the sheer number of documents in print, but also on the wide range of what is available. The government is comprised of agencies that regulate areas such as commerce, agriculture, and education, and each of these agencies publishes pamphlets, monographs, and handbooks.

In addition to the information you would expect government agencies to provide, they also produce materials on less obvious topics. The government monitors much more than public policy issues. For example, consumer affairs publications, covering unexpected subjects like guides to making home repairs, nutrition and exercise, or planning a trip overseas, are available.

Many government publications are offered to the public, either directly, through the United States Government Printing Office (G.P.O.), or through libraries. And most are either free of charge, or sold at a relatively low cost. When dealing with government resources, however, the old rule applies: You won't get it unless you ask for it. Virtually thousands of publications are in print, and again, being specific about what you want will work to your advantage.

The Big Challenge: Finding Out What's Available

Though headquartered in Washington, DC, the federal government is relatively decentralized. Information, like the policy-makers themselves, is scattered among departments and agencies, many of which have regional offices outside of Washington. There are a few time-saving ideas you may want to consider ahead of time as you approach your search for government information.

First of all, as always, take a close look at your research plan. Exactly what are you looking for? Is there a specific question, or questions, you want answered? Or are you seeking a perspective on an issue, as in some aspect of public policy? This is an important distinction when dealing with the government, because some departments are responsible for policy, like the Congress, while others are focused on both policy as well as providing specific services, like the Commerce Department. Making this distinction will help you as you begin searching through various general and agency-specific catalogs.

Another obvious use for your research plan is to help answer the question: Who would be interested in keeping this information? While the breadth of information offered by each specific agency might very well surprise you, you will still be best off starting with the obvious choices, as in looking to the Department of Commerce for business statistics, and so forth. Available information from the federal government is centralized. Sort of. While the G.P.O. is often the place to start for ordering any kind of information from the federal government, information may still be available from specific agencies directly. It can't hurt to try. And if you want to get in touch with someone personally, you will have to contact the agency directly. It never hurts to go to the source.

Even government information housed in a library may not be broad-based enough to answer all your needs. So taking the time to think about your target source, before your search, will save you time later.

Where to Start

The best place to start in searching for government publications is your local library. This saves you what could be an extensive time delay as you order, and then wait for, government periodicals. And publications at your library can be perused free of charge, which may or may not be the case with materials ordered through the government.

Libraries often carry large numbers of government documents, either because a diligent librarian has carefully collected them, or because the library itself has been designated as a depository through the Federal Depository Library Program.

Federal Depository Library Program

The Federal Depository Library Program was established by Congress to provide free access to government publications. Through this program, approximately 1400 libraries—public, academic, state, and law libraries—maintain large collections of government publications, thus serving as a link between the public and the federal government. Because these collections are diverse, based on the needs of the local library, you won't find every possible government document in print available at each of the 1400 depositories.

However, 53 libraries nationwide have been designated as regional depository libraries, and are distinguished from the smaller, selective depository libraries. These libraries maintain a complete collection of documents, and can be of assistance in locating documents that are either not available through a selective depository library, or are otherwise out of print.

To locate a federal depository library, the best place to start is your local library. It may participate in the program as a selective depository, or can direct you to the closest participating library. The 53 regional depository libraries are listed in the back of this book. For a complete list of all depository libraries, you can write to this address:

Federal Depository Library Program
U.S. Government Printing Office
Superintendent of Documents
Stop: SM
Washington, DC 20402

Chances are, your library can help you obtain any government document that you need. However, you also have the option of obtaining them directly from the Superintendent of Documents of the U.S. Government Printing Office.

U.S. Government Printing Office

The Superintendent of Documents of the United States Government Printing Office is the official sales outlet for copies of government publications. Publications available through the G.P.O. include pamphlets, periodicals, brochures, and books—over 14,000 titles in all, which is a lot of documents. You can find the specific titles of available items regardless of whether or not you have ready access to a federal depository library. And if the documents are not readily available in your library, you can make direct contact with the G.P.O.

Most libraries have various sources that serve as references to government publications. These sources can be the best place to start, because you can get an idea of what is available within your specific area of interest, and you can obtain a list of the relevant titles. This saves time as you look to see what the library actually has in stock. The standard listing of government publications is as follows:

Monthly Catalog of United States Government Publications

As its title implies, this catalog is issued monthly by the Library Programs Service of the Superintendent of Documents, U.S. Government Printing Office. Medium- to large-size libraries will carry it. The *Monthly Catalog* contains a listing of some, though not all, government documents, organized in Superintendent of Documents classification number order (keep in mind that this classification system is unique to the Superintendent of Documents). Each listing references the government author and the name of the issuing agency. The *Monthly Catalog* also contains indexes, including:

Author index

Title index

Subject index (based on Library of Congress Subject headings)

Series/Report index

Stock Number index (based on the Superintendent of Documents sales stock number)

Title Keyword index (an alphabetical list of truncated titles)

The sample entry on page 85 will give you an idea of what you might find in the *Monthly Catalog*.

Because the *Monthly Catalog* is not copyrighted, it is also available through a variety of CD-ROM producers. Check with your librarian. Some of these include:

Government Documents Catalog Service (acronym: G.P.O.), published by Auto-Graphics, Inc. This is an enhanced version of the complete *Monthly Catalog* of the U.S. Government Publications Office, with full Boolean search and record downloading capabilities.

G.P.O. on SilverPlatter, published by SilverPlatter Information Inc., with citations on government publications such as books, reports, studies, serials, maps and more, all from the *Monthly Catalog*.

Government Publications Index on InfoTrac, published by Information Access Company, with indexing to public documents generated by legislative and executive branches of the U.S. government beginning with 1976.

In addition to those listed above, your library may also carry a wide variety of alternate, and more specialized, references to government publications.

Figure 5–1

SAMPLE ENTRY

Monthly Catalog descriptive cataloging entries follow the precepts of the *Anglo-American Cataloguing Rules,* 2nd ed., 1988 revision, the Library of Congress Rule Interpretations, the *GPO Cataloging Guidelines,* and the several pertinent OCLC format documents. All name and series authorities are in AACR2 format, and are established through the Library of Congress National Coordinated Cataloging Operations Project (NACO). The subject headings used in the GPO cataloging are derived from the *Library of Congress Subject Headings,* 14th ed.

The following sample entry is an artificial, composite record, designed to illustrate the major features of a *Monthly Catalog* bibliographic citation.

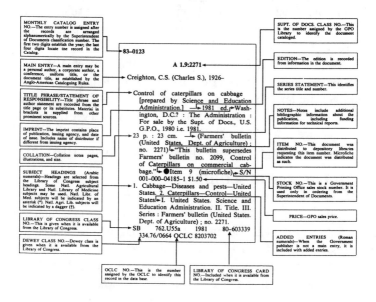

PRELIM. 7

Publications Reference File

The U.S. Government Publications Office offers a *Publications Reference File* (P.R.F.), which is a catalog of all publications and subscription services currently for sale through the Superintendent of Documents. The catalog is available on both microfiche and machine-readable magnetic tape. The microfiche service consists of bimonthly listings. This publication also lists stock numbers, as does the *Monthly Catalog*. Each government publication is identified by a unique stock number, which is required when placing an order.

To use the P.R.F., you can look up the subject, title, or keyword in the alphabetical listing, and then peruse the entries under the subject heading. If you are interested in ordering a specific publication, check its entry closely to make sure it is "In Stock."

You can also search the P.R.F. online, through DIALOG.

DIALOG and DIALORDER

DIALOG Information Services, Inc., offers a computerized reference system, with information on all U.S. Government Printing Office sales items, subject bibliographies, and catalogs listed on the *Publications Reference File*. DIALOG subscribers can place an order through DIALORDER. Check with your librarian about this service.

Out-of-print G.P.O. Sales Publications Reference File

The *Out-of-print G.P.O. Sales Publications Reference File* contains the historical records for publications that were once available through the G.P.O., from as far back as 1972. It is supplemented every year.

G.P.O. References Available to Individuals

In addition to the references above, which are most likely to be available in a library, the G.P.O. publishes indexes

Figure 5–2: Sample Record (showing a typical entry on the PRF)

1—KEY PHRASE:
MARKETING IN CANADA OBR 79 35

STOCK NO: 003-000-90670-1
....5

2—STOCK STATUS: IN STOCK - WAREHOUSE & RETAIL
(PRICED)

LOCATION: U9 6

3—STATUS CODE: 04   STATUS DATE: 01/10/80

SUB LIST: OBR 7
CATALOG NO: C 57.11:79-
35——————8

4————

9———TITLE: Marketing in Canada, OBR
                         79-35
10———AUTHOR: Fernandez, Kenneth L.
11———DOCUMENT   Commerce Dept., Industry
SOURCE: and Trade Administration
12———IMPRINT: 1979: 36 p.1 ill.
13———DESCRIPTION: Overseas Business Reports
                         79-35, Issued with perfora-
                         tions, Prepared by Kenneth L.
                         Fernandez, Office of Country
                         Marketing, International
                         Marketing Information
                         Series, Item 231-B.
14———NOTE: Supersedes C 57.11:76-02,
                         S/N 003-000-90465-2 and
                         C 57.11:78-07, S/N 003-000-
                         90593-4, Weight: 3 oz.
15———SB NOS: SB123 SB125 SB278
16———BINDING: Self Cover, Stitch; Paper,
17———PRICE: 01/09/80   Discount 18
                              Each
                         $1.25 NON-PRIORITY-
                         DOMESTIC
                         $1.60 NON-PRIORITY-
                         FOREIGN

Parts of the Record

(1) **Key Phrase** Any heading that indexes the publication and sorts on the microfiche. The term "key phrase" refers to any access point: stock number, catalog number, title, author, series, subject heading, as well as key words from the title.

(2) **Stock Status** Tells whether or not an item is available for sale from GPO. Most publications listed are available, but some are forthcoming or out-of-stock.

(3) **Status-Code** Numerical symbol for the stock status.

(4) **Status-Date** Date the status of the publication was changed.

(5) **Stock Number** The unique 12-digit hyphenated number (000-000-00000-0) that GPO Sales uses to identify a publication or subscription. This number should be used when ordering a publication.

(6) **Location** Symbol for the unit in the GPO retail warehouse where copies of the item are stored.

(7) **Sub List** Symbol used by GPO Sales to identify a subscription, or a publication available on standing order service.

(8) **Catalog Number** Superintendent of Documents classification number. Many Depository Libraries use catalog numbers to arrange documents on shelves in their collections.

(9) **Title** Name of document. Usually taken from the title page. May be taken from the cover, envelope, or mailing carton of items without a title page.

(10) **Author** Person(s) who wrote the document. May also refer to editors, illustrators, compilers, or task force leaders named prominently in the publication.

(11) **Document Source** Name of the Federal agency that issued or released the document. Often it is what librarians refer to as the "corporate author."

(12) **Imprint** Gives the year the publication was printed, the number of pages, and related information.

and catalogs that are available to individuals, and are generally free of charge. While these publications are likely to be available in your library, you can also obtain your own copies. These publications are listed below:

Subject Bibliographies The G.P.O. publishes more than 230 *Subject Bibliographies*. These bibliographies are based on a single subject, or a field of interest, and list publications and subscriptions sold by the G.P.O. Each entry is listed by title, with the G.P.O. stock number (essential for ordering!) and the price. Some of the entries also include a brief description of the publication or subscription, as well as ordering information, and the date of publication.

Also available from the Superintendent of Documents is a *Subject Bibliography Index*, which lists all of the specific *Subject Bibliographies* that are available. You can obtain a free copy of this index by writing:

U.S. Government Printing Office
Superintendent of Documents
Stop: SSOP
Washington, DC 20402-9328

U.S. Government Books Also available free of charge is *U.S. Government Books*, an annotated and illustrated catalog of almost 1,000 new and popular books available through the government. This may be obtained by writing to:

FREE CATALOG
Box 37000
Washington, DC 20013

The Consumer Information Catalog The federal government is a major publisher of free and low-priced consumer publications. These titles are listed in the *Consumer Information Catalog*, issued by the General Services Administration's Consumer Information Center. To obtain a copy of this free catalog, write:

Consumer Information Center
Pueblo, Colorado 81009

Government Periodicals and Subscription Services   This is a catalog of all Superintendent of Documents subscription services. It is identified as Price List 36, and is available by writing:

U.S. Government Printing Service
Superintendent of Documents
Mail Stop: SSOP
Washington, DC 20402-9328

New Books   An annotated bimonthly listing of all new titles entering the G.P.O. sales program during the preceding two months is available in each issue of *New Books*. To be placed on the free mailing list, write:

New Books
U.S. Government Printing Office
Superintendent of Documents
Mail Stop: SSOM
Washington, DC 20402-9328

How to Order G.P.O. Publications   When ordering directly from the G.P.O., you have a few options: mail, telephone, and online. Order forms are easy to come by—most libraries have them, or you can photocopy the one in the Appendix, in the back of this book. Remember to print clearly, and to make sure you identify the correct stock number of your publication.

You can also order by telephone, with a major credit card, by dialing (202) 783-3238. Again, be sure to have the correct stock numbers at hand. When you call, be prepared to stay on hold for a while, as the staff is extremely busy.

In either case, be prepared to wait—*weeks*—for your order to arrive. Both order processing and order fulfillment can be time-consuming. If your needs are immediate, consider getting in touch with a Depository Library, either through your local library, or by contacting the Regional Depository in your state.

Online orders, as discussed previously in this chapter, are available through DIALOG (check with your librarian).

Caution

While more than 14,000 titles are available through the G.P.O., keep in mind that this is still a *fraction* of what is actually published by the government. Again, going through specific departments and agencies is something that you should consider.

U.S. Government Bookstores

The U.S. Government Printing Office operates 24 bookstores, located in major metropolitan areas around the country. These stores carry many of the more popular G.P.O. publications, as well as ones of local interest, and they will special order other books offered by the government. A list of these bookstores is included in the Appendix.

Beyond the G.P.O.

Many, many government publications, and other sources of information, are not included within the pages of a G.P.O. catalog. These include items published by various federal agencies, such as the Departments of Agriculture and Education, the Bureau of Census, and the Department of State, as well as federal archives. Each of these offices publishes materials, including booklets and periodicals, that may or may not be listed in the *Monthly Catalog*. It is not impossible to locate these sources; in fact, many are relatively accessible. The trick is to find a direct route.

You can always look in the federal government pages of the nearest telephone directory, particularly that of a major metropolitan area. Federal agencies have regional offices, and this can be the most direct route. A regional office can usually mail you a publications list, and you may also find someone who can talk with you about what you need. Of course, you can also contact the Washington, DC, office of a federal agency. Below are some of the agencies that are most likely to offer publications and offer other assistance.

Library of Congress

The Library of Congress (LC) is the biggest library in the country, and certainly supported by your tax dollars, but it is not necessarily a "public" library in the usual sense of the word. You can visit the Library of Congress and conduct research, but it was not created to be a readily available resource for the average library patron.

A few Library of Congress publications are available, including folk, music, and literary audio recordings, as well as video tapes. For more information write to this address:

Library of Congress
Motion Picture, Broadcasting and Recorded Sound Division
Public Services Office
Washington, DC 20540

The LC also publishes an illustrated brochure of the greeting cards, calendars, notepaper, posters, and other items it has available for sale. For a copy of this brochure, write:

Library of Congress
Office Systems Services
Printing and Processing Section
Washington, DC 20540

The LC also publishes books and pamphlets on various topics. Check in your geographical area for a regional or selective depository, or in a G.P.O. list of publications. Also talk to your librarian about Library of Congress publications. Generally Library of Congress publications need to be ordered directly from the LC. The LC's catalog is called *Library of Congress Publications in Print*. To reach the Library of Congress, write:

Library of Congress
Public Affairs Office
10 First Street SE
Washington, DC 20540

Department of Agriculture

The Department of Agriculture offers reports, general publications, and specialized bulletins. To reach them, write or call:

Office of Communication
Fourteenth Street and Independence Avenue SW
Washington, DC 20250
Telephone: (202) 447-2791

Bureau of Census

The Bureau of Census offers a wide variety of census reports, by region and industry, for example, as well as a number of bulletins, handbooks, manuals, and guides. *Statistical Abstract of the United States*, the Bureau's major publication, is an annual, single-volume compilation of U.S. statistics on all subjects. To request a publications list, contact them at:

Public Information Office
Bureau of Census
Department of Commerce
Washington, DC 20233
Telephone: (301) 763-4640

National Archives and Records Administration

The National Archives and Records Administration is concerned with collecting and organizing a wide range of historical records and related information, and publishes handbooks and bulletins. The agency also offers a "Reference List of Audiovisual Materials Produced by the United States Government," a compilation of audiovisual materials produced by numerous federal agencies in subject areas that include medicine, education, and science. To contact the National Archives, write to this address:

National Archives and Records Administration
Seventh Street and Pennsylvania Avenue NW
Washington, DC 20408

Department of State

The Department of State offers publications concerned with foreign affairs, currency, international travel, lists of embassies and diplomats, and related topics. For information:

Office of Bureau Services
Bureau of Public Affairs
2201 C Street NW
Washington, DC 20520
Telephone: (202) 647-6575

National Technical Information Service

The National Technical Information Service (NTIS) provides access to U.S. and foreign government sponsored research and development and to engineering research results, announces summaries of completed and ongoing U.S. and foreign government sponsored research and development and engineering activities, and provides technical reports on these topics. NTIS also manages the federal Computer Products Center, which provides access to software, data files, and databases provided by federal agencies, and also manages the Center for the Utilization of Federal Technology, which runs an active inventions licensing program for the U.S. government. NTIS offers U.S. firms access to foreign government research and engineering programs. A catalog of publications can be obtained by calling or writing:

National Technical Information Service
U.S. Department of Commerce
Springfield, VA 22161
Telephone: (703) 487-4650

NTIS offers an online version of its bibliographic tool for libraries and information centers, called *Government Reports Announcements & Index*, a semimonthly indexing and abstracting service containing current citations of all publications received by NTIS. It is accessible through online services such as DIALOG.

Locating Government Agencies

Because the federal government is made up of a multitude of agencies and departments, finding the one that has the information you need may not be an easy task. It may be most expedient to refer to one of the directories that list agencies and their publications. Many of these directories will be available in your library. Some of the major directories in this area include:

United States Government Manual, published annually by the U.S. government. As the official handbook of the federal government, it describes the purpose and programs of government agencies and departments, including addresses, personnel, organization charts, and histories.

Federal Regulatory Directory, published by Congressional Quarterly, includes extensive profiles of large regulatory agencies and summary profiles of a number of other agencies.

And to keep up with the ongoing activities of government agencies:

National Journal, published by Government Research Corporation, is a weekly publication on the policies of government agencies. Each issue is indexed by personal name and private and government organizations.

Other Indexes to Government Publications

Indexes are also available that allow you to find not only the names of government publications, but also to look up specific articles. Some examples include:

American Statistics Index, published monthly, and compiled annually and quinquennially by Congressional Information Service, Inc. A comprehensive guide to U.S.

Government statistical information that is also available online and in CD-ROM format.

Guide to U.S. Government Publications, edited by Donna Andriot, and published annually by Document Index of McLean, Virginia. The *Guide* is an annotated compilation of the important series and periodicals currently being published by the various U.S. Government agencies, as well as important reference publications issued within the various series.

While you're seeking out information resources in the government, you may also want to consider going to the policymakers themselves.

Contacting Members of the U.S. Congress

Each member of Congress operates his or her own office to handle communication with his or her constituents. Each member sits on one or more committees, focused on issues ranging from national defense to child welfare. Congressional offices often offer pamphlets and reports that are focused on a specific topic. Also, the representatives from your own area, or a Congressperson from another state who sits on a committee that you are interested in, can offer you additional assistance. This might include helping you to get into contact with experts or obtaining publications. It never hurts to try.

Congressional offices in your own city, or the nearest metropolitan area, are the best place to start. Staff people in these offices are focused on serving the local constituents, and are more likely to have time to provide information. However, Washington offices are also set up for this purpose.

To contact a member of Congress, check your library for one of the following publications:

Official Congressional Directory, published annually by the U.S. Congress. It includes biographical information about Congress members; committee and subcommittee listings; foreign representatives and consular offices in the U.S.; maps of Congressional districts; state delegations; and other reference information.

Congressional Staff Directory, published by Staff Directories, Ltd., includes biographies of the staff and House and Senate assignments to committees and subcommittees.

Congressional Yellow Book, published by Monitor Publishing Co., is a directory of members of Congress, their committees, and their key aides.

The Almanac of American Politics, edited by Michael Barone and Grant Ujifusa and published by National Journal, includes biographical data on members, committee assignments, and ratings of performance by special interest groups.

The Congressional Information Service publishes an index, available in most libraries. The *Congressional Information Service Index* is organized by subject and name, and indexes congressional publications, including hearings, documents, reports, and public laws.

Congressional Record is a chronicle of the daily activities of Congress, with verbatim testimony from hearings. Biweekly and final indexes are available. The *Congressional Record* is most likely to be available at depository libraries.

You can also obtain up-to-date information on the activities of Congress through LEGI-SLATE, an online service covering Congress and federal regulations. It is considered to be one of the best sources of congressional information, and also includes many full-text entries. This service may be available in your library.

Government-related Publications

The Washington, DC, area, both inside and outside the Beltway, is replete with large and small organizations that monitor the federal government and its elected officials, agencies, and policies. These organizations publish newsletters, directories, and guidebooks. While some of these publications are both highly specialized and expensive, many are offered by associations and nonprofit organizations that will sell them at minimal cost, or even free of charge. Such groups employ experts who may be available to answer questions.

These non-federal government organizations are not very easy to locate. The best place to start is your library, to see if any of the newsletters and journals of these organizations are available.

One of the best guides to organizations in the Washington area, both in- and outside the government, is:

Washington Information Directory, John J. Russell, Managing Editor, and published annually by Columbia Books, Inc., of Washington, DC. *Washington Information Directory* is a comprehensive directory of the key institutions and leaders of the National Capital area. The organizations listed in the book are organized by headings that include national government, local government, international affairs, the media, business, national associations, labor unions, the bar, foundations, education, cultural institutions, and others. *Washington Information Directory* includes a combined index of organizations and individuals.

In addition, organizations that offer publications and services related to government, both within and beyond the Washington area, are listed in:

Encyclopedia of Governmental Advisory Organizations, edited by Donna Batten, published by Gale Research Inc. This reference book lists permanent, continuing, and ad hoc U.S. Presidential Advisory Committees, congressional advisory committes, public advisory committees, interagency committees, and other government-related groups.

Government Research Directory, also available through Gale Research. This publication provides contact information and detailed organization and mission descriptions of research programs and facilities operated by or for the U.S. government.

Government-related information that you might receive from a Washington-based organization ranges from national politics, such as information available through political think-tanks, to international issues, available through groups with a focus on a specific country.

Organizations with an interest in the workings of the government are located outside of Washington as well. An example is:

Public Affairs Information Service, Inc. (PAIS) was founded in 1914 by a group of librarians, and was chartered as a nonprofit educational corporation in 1954 by the Regents of the University of the State of New York. It is housed at the New York Public Library.

PAIS produces publications that include:

PAIS International in Print, a subject index to worldwide English-language, French-language, German-language, Italian-language, Portuguese-language, and Spanish-language public policy literature. The subject headings and notes are in English. Prior to 1991, this was published in two parts: *PAIS Bulletin* and *PAIS Foreign Language Index*.

PAIS International Online, an enhanced compilation of the material in PAIS's printed indexes.

PAIS on CD-ROM, a CD-ROM version with enhanced searching capabilities of PAIS's other publications.

PAIS Subject Headings, a listing of the controlled vocabulary terms used to index the other PAIS publications.

PAIS is an excellent source for information on Congressional hearings and committees in addition to books and periodical articles. Generally, PAIS publications are best accessed through libraries.

State and Local Resources

You are surrounded by what might be extensive sources of information through your state and local government. These resources might include agencies in areas such as consumer protection services, cultural affairs, and environmental protection licensing. Counties often have their own historical societies. And many local govenrments have formal information and referral services, staffed by professionals who can either answer questions or direct you to other resources in your areas. Your local chamber of commerce, for example, can help direct you to business people. Before you look to Washington for assistance, you might be surprised at what you can find in your own state and county.

A librarian at your local library can explain local information resources and help you get in touch with them. Your library may also have a guide to local and state resources, either published formally, or compiled by the staff. You can also check in your telephone book under state and local government listings. Look either for specific departments, such as health or transportation, or for general public information numbers.

Most states have a state library, which is accessible to state residents. For specialized information, such as various licensing requirements, a state library may be the best resource. Your local library probably has direct access to the state library, through interlibrary loan, or possibly computer gateways or online databases. While you can call or visit your state library on your own, it may be easier to contact a librarian at your local library.

Your own state universities are wellsprings of information, with comprehensive libraries, research institutes, and faculty members with expertise in specialized areas. Additionally, agencies in other states may be willing to answer questions and send information when appropriate.

For information about state agencies, look to:

The National Directory of State Agencies, JoAnne DuChez, Managing Editor, published annually by Cambridge Information Group Directories, Inc. This is a comprehensive guide to state agencies and their staffs. It is organized state by state as well as by function, with contact names, addresses, and telephone numbers.

Reference books are also available that cover the resources of one specific state, describing departments, political groups, and state officials, along with statistics and historical information. Most likely your library has a book like this for your state.

Using ERIC

ERIC, the Educational Resources Information Center, is a national information system providing users with access to an extensive body of education-related literature. Established in 1966, ERIC is supported by the U.S. Department of Education, Office of Education Research and Improvement. The ERIC database, the world's largest source of education information, contains nearly 700,000 abstracts of documents and journal articles on education research and practice. The information is available at about 3,000 locations worldwide. The ERIC database can be accessed online, through CD-ROM or print and microfiche indexes.

The ERIC system, through its sixteen subject-specific clearinghouses and four support components, provides a variety of services and products, including research summaries, bibliographies, reference and referral services, computer searches, online database access, and document reproduction. Through ERIC, you can access information on a wide range of topics, such as Adult Literacy, Computer Use in Education, Health Education, and National Education Goals.

ERIC indexes two types of information: articles from journals that are not published by ERIC, and ERIC documents. ERIC may be available at your local library, or at a nearby college or university library. If not, your librarian may be able to advise you on how to obtain ERIC materials. To contact ERIC, write or call:

Educational Resources Information Center
U.S. Department of Education
Office of Educational Research and Improvement
555 New Jersey Avenue NW
Washington, DC 20208-5270
ACCESS ERIC Toll Free Number: 800-USE-ERIC

Your Government Works for You

Don't underestimate the kinds of information that you can gain through the federal, state, and local government. Not only are a variety of publications available, but policy is formulated with the guidance of experts, and making an individual contact is not out of the question (see Chapter 8). The key is patience. Each government office has a constituency of virtually millions of people—at the federal level, every man, woman, and child in the country. Do your homework beforehand, clarify your questions, and when possible, obtain the specific names and identifying numbers of publications.

Thank you to Catherine M. Dwyer, Government Documents Librarian, SUNY–Albany, for her comments on this chapter.

Tricks Librarians Use

1. Obtaining additional contacts . . .
Statistical Abstract of the United States is a comprehensive guide to government statistics. But an additional benefit is at the end of each statistical table. The document and/or agency from which the information was obtained is referenced. You can then look this agency up in a directory and contact it directly for additional information, or you can check the original document for more information.

2. Scoping out the territory . . .
The G.P.O.'s *Publications Reference File* is organized by keywords. If you have a broad topic in mind and want to narrow it down, you can look it up and, by perusing related keywords, get some ideas about

---

related subareas. For example, under "geography," you might discover some related specialized areas to pursue. Additionally, by using the *Publications Reference File*, you also get an idea about the kinds of government publications that might offer helpful information.

3. *Using Government Publications*, by Jean L. Sears and Marilyn K. Moody, published by Oryx Press, is a comprehensive guide to the ins and outs of government publications. Volume I is titled *Searching by Subjects and Agencies*, while Volume II is *Finding Statistics and Using Special Techniques*. Both volumes are organized by subject, and include various search strategies as well as resources.

4. *The Federal Data Base Finder: A Directory of Free and Fee-Based Data Bases and Files Available from the Federal Government*, by Matthew Lesko, published by Information USA (1990) lists a multitude of databases and files available from the independent agencies and the legislative, executive and judicial branches, as well as the National Archives and National Technical Information Service. These databases cover diverse subjects, including a listing of U.S. motion picture theaters, missing works of stolen art, and infant formula nutrients. The book is indexed by topic.

5. *Persistence!* When contacting government agencies, it may require numerous attempts before you actually reach a "live" voice. And from there, you may be transferred a few times before you reach the person you need. Be persistent. And patient.

6

Searching Off the Beaten Track

Regardless of your topic, many valuable resources are available outside of the walls of your local library. This chapter leads you off the beaten track . . . to organizations, museums, think-tanks, and other places that can enrich your fact-finding.

Expanding Your Horizons

Somewhere out there is the exact resource you need. If it's a book, it may or may not be in your library, depending how extensive the holdings are. If it's a journal, depending on how obscure it is, your library may not have even heard of it. And if the information you need is of a highly specialized or timely nature, or related to popular culture, you will most likely find your library to be a limited source.

Think back to the movie example in Chapter 2. The library was certainly the best place to start—with indexes, almanacs, directories, history books, and a limited number of magazines. However, the most in-depth information was gained through organizations and archives that serve the film community. This will often be the case in other kinds of searches. The library can often be the starting place where you can look to find out where you need to go next.

Professional and Trade Associations

Professional and trade associations are created to provide professional development and networking opportunities, and to enhance the status of members of a trade or profession. Some of the better-known trade associations include the American Medical Society, the Petroleum Institute, and the Direct Marketing Association. Some of these associations actually conduct collective bargaining on the part of their members, like the American Federation of Teachers, while most of them conduct various political activities, including lobbying. Because of the strong political orientation of professional and trade associations, many of them are located in the Washington, DC, area.

Some of the reasons for looking to a professional or trade association in your fact-finding are obvious, while others are not. Keep in mind the research plan from Chapter 2. Remember that question about who might be interested in collecting certain kinds of information? In the process of serving their members, associations document the progress of the profession by collecting large amounts of information—statistics, history, new developments, and opinions. And this information is more broad-based than you might expect.

Associations that serve professional groups exist in part to ensure that the profession is represented in a positive light to the public. To accomplish this, many associations offer brochures and other publications that may be requested free of charge, or ordered through a publications list, for a low price.

Professional and trade associations are veritable storehouses of information. Some resources are privy only to members and will be difficult, though not impossible, to obtain, while others are readily available to the public.

Journals and Newsletters

Associations generally publish a magazine and/or a newsletter, both of which may or may not be available to nonmembers. Journals are usually oriented toward current issues in the field, while newsletters focus on news about the association's activities and its members. Associations will often send out a copy of either of these, even if you are not a prospective member. Also, you can most likely obtain a copy of the journal's annual index, and then request reprints of articles.

Conference Proceedings

Associations also hold a national annual conference, for which a schedule of events as well as conference proceedings, with abstracts of any papers that were presented, is published. You may obtain a copy of the conference proceedings from the most recent annual meeting, though a fee may be charged. If conference proceedings are available to members only, they may still be available through interlibrary loan, if your local library doesn't own them.

Other Publications

As part of their lobbying efforts, professional and trade associations distribute publications called "white papers," which formalize the position that members of the association hold regarding, for example, impending legislation. They also offer handbooks and specialized information for their own members. Much of this material is for sale, to both members and the general public. Classroom materials, including videotapes and study guides, may also be available.

Library or Clearinghouse

Many associations also maintain a library for members, with books, journals, and other publications of interest to the profession. Most likely, you cannot borrow these materials as an outsider. However, the librarian may be willing to send you photocopies of articles, suggest where you might locate them yourself, or even answer specific questions that you might have.

Locating Associations

The best place to locate associations is within your own community. Look through community resource books, many of which will be in your library. Also check your local telephone book, under the heading of your particular interest, such as business or education, as well as under the general headings of "association," "trade association," and "organization." Local associations are often affiliated at the national level and, even if they aren't, you may find the information you need at the local level.

National professional and trade associations can be found in directories, including:

Encyclopedia of Associations, edited by Deborah M. Burek, published by Gale Research. *Encyclopedia of As-*

sociations is a guide to national and international associations, organized under headings that include legal, public administration and military, environmental and agricultural, cultural, educational, chambers of commerce and trade and tourism, and others.

Encyclopedia of Associations Series on CD-ROM is a CD-ROM database with 100,000 descriptive entries, including national associations in the U.S.; regional, state, and local U.S. associations; international associations; and periodicals issued by national associations in the U.S. A wide range of searches can be performed through the entire file, with 15 searchable indexes.

Encyclopedia of Associations Series Online is available through DIALOG Information Services, Inc., with national, regional, and international organizations.

Because so many associations are located in Washington, DC, looking under the "Association" heading in the Washington, DC, Yellow Pages is a great way to find out the names of associations. You'll find numerous pages of associations, with street addresses but without zip codes.

Contacting an Association

Associations, even when they serve a specific professional group, exist to serve. Still, associations are in many cases large organizations, with hundreds of employees. Reaching the correct person, or even department, and then obtaining the information you need, will require some careful planning.

Being as specific as possible is the key to routing your request through an association, particularly at the national level. If the directory you are using to locate the association also includes the names of key people, such as public relations manager, publications manager, or public information officer, write those names down, with the correct spelling. When you are later making contact with the association, refer to these people directly. Even if you don't reach them, you will be connected with their assistants, or associates, who can help you move in the right direction.

If your budget allows, a telephone call is the most expedient way to reach an association. And if you end up in a blind alley by reaching the wrong association, for example, you can then ask for advice or a referral. Associations also respond to written inquiries.

In either case, be specific in your request. If you simply want information about the organization so that you can decide if it might be helpful at a later time, then simply request a membership packet. If you are looking for specialized publications, ask for a publications list, and a sample of the organization's journal. If you have a specific question, address your request to the public relations department or public information office, where your question will at least be routed to the correct person.

Nonprofit Organizations and Societies

Nonprofit organizations and societies are similar to professional and trade associations in their overall structure and scope of activities, with memberships that are often both national and regional in scope. Generally, an organization or society is dedicated to a cause, an activity, or a discipline. Examples include organizations that promote the arts, such as opera or dance, or that are dedicated to the well-being of a certain group, such as the elderly or disabled. Other organizations are focused on political causes, such as an area of foreign policy. Academic societies may include members from a variety of professions who are interested in a specific discipline, such as astronomy. Societies like the Gerontological Society are focused on both academic and professional issues. Other societies are organized around a specific interest, like stamp-collecting. And others are created to offer support for members of specific ethnic groups.

Organizations and societies run the gamut from large to small. A stamp-collecting society, though national in scope with an annual conference and a newsletter, might be managed from someone's kitchen. At the other end of the spectrum, the American Association of Retired Persons (AARP) is a large national organization, with extensive lobbying activities, a monthly magazine, and chapters in towns and cities around the country. As with professional associations, many of the national organizations are based in Washington, DC.

Organizations and societies can be excellent sources of information, specifically because they are created to generate relevant information. Many offer journals and newsletters, as well as a variety of other publications, that may be requested or purchased. Smaller groups, like political groups or stamp-collecting clubs, may not have the funds to do a lot of extensive mailing, and will instead invite you to pay a small membership fee.

Locating and Contacting Organizations and Societies

At the local level, community resource guides and the telephone book are the best place to locate organizations and societies. And, the *Encyclopedia of Associations* will be an excellent resource for locating groups of this type at the national level.

Another directory to check out:

National Directory of Nonprofit Organizations, published by The Taft Group. This directory lists nonprofit organizations in the U.S., arranged by activity groups such as business and professional; advocacy; cultural, historical or other educational activities; litigation and legal aid activities; and scientific research activities. For each organization listed, address, major activities, and other key data is supplied. A geographic index is included.

You can also locate regional organizations through: *Regional, State, and Local Organizations*, also published by Gale Research as part of the *Encyclopedia of Associations* series. It is a guide to U.S. nonprofit membership organizations with interstate, state, intrastate, city or local membership. It is published in five regional volumes.

Nonprofit organizations should be approached in a similar manner to professional and trade associations, through either a telephone call or a letter. Again, you will have the best results with specific questions.

A slight caution: many organizations, particularly ones political in nature, have a bias. You'll want to make sure you're aware of what that bias is, and how it might be affecting the information you receive. And you may want to contact a variety of organizations to gain a balanced view.

Foundations

Foundations are non-profit organizations that give money to a specific cause, or causes. Some are created by wealthy families to disperse funds on a yearly basis, such as the Rockefeller Foundation and the Ford Foundation. Others are created by companies, like the ARCO Foundation and the AT&T Foundation. In addition to these more well-known examples, there are literally hundreds of large and small foundations in the U.S., as well as foundations in other countries.

A good source of information on foundations is The Foundation Center, the nation's largest information center devoted exclusively to foundation and corporate fundraising. The Foundation Center has two national libraries, in New York City and Washington, DC, which house documents and publications on foundations and corporations and their grants. Services include an online database of funding sources, accessible through many libraries (for a fee). Many of The Foundation Center's services are limited to members.

To contact them, write:
The Foundation Center
79 Fifth Avenue
New York, NY 10003-3050

A good resource for locating foundations is:
The Foundation Directory, compiled by The Foundation Center, is the standard reference work for information about private and community grantmaking foundations. Published annually, it lists four categories of foundations: independent, company-sponsored, operating, and community. Each entry in *The Foundation Directory* is complete with funding sources, purpose and activities, publications, and key personnel.

Foundations are constantly in the process of making decisions about where to spend their money. They need to know what societal issues they need to involve themselves with, which organizations are focused on these causes and what they're doing, and what the trends are. And because foundations are also under public scrutiny, they are also good communicators.

Many of the larger foundations publish annual reports and other literature that describe their programs and express their viewpoints. Some even publish formal reports from studies that evaluate the results of some of their programs. For example, if you are interested in the Amazon rain forest or some other aspect of ecology, or the homeless, or African famine relief, a foundation that has funded, and then evaluated, programs in this area might be an excellent source of information.

Locating and Contacting Foundations

Because many foundations are funded by families and companies, they tend to be located close to their founders. The best place to start is your telephone book, checking the Yellow Pages under the heading of "Foundation," as well as in community resource guides.

Also, check your library for a foundation directory, including:

Source Book Profiles, edited by Francine Jones, and published by The Foundation Center, has descriptions of foundations in the U.S., arranged alphabetically, by subject, and geographically.

The International Foundation Directory, edited by H. V. Hodson and published by Europa Publications, describes foundations around the world.

Societies have their own public relations/public information departments. You can call or write to request an annual report that lists the projects the foundation funds. It is also helpful to briefly describe your specific area of interest so that, if there is a match, you can obtain your information more quickly.

Museums and Galleries

For all of the large, well-known museums—the Smithsonian Institute in Washington, DC, Museum of Modern Art in

New York, Museum of Science and Industry in Chicago to name but a few—there are literally hundreds of specialized museums and galleries throughout the U.S. Many are community-oriented, featuring local history and artifacts, and the works of artists in the area. Others are focused on specific periods of history, styles of art, famous people, or the work of a specific artist. Chances are a museum or gallery exists, somewhere, with exactly what you are looking for. Museums can be organized around such diverse interests as computers and technology, Rodin, the Salem witchcraft trials, the movie industry, the Civil War, notorious criminals, Barnum and Bailey's Circus . . . the subjects are really almost endless.

Museums and galleries can provide you with the obvious—in-depth information that directly relates to your area of interest, and even a chance to experience the "look and feel" of a period of history, an artist, or an industry. Yet, museums and galleries can help you with the not-so-obvious aspects of your fact-finding, like background information. For example, if you're interested in a period of history, such as World War II, you might want to also consider the art that was created during that period, or the architecture, and also take a look at a local museum to better understand how it affected your own community. A computer museum might provide an opportunity to gain firsthand experience in a technology that holds your interest.

Museum curators are interested in the nuances of their specialization, the details that add flavor and character, and that grab the interest of patrons. These include pieces of trivia about a famous person or event, or a little known benefit of a technology. And they maintain the facts and figures that may be missing from books. Often this information is published in the museum's own publications, available through the museum bookstore, and usually through mail order. Some larger museums, like the Smithsonian, have bookstores with an extensive range of publications. Smaller museums will often offer publications focused on local history and other specialized concerns.

Museum curators will sometimes field questions, by telephone or through a letter. Some museums have developed a formalized process for answering research questions, and may even provide these services for a fee. Others will answer questions on an ad hoc basis. This will be discussed more in Chapter 8, "Dial an Expert."

Museums and galleries, both public and private, can be the missing link to finding that last detail to add spice and authenticity to your results.

Locating Museums and Galleries

As always, the best place to start in your search for museums and galleries is within your own community. If your topic is of local interest, a community resource guide or the Yellow Pages will list museums and galleries that you may want to visit.

If your topic is more specific, like an area of technology or a historical event, you may want to seek out a directory that describes museums and galleries at the national, and even international, level. Your local library should have access to directories such as:

The Official Museum Directory, published by the American Association of Museums with Macmillan Directory Division. It features profiles and statistics on museums around the U.S., and lists the official museum organizations in foreign countries as well. The directory, published annually, is arranged geographically and includes a subject index.

Contacting a Museum or Gallery

Because museums and galleries vary greatly in size and in the services they offer, each of them has its own organizational structure. If you have located an institution through a directory, make sure you take note of the name of the public information, public relations, or publications manager. Telephone inquiries, or letters, should be addressed to this person.

If you want more than a publications list and a brochure, going straight to the department may get you a step closer to what you want. Again, asking for a specific department, or preferably a person, will speed your communication. Don't be afraid to address a specific question to a museum curator—curators are in the business of asking questions themselves, and may have some valuable insights. And if they don't have an answer, they may be able to give you a referral.

Colleges and Universities

Colleges and universities are rich in resources, any of which can be mined in the process of your search for facts. Academic departments cover subjects from English to Computer Science to Marketing. Research institutes focus on anything from East Asian History to biomedicine. And don't forget historical and cultural archives, art galleries, various government- and corporate-funded research projects, as well as extensive libraries.

While your use of college and university facilities may be limited if you are not a student, institutions of higher learning are relatively accessible. Galleries generally have visiting hours for the public, as do archives, especially if they include displays. You may even be able to use the library, even if you can't borrow materials.

These are the obvious resources. Here are some other college and university resources to consider:

Bookstores
College bookstores are filled with obscure books, many of which may be assigned reading for a specific course. By browsing through the books in the academic area of your interest, you may find textbooks and books chosen for supplementary reading that you can't find anywhere else. Also take a look at the magazine section.

Academic Departments
College catalogs often include the names of the faculty members in each department, as well as a brief description of their areas of interest. You may find a match. For example, you may have an interest in marketing opportunities in the Eastern bloc nations, and discover the name of a member of the marketing department of a local school who has the same interest. From there, it's only a matter of contacting him or her (read about this in Chapter 8). Even if a faculty member doesn't have time to talk with you, he or she may have published papers in your area of interest, or know of a journal, or a colleague, that you might consult. It's always worth a try.

Research Projects
The bulk of federally funded research is located on the campuses of major universities, and many corporations also fund university research. While some of this research is secret, other projects, in areas such as science and medicine, result in research papers that are widely distributed, as well as published in academic journals. You can request copies of these papers, or a bibliography. While some research projects will be listed and described in the academic catalog, others will not be described in detail. Individual academic

departments are the best places to start. Also, most universities have an office that monitors research grants, and an information officer in that department may be able to send you a description of research projects in progress. You can also check with the public relations department.

University Presses
Many universities have their own presses that publish books frequently written by members of academia for an academic audience. Often these books are too specialized for mainstream publishers. Most university presses offer a catalog of books, with descriptions and ordering information.

Locating Colleges and Universities
The best advice for locating college and university resources is to start locally, and be prepared to go national. In many cases, your own local and state universities will have the information you need, particularly if it is a matter of obtaining library resources, or contacting a faculty member. And in the case of public institutions, these resources are more available to taxpayers in their own state.

Specialized institutes, archives, and government-sponsored research projects can be located anywhere, so be open to contacting colleges and universities in other states. However, these resources can also be national and international in scope.

Your local library most likely maintains a file of college catalogs for institutions of higher learning within your own state. By carefully going through the pages of each one, you'll gain a feel for the kinds of institutes and archives that might be of interest to you. If you are looking for investment opportunities in the movie industry, for example, a university with a graduate film department or an active film institute might be a good starting point for you. Also check specific academic departments. For example, if you are interested in Asian art and you come across a school with a large number of course offerings, and even a specialized major, in that area, this will be a helpful department to contact. By thumbing through the catalogs, you'll be surprised at the resources and new ideas that jump out at you.

For directories, or even catalogs, of schools across the country, you have a few media options: CD-ROM, online, and microfiche, depending on what your library has to offer. CD-ROM directories list colleges and universities, with addresses and other key information, but generally do not include the actual catalogs. CD-ROM directories include:

College Blue Book on CD-ROM, published by Macmillan Publishing Company. It contains the full text of five volumes of the *College Blue Book*, which is published in hardcover. The volumes include I: Narrative Descriptions; II: Tabular Data; III: Degrees Offered by College and Subjects; IV: Scholarships, Fellowships, Grants, and Loans; and V: Occupational Education. Volume III is especially useful for locating the names and addresses of colleges to contact.

Peterson's College Database, published by Peterson's Guides, Inc. This is a full text database containing profiles of all accredited, degree-granting colleges and universities in the U.S. and Canada.

Peterson's Gradline, published by Peterson's Guides, Inc. It profiles graduate and professional programs in 300 academic disciplines, which are offered by colleges and universities in the U.S. and Canada. It includes names and addresses of institutions, faculty and their research specialties, degree levels and specific concentrations, research facilities, financial aid, and more.

Both of the CD-ROM offerings by Peterson are also available online, through services such as DIALOG, BRS and Compuserve.

Your library may also include a collection of catalogs on microfiche, or a print collection of recent college catalogs. Keep in mind that this information may not be up to date and, in that case, you should also consider contacting the institutions themselves.

For the names of research institutes that serve your area of interest, also consider the use of directories, many of which your library may currently own. An example of major directories of this type include:

Research Centers Directory, edited by Karen Hill and published by Gale Research. The directory is a guide to over 12,000 university-related and other nonprofit research organizations established on a permanent basis. Organizations are arranged by subject areas, including agriculture, behavioral and social sciences, business and economics, education, government and public affairs, law, and physical and earth sciences, to name a few. It is updated annually.

Contacting Colleges and Universities

Being as specific as possible is the key to successfully contacting colleges and universities, both in terms of getting in the door, and getting your questions answered. As you go through catalogs, jot down names whenever you can. If it's an academic department you're interested in, and you're not sure of a specific faculty member, the department chair's name will be sufficient as a starting point. If it's an institute, go for the name of the public information or public relations manager. If it's a research project, start with the project director or principal investigator.

Calling or writing will probably be equally effective in dealing with academic institutions. Faculty members have limited office hours and are very difficult to reach. Your contacts at institutes, or on research projects, spend a large portion of every day in meetings. A carefully worded letter, with a follow-up phone call, would be your best approach. This process is further described in Chapter 8.

Think-Tanks

Think-tanks are organizations in which individuals with a specific area of interest—public policy, education, science— conduct research, write, and, as the name implies, think. Generally, think-tanks are funded through grants from corporations and the government. The Rand Institute in California is probably the most well known example of a think-tank. The Brookings Institute and the Heritage Institute, both public policy think-tanks in Washington, DC, are also well-known examples.

Like university-associated research institutes, individuals at think-tanks write extensively. Their output includes research reports, opinion or "white" papers, pamphlets, brochures, books, and newsletters. Many of these publications can be purchased, and a publications list with ordering information can generally be obtained by calling or writing.

The best way to locate a think-tank related to your area of interest is to refer to the *Research Centers Directory*, described above.

Some think-tanks will be more helpful than others, depending in part on their funding source, and how strongly they are mandated to provide information to the public. To make contact, start with the public information officer or public relations manager, by telephone or letter, and ask for information about any services the institution might offer. This will at least get you a brochure and a publications list, if one is available.

Advertisements

Don't underestimate the information you can glean from advertisements. They can provide you with instant referrals to other information sources. For example, a Civil War magazine (yes, there are even magazines about the Civil War) might include advertisements about specialized museums, private collections, and books. A business magazine will include advertisements about online databases, newsletters, and information-gathering services. Even nonprofit organizations use advertising as a means of getting the word out about their services and publications.

Specialized journals and magazines, even academic journals, are particularly good sources for advertisements that will help you to find that off-the-beaten-track publication or service that will give you the details you can't find in the standard information sources. It's also a good way to find out about unique bookstores, archives and university programs. And don't forget to comb through these journals' classifieds—they can be a real gold mine for finding individuals with specific interests and needs that may correspond with your own.

Rewards Off the Beaten Track

One of the watchwords for state-of-the-art fact-finding is flexibility. Information is everywhere. Virtually any organization or institution is a stronghold of facts and figures, much of which can be available to you, simply by asking for it. The key is to be open-minded, and consider all the options, even when it means going into previously uncharted territory. And then, all you need to do is ask.

Tricks Librarians Use

Subject Collections, compiled by Lee Ash and William G. Miller, and published by R. R. Bowker Company, is a guide to special book collections and subject emphases as reported by university, college, public, and special libraries and museums in the United States and Canada.

7

Unlocking
Business Secrets

The business world thrives on information, and the corresponding resources are amazingly plentiful. So when your
fact-finding includes business-related information, you literally have a wide range of resources at your fingertips. In
this chapter, the alternatives for locating business information are described.

Business Information Is Everywhere

As they make decisions, business people rely on facts from
a variety of sources. While they draw heavily on the obvious
examples of economic statistics, industrial research, and
company information, business people also use information

that is not normally associated with business. For example, history, psychology, and popular culture are considered foundations for decisions about product and company direction. Many companies employ their own research departments to collect information. While the people who work in these departments may actively conduct their own research, they generally look to outside sources for facts and figures. As a result, an entire industry has emerged to meet the information demands of business. Companies and research groups offer indexes, journals, reference books, online databases, newsletters . . . the whole gamut of state-of-the-art resources. With some diligent searching, many of these resources will be available to you.

You'll find the business information options to be so extensive that they're almost mind-boggling. However, they also vary widely in terms of quality, timeliness, and accessibility. Some publications go into more depth than others, and the ratio of primary to secondary sources varies greatly. Primary sources are based on original research, while publications using secondary sources are basically reporting on what has been published elsewhere. This kind of information is subject to the interpretation of the writer, and is otherwise "watered down," and possibly missing key facts from the original document. Business information also goes out of date quickly, so you need to be careful if you are using a source that was published a few years ago. In terms of accessibility, some publications are available to the public, while others, due to either cost or restrictions of potential readership, may or may not be as readily available to you.

Stay on Target

Because of these possible limitations, your goals will be better served if you keep your options open. Again, this goes back to your research plan. Take the time to carefully consider what you need to find—specific facts, dates, statistics, historical or company information, opinions—and carefully word your research questions. The more targeted you are, the less time you will waste. One resource, such as a CD-ROM index to journals, may be organized so that you can get to your needed reference quickly, while another resource, such as a reference book, may offer some, but not enough, of the information you need.

While the resources are plentiful, taking time to ask yourself "Who would collect this information?" will also help you to save time. With a variety of organizations—including trade associations, industry groups, and research firms just to name a few—that are collecting and disseminating business information, you'll get faster results by starting with the most likely source.

As always, planning ahead helps you as you undertake your work. Your library may have some business information resources, but not others, so be ready to consider as many alternatives as possible. If your questions are targeted, your librarian will have a much easier time in guiding you through this process.

Business Fact-Finding Options

Business information resources are unlimited both in terms of the kinds of information available as well as the medium in which they are published. Below are some of the options to consider, some guidelines for use, and a few examples. More in-depth examples are included later in this chapter.

Magazines

Business magazines offer news, opinions, and feature articles on industries and trends. These magazines include *Busi-*

ness Week, *Forbes*, and *Fortune*. While much of what appears in these magazines is valuable information, keep in mind that publishers, editors, and advertisers all have their own viewpoints and biases, which may be indirectly reflected in the editorial content. When gathering facts from an article in a business magazine, particularly if it reflects the opinions of the writer, it is advisable to check a second source to gain a more balanced perspective.

The major indexes to articles in business magazines are:

Reader's Guide to Periodical Literature
Business Periodicals Index
Business Index

Journals

Business journals are generally written for a more specialized audience, such as members of a specific profession, like accountants; executives or upper level managers across industries; or practitioners in specific industries, such as aerospace or petroleum. Some specialized journals are published professionally and, therefore, carry advertising. Others are subscriber supported, or published by a trade organization, and may or may not carry advertising. In any case, certain biases may be reflected.

Some of the better known business journals include:

Journal of Accountancy
American Economic Review
Journal of Management
Journal of Advertising Research

Based on the specialized nature of journals, they are especially good for up-to-date, highly specific information. For example, if you want to know about a subspecialty of a field like marketing, or you need an in-depth perspective on how current legislation will affect an area of industry, a journal article may well give you the details you need. Journals are also good references to other information—their classified ads are full of ideas for further study, as well as other potential information resources, including books and specialized libraries and publishers.

Your library may carry some of the major journals; you may want to start by simply looking through *Ulrich's* to obtain the names of these publications. It can be helpful simply to peruse a few of the journals that represent the field you are interested in to gain an idea of the level at which the journal articles are written, and to gather ideas for other resources to pursue. Indexes to business journals include:

ABI/Inform, an index to business and management journals, which also provides abstracts of the articles indexed. It is also available on CD-ROM and as an online database.

Business Periodicals Index, published by H. W. Wilson, which covers business and management journals in such diverse areas as accounting, advertising, banking, communications, economics, finance, industrial relations, insurance, marketing, and personnel. It is also available as a CD-ROM and an online database.

Predicasts F&S Index United States, which is indexed by U.S. company names, includes business, industrial, and financial periodicals.

Online Databases

The business community has been particularly aggressive in using online databases. Not only did business people recognize the potential of databases early on, they also had the requisite computer resources, as well as the funds, to get started. While costs have declined, and use of online services has spread to the nonprofit sector and to homes, the bulk of online databases are still business-oriented. Some of the online databases are available only to businesses while others are readily accessible by libraries.

Business databases offer a variety of information, including statistics, corporate profiles, and industry overviews. Some even have up-to-the-second information, and are connected to the wire services that newspapers and other news organizations access.

Here are some of the major business databases that may be available in your library.

Disclosure

Disclosure Incorporated offers a variety of online databases and other business information services, including:

Disclosure Database, which contains information and approximately 230 financial data items on more than 12,000 publicly owned companies in the United States, and whose securities are traded on the American Stock Exchange, New York Stock Exchange, NASDAQ, and over-the-counter. The information in this database comes from SEC filings, annual, 10K and 10Q reports, and related sources.

Disclosure/Spectrum Ownership, a database that offers detailed and summary stock ownership information on publicly held companies in the United States.

Disclosure offers databases in addition to those described above. Your library is the best place to access information from Disclosure, but you can also contact the company directly:

Disclosure Incorporated
5161 River Road
Bethesda, MD 20816
Telephone: (301) 951-1300

Predicasts

Predicasts is a widely used source of business information, with databases containing more than 11 million records, including abstracts, full-text records, forecasts and statistical series, news releases, newsletters, and annual reports. Information is available on subjects relating to business, technology, and industry. Online databases offered by Predicasts include:

PROMT (Predicasts Overview of Markets and Technology) is a multi-industry database for information on companies, products, applied technologies, and markets, containing abstracts and full-text articles. Sources include U.S. and international trade and business journals; U.S. and international daily newspapers and regional business publications; corporate news releases; highlights from corporate annual reports; U.S. and international investment analysts' reports and industry studies; research studies; trade and business newsletters; and government publications. PROMT is updated every business day.

MARS (Marketing and Advertising Reference Service) offers information on the advertising and marketing of consumer products and services, including advertising campaigns and budgets, new products, market size and share, marketing strategies, ad agency activities, consumer research, and regulation. Areas covered in the database include food and beverages, personal care products, travel, consumer electronics, health care, and others.

NPA/Plus (New Product Announcements/Plus) offers access to the full text of company news releases that describe a broad range of business events, including new products and technologies, license and sales agreements, new or expanded facilities, capital expenditures, contract awards, and corporate financial results.

PTS Newsletter Database contains the full text of more than 500 of the most important business and industry newsletters published in the United States, Europe, Latin America, the Middle East, and Asia. These newsletters are focused on industries and subjects such as biotechnology, medicine and health, manufacturing, financial services, international trade, and telecommunications.

In addition to those listed above, Predicasts also offers other business-related databases. You are most likely to access a Predicasts database through your library. However, you can also contact the company directly for further information:

Predicasts
Online Services Department
11001 Cedar Avenue
Cleveland, OH 44106
Telephone: (800) 321-6388
          (216) 795-3000

Other online databases include:

Corporate Affiliations, offered by National Register Publishing Company. It is a directory file containing business profiles and corporate linkage for 80,000 parent companies. It combines information from the print directories *Directory of Corporate Affiliations* and *International Directory of Corporate Affiliations*. Each record includes name, address, telephone number, business description, executive names, and corporate family hierarchy. *Corporate Affiliations* is available through DIALOG.

Management Contents, from Information Access Company. It indexes and abstracts articles in business and management periodicals, as well as some proceedings, study courses and books.

Company Intelligence, from Information Access Company. It is a daily-updated database that combines directory information and news on 150,000 U.S. companies, as well as noteworthy companies from around the world.

Business Dateline, from UMI/Data Courier. It contains the full text of articles from regional business publications from throughout the U.S. and Canada.

BusinessWire, from BusinessWire. It contains the unedited text of news release from news sources that include companies, public relations firms, government agencies, political organizations, colleges and universities, and research institutes. Most are business/financial in orientation.

These are only a sampling of online resources with business information. You can find out about others through the database collections index of the online service you are using, such as DIALOG or CompuServe. Other online resources are also discussed in this chapter, as well as in Chapter 14.

CD-ROM

As with online databases, the business community has also been a major user of CD-ROM-based indexes and databases. While much of the information available on CD-ROM is also offered in print, CD-ROM can streamline your search. Examples of major business-oriented CD-ROM offerings include:

Compact D/SEC (formerly *Compact Disclosure*), a CD-ROM database containing financial and management information on public companies with at least $5 million in assets and 500 shareholders in one class of stock. Information is obtained from SEC documents.

DIALOG OnDisc: Thomas Register, provided by Thomas Publishing Company and published by DIALOG Information Services. It is a CD-ROM version of the *Thomas Register of American Manufacturers*, and contains company descriptions and profiles. Product indexing provides access by product classification and trade names.

Dun's Million Dollar Disc, from Dun's Marketing Services. It is the CD-ROM equivalent of the *Million Dollar Directory* and *Reference Book of Corporate Managements*. It contains listings of top public and private companies with locations, telephone numbers, and other vital information.

ABI/INFORM, which provides full-text coverage of more than 250 publications. It spans business magazines and journals from a wide range of industries and subject areas.

InfoTrac Business Index, from Information Access Company. It covers popular business magazines, news magazines, and journals, and is a resource for locating information on both public and private companies.

MarketPlace Business, from MarketPlace Information Corporation. It is a database of marketing information focusing strictly on businesses, including name and address, telephone, key contacts, annual sales, and other information.

The Banker's Almanac, from SilverPlatter, contains directory information on banks that operate internationally, with names and addresses, contact names, ownership information, summary balance sheets, world and country rankings, and other facts.

Predicasts F&S Index Plus Text, from SilverPlatter, brings together trade and business journals, periodicals, and government publications to cover industries around the world. Most records feature full text or abstracts.

The American Business Phone Book, from American Business Information. It lists the telephone numbers of more than nine million businesses.

The CD-ROM offerings for the business community are expanding at a rapid pace and those listed above are only a sampling. More CD-ROM options are also discussed in Chapter 12.

Newsletters

Business newsletters are both a big business as well as a cottage industry. Some of the larger publishers, such as *American Banker—Bond Buyer*, offer newsletters on topics from Eastern Europe's trade opportunities to California's public finances. Smaller, more specialized newsletters, focused on topics such as investment hints, global agriculture, or pending federal legislation, are often edited and published by an individual or a small group of people. Because newsletters are highly focused on one niche of business, locating one in your area of interest may open up a new realm of facts and potential alternate sources of information.

A few words of caution about newsletters are in order. Because they're so specialized, they may not be available at your local library. They are generally rather expensive, and subscribing to one may be prohibitive. Also, some newsletters are sent to a restricted list of subscribers, based on their coverage. Any or all of these cautions may keep you from having access to a newsletter. But it can't hurt to try.

Names and addresses of newsletters can be located by consulting:

PTS Newsletter Database, from Predicasts, described previously under "Online Resources."

Newsletters in Print, published by Gale Research (discussed in Chapter 6). Because this reference book is organized by topic, it is easy to locate the newsletters relevant to your area of interest. It is also available online, through DIALOG.

Also check for the titles of newsletters in *Ulrich's*, described in Chapter 6.

The best way to contact a newsletter is to write a letter to the publisher, briefly describe your fact-finding need, and to request either a back issue that addresses your question, or a sample copy of the newsletter. While some will be more helpful than others, and all are most likely very busy, you may reach a publisher who understands that you are a future subscriber, and will be willing to help.

Newspapers

Newspapers are full of business information. This includes the business section of your local newspaper, national dailies such as the *New York Times*, and national business newspapers such as the *Wall Street Journal*. Also, many communities offer local business newspapers. *PROMT* and *Trade & Industry Index*, described previously, offer indexing to regional and local business newspapers. Look to newspapers for up-to-date news, feature articles that may describe an industry or market from an in-depth perspective, and editorials.

You may want to start with your local newspaper and check if your library has an index to back issues. Also check with national newspaper indexes, such as those available for the *New York Times*, *Washington Post*, and *Wall Street Journal*.

Some local business publications publish their own indexes. *DIALOG* offers an online database that serves as an index to local and regional business newspapers. For example, *Trade & Industry Index* indexes and abstracts over 100 local and regional business publications. *Business Dateline*, also available through *DIALOG*, contains the full text of articles from U.S. and Canadian regional business publications.

Reference Books, Directories and Indexes

An absolute plethora of reference books, directories, and indexes have been published for business and industry. Some are general in nature, and list facts and resources across industries. Others are more specific, and are organized, for example, by industry, geographical area, or profession.

Reference books and directories are full of interesting facts, background information, statistics and ideas with which to pursue your research. For example, if you are looking for statistics on a certain industry, such as banking, a reference book can offer exactly what you need in a single resource. Directories are a likely source of company names, key facts, and lists of executives. Depending on the scope of the reference book, it might also direct you to other, more in-depth resources.

Examples of reference books and directories for the business community include:

Million Dollar Directory, published by Dun's Marketing Services. It consists of a geographic cross-reference volume listing businesses by state and city, with full entries found in the alphabetical volumes. An industry cross reference is also available.

Standard & Poor's Register, which contains a volume listing corporations, another with directors and executives, and a third with miscellaneous directories.

The information in both the *Standard & Poor's Register* and *Million Dollar Directory* is brief, and provides the essentials without in-depth coverage.

Worldwide Franchise Directory, published by Gale Research, offers in-depth profiles on more than 2,000 franchise opportunities, including U.S. and Canadian companies, as well as those based in other countries.

Business Rankings Annual, compiled by the Business Library Staff of the Brooklyn Public Library, and also published by Gale Research. It lists companies, products, services, and activities, compiled from a variety of published sources, grouped by subject.

Reference Book of Corporate Managements, published annually by Dun's Marketing Services. It lists executives, with a brief description of their experience and education backgrounds, from companies across a wide spectrum of industries.

Small Business Sourcebook, edited by Charity Anne Dorgan and published by Gale Research (1989), is an annotated guide to live and print sources of information and assistance for 163 small businesses, with a detailed listing of similar sources for the small business community in general.

The Source Book of Franchise Opportunities, by Robert E. Bond and Christopher E. Bond, published by Dow Jones–Irwin (1991). It lists franchise opportunities by business categories that range from Automotive Products and Services to Travel.

Job Hunter's Sourcebook, edited by Michelle LeCompte and published by Gale Research (1991). It includes information on specific fields, as well as general sources of job-hunting information.

Marketing Information: A Professional Reference Guide, edited by Jac L. Goldstrucker and published by the College of Business Information at Georgia State University (1987). It contains names, addresses, and telephone numbers of associations, businesses, agencies, and other organizations in the marketing field, as well as an annotated bibliographic guide to marketing books, periodicals, and other publications.

Business Information Desk Reference, by Melvyn N. Freed and Virgil P. Diodato, published by Macmillan (1991). It is a handbook for locating specific business subject matter, and covers a range of business areas.

Other reference books are discussed later in this chapter, under "Business Issues and History."

Market Research Reports

Corporations rely heavily on market research. Much of this is primary research, designed and conducted by research firms to their clients' specifications. Primary research is generally proprietary, and not released outside of the company. Other market research is secondary, conducted by firms who in turn publish reports, which are then offered for sale to the companies that would benefit from it. Secondary research is usually targeted toward specific industry segments, such as insurance or manufacturing, or it can be focused on a specific topic, business issue, or profession. For example, research reports that outline future trends in an industry, or the concerns of a professional group, are secondary research.

If you are interested in statistical information concerning issues and future trends, chances are that a research report could be helpful. Unfortunately, locating the one you need will not be so easy. Begin by looking in your library. The business section may have a file of research reports. You can also contact, through a telephone call or letter, the firms that offer this research directly and explain the specific questions you are researching. After a major study is conducted, an abbreviated report is often compiled and distributed for marketing purposes, explaining the study and its key findings. You may be able to obtain one of these reports, and it may have enough of the information you need. You may also be able to obtain a copy of a report from a study that is now outdated.

A good online source for market research reports is:
Arthur D. Little/Online, offered by Arthur D. Little Decision Resources. It is derived from the publications of Arthur D. Little Decision Resources, plus the nonexclusive publications of Arthur D. Little, Inc., its divisions, and subsidiaries. The database includes industry forecasts, technology assessments, product and market overviews, public opinion surveys, and management commentaries. Industries and technologies covered include the chemical industry, health care, biotechnology, food processing, environmental issues, and the information processing and telecommunications industries. It is available through DIALOG.

To obtain the names of research reports and the firms that produce them, you can consult:

Conference Board Cumulative Index, a subject index to studies, pamphlets, and articles that have been published by the Conference Board, a business research firm. Areas covered include consumer research, corporate relations, economic and policy analysis, human resources, international business, and management.

The U.S. government also conducts business-related research through the various agencies that are described later in this chapter. One of the most useful of these surveys is the *U.S. Industrial Outlook*, published annually by the Department of Commerce. The *Outlook* includes the government's economic prospects for 350 key industries.

Business Organizations

A wide range of organizations exists to provide services to the business community. These include trade and industry associations, as discussed in Chapter 6. These groups offer newsletters and journals, as well as other reports, brochures, and books, many of which are available to the public.

Some other organizations to consider include:
United States Chamber of Commerce
1615 H Street NW
Washington, DC 20062
Telephone: (202) 659-6000

The United States Chamber of Commerce is the world's largest business federation and publishes *Nation's Business* and *The Business Advocate*.

United States Trademark Association
6 East 45th Street
New York, NY 10017
Telephone: (212) 986-5880

The United States Trademark Association is an international membership organization committed to promoting trademarks as essential to commerce through the world. It offers a variety of services and publications.

For a comprehensive list of business organizations, refer to *International Associations*, published by Gale Research.

Business Facts from the Government

The U.S. government, through a variety of agencies, both regulates and nurtures business. Almost all of these agencies offer a variety of publications, most of which are available through the U.S. Government Printing Office. These agencies are briefly described below.

Federal Trade Commission

The responsibility of the Federal Trade Commission (FTC) is to maintain American competitive enterprise. Activities revolve around public policy in areas such as trade, advertising, pricing, packaging and labeling, and credit disclosure. For a list of publications, referred to as *Federal Trade Commission—"Best Sellers,"* or other information, contact:

Federal Trade Commission
Public Reference Section
Washington, DC 20580
Telephone: (202) 326-2222

Securities and Exchange Commission

The Securities and Exchange Commission (SEC) is responsible for administering and enforcing federal securities laws and regulating the activities of publicly traded companies, to protect investors and ensure that securities markets are fair.

Various bulletins, pamphlets, and other publications are available by contacting:

Securities and Exchange Commission
Office of Public Information
450 Fifth Street NW
Washington, DC 20549
Telephone: (202) 272-2650

The SEC also operates a public reference room and a library, in Washington, DC. They may be contacted by writing to the above address or by calling (202) 272-7450 (Reference Room) or (202) 272-2618 (Library).

The SEC is also discussed later in this chapter, under "Facts from the SEC."

Small Business Administration

The Small Business Administration (SBA) was created to assist America's entrepreneurs in creating small businesses. SBA offices are located in major cities around the U.S., and are listed under "U.S. Government" in the telephone directory. A publications list can be obtained by contacting:

Small Business Administration
Publications Center
Post Office Box 30
Denver, CO 80201-0030

Department of Commerce

The Department of Commerce supports U.S. international trade, technological advancement, and economic growth through a variety of programs. Concerns of the Department of Commerce include unfair foreign competition, increased scientific and technological development, patents and trademarks, promotion of travel to the U.S. by foreigners, and minority business growth. Services include maintaining economic and social statistics, providing information, and conducting research.

The Department of Commerce offers an annual list of publications, which can be obtained through the U.S. Government Printing Office. The list includes reports and data on business and economic topics, along with a subject index. The department also publishes a weekly *Business Service Checklist*, announcing recent publications issued by the various operating units. Write or call:

Superintendent of Documents
U.S. Government Printing Office
Washington, DC 20402
Telephone: (202) 783-3238

The Public Affairs office, which includes information activities, can be contacted at (202) 377-3263. Also check your local telephone book for regional offices. The international business activities of the Department of Commerce are discussed in Chapter 10 under International Business.

Department of Labor

The Department of Labor is responsible for the welfare, including working conditions and employment opportunities, of the wage earners of the U.S. Areas of concern also include wages, pension rights, job training, collective bargaining, and economic trends.

The Department of Labor's Office of Information and Public Affairs offers a variety of brochures and other publications, listed on *Publications of the Department of Labor*. To obtain a copy of this publications list, along with ordering information, contact:

Office of Information and Public Affairs
Department of Labor
Room S-1032
200 Constitution Avenue NW
Washington, DC 20210
Telephone: (202) 523-7316

Additionally, the Bureau of Labor Statistics, which is an agency of the Department of Labor, offers periodicals that include *Monthly Labor Review, Consumer Price Index, Occupational Outlook Handbook*, and others. You can find out more about these publications by contacting:

Information Office
Bureau of Labor Statistics
441 G Street NW
Washington, DC 20212
Telephone: (202) 523-1221

The Department of Labor also maintains regional offices around the country. Check your local telephone book for the nearest office.

Federal Reserve System

The Federal Reserve System is the central bank of the United States, and is charged with making and administering policy regarding the nation's credit and monetary affairs. The Federal Reserve regulates and supervises banking functions that keep the banking industry reliable and stable. Publications include *The Federal Reserve System—Purposes and Functions*, and a series of pamphlets. The Federal Reserve Board may be contacted through:

Federal Reserve System
20th Street and Constitution Avenue NW
Room MP-510
Washington, DC 20551

Locating Business Information

While business information resources are readily available, you can save time, and increase the quality of the information you obtain, by using these strategies for targeted business fact-finding.

Finding and Using Business Statistics

Business people love statistics, and for better or worse, many business decisions are based on quantitative facts—averages,

averages, percentages, and standard deviations. Companies look at numbers to make product decisions; for example, numbers measure preferences for one product feature over another. They also look at lifestyle trends, what people's daily lives will be like over the next few years, and what products and services they will need to help them achieve their goals. Companies also look at economic trends—how disposable income will grow, for example. And companies also use statistics to track how they stand in relation to their competition, by measuring market share.

Statistics are quoted everywhere, particularly in the media. Sometimes these numbers are collected by the individual medium itself, as when, for example, a major newspaper conducts its own telephone survey, or uses a research service to conduct it for them. Other times, the reporter has obtained a research report, and is quoting it in the article. In either case, when statistics are quoted in an article, the writer will indicate the source of the statistics.

To find statistics used in the media, look in an index to a major local newspaper, or the *Wall Street Journal*. Go for articles that are directly related to your topic; look under subject headings, rather than under "statistics." When you encounter statistics in an article, keep the following points in mind:

1. Who provided the numbers? If the reporter is quoting from an outside source, such as a research institute, indicate this in your notes. You may want to examine the source directly to make your own decisions about the statistics, without the reporter's bias. Also, you may find other facts that were not included in the article.

2. How recent are the numbers? Avoid using old statistics by checking to see if the original source of the statistics has conducted further research. If you are referring to

an older publication, check in later issues for articles that may provide updated numbers.

While publications are a ready source for statistics, they are also the easy way out in many cases. The writer has already interpreted the statistics once, and is in turn feeding the interpretation to the reader. Again, this goes back to the concept of secondary source. The statistics have already been interpreted once, and by using the same data, you run the risk of adding yet another slant and misinterpreting the information. If you are using the statistics for your own purposes to gain general understanding of the topic in question, then gleaning them from an article may be enough. But if you are in turn reporting the statistics to someone else, it is definitely advisable to go to the original source. If the writer has mentioned the source without noting its location or any other identifying information, you can look it up in a directory of organizations or research institutes.

Other sources of business statistics exist, including reference books related to your specific area of interest, as well as indexes to sources of statistical information.

Consumer Product & Manufacturer Ratings, 1961–90, published by Gale Research, has extensive data and quality analyses on consumer products and the companies that manufacture them.

American Salaries and Wages Survey, published by Gale Research, includes a wide range of salary statistics.

Also remember that the Bureau of Labor Statistics and the Department of Commerce are excellent sources of business-related statistics. Check your library for *Statistical Abstracts.*

Organizations and associations are other sources of statistical information. Let's go back to that question from your research plan, discussed in Chapter 2: "Who would be interested in statistics on your topic?" If you want to know about trends in the diagnosis of mental illness, you might contact the American Psychological Association. For statistics on the elderly, you could look to the Gerontological Society, or the American Association of Retired People. For financial statistics, the American Banking Association might be the place to start. Organizations like this, as discussed in Chapter 6, are generally located in Washington. However, you might find a local chapter in your own city. Or, in the case of professional groups such as psychologists or bankers, you might also find independent groups established in your vicinity.

Statistics are everywhere. You are only limited by your willingness to do the digging that is sometimes necessary to find the source you need.

With Statistics, Consider the Source

One of the first things that students of statistics learn is how statistics can be used to "lie." Almost any set of numbers can be interpreted one way or another, depending on the bias of the researcher. For example, suppose you saw statistics on the per capita use of a product, such as milk or red meat, that showed a slight decline over the previous year. Based on those numbers alone, you might assume that milk shakes and hamburgers are on the way to extinction. However, this research might have been conducted with individuals in a certain age group only. Or, when compared to an even sharper decline the year before, the numbers indicate that the worst is over. You might even guess that consumption is on the upswing.

The key is to consider not only who is reporting the statistics, but also who is conducting the research. If the study above was conducted by an organization of vegetarians, you might want to consider other sources as well. Everybody has her or his own bias, even researchers, and your best protection is to either look for statistics from a variety of sources, or try and locate independent research organizations that are not funded by any particular industry groups.

Working with Company Information

When seeking financial information, you have a variety of options, depending on your specific needs. The facts you need to find a good investment opportunity will be different from those required for researching the history of the garment industry. You may want to focus your search on specific companies or on specific industries. You may be looking for balance sheet numbers, corporate history, industry outlooks, or some combination of these factors.

In any case, as always, start out with a clearly defined focus, and don't hesitate to explore all the alternatives, including those offered through CD-ROM and online databases.

Facts from the SEC

Company information can be gained from a variety of sources, particularly if the company is public, and listed on one of the stock exchanges. Public companies come under the jurisdiction of the Securities and Exchange Commission (SEC), an agency of the U.S. government. The SEC imposes strict guidelines on public companies regarding the dissemination of financial information. For example, companies have to issue press releases in advance of any "material" event, that is, events that might affect the price of the stock. Examples of material events include major contracts, quarterly or annual revenue figures, personnel changes at the executive level, and potential takeovers or consolidations, to name but a few. These press releases are public information, and are usually released by the company over wire services, such as BusinessWire (also available through online database), as described below.

The SEC also requires that public companies file quarterly and annual statements of earnings. The quarterly statement is referred to as the 10Q, and the annual statement is the 10K. These statements include not only earnings (or losses), but other pertinent data from the balance sheet as well.

Your local library may have a collection of 10Q and 10K statements, at least for companies in your regional area, though the collection may not necessarily be up to date. You can obtain the 10Q and 10K for a public company from the SEC. Copies of these statements are also available by making a direct contact, by telephone call or letter, to the company you are interested in.

Another source of SEC financial statements is available online:

SEC Online, offers a full-text database of financial reports filed by public corporations with the Securities and Exchange Commission. Companies on the New York, American, and National Association of Securities Dealers stock exchanges are included. SEC Online is offered through DIALOG, Dow Jones, LEXIS/NEXIS, and other online database services.

Keep in mind that, unless your interest in a specific company is purely financial, and you are adept at reading balance sheets, you will want to look for something more than SEC statements. A good place to start is the annual report.

Annual Reports

An annual report, if well-written, tells the story of a company. It identifies the company's values, what motivates its management, and how employees are treated. It also describes the company's products and services in a way that clarifies why customers purchase the company's offerings, and how, in turn, customers benefit. The annual report should also indicate what the company expects for the future.

Public companies are required by the SEC to issue an annual report. Some are slick, glossy publications with interviews and product information, and are illustrated with color photographs and designs. Others are basic, with only the essential information. The SEC has strict guidelines regarding the content of annual reports.

Annual reports are often available through your library, particularly for companies in your geographical area. You can also obtain an annual report directly from the company. To obtain the exact name of a company, with its address, telephone number, and other pertinent information, use a reference book such as *Million Dollar Directory* or *Standard & Poor's Register*, or an online database such as *Disclosure*, all discussed earlier in this chapter.

When requisitioning a company's annual report, address your written or telephone request to the Investor Relations Manager. You don't need a specific reason for requesting an annual report, and public companies are generally willing to comply. Private companies may or may not issue annual reports; they are not required to by law. For information on a private company, address your request to the public relations or marketing department. Most likely, a company brochure is available.

Stock Analyst Reports

Major brokerage firms have analysts on staff who conduct their own research, and write reports that are distributed to their own brokers, as well as to clients. Each analyst is generally focused on one or two industries, such as entertainment or technology, and issue reports that cover industry trends, as well as reports on specific companies. Though written from an investment perspective, these reports also explain products and technology in understandable terms, provide company history, and include a discussion of company strategies and prospects. Keep in mind that these reports can sometimes reflect the bias of the brokerage firm, particularly if that firm also has a financial interest in the company. Still, analyst reports can be invaluable in adding a new perspective to what a company or industry is saying about itself.

To obtain an analyst report, you can contact stockbrokers in your own community and ask if they have issued a report on the industry or company in which you are interested. If a local office can't help you, you can also ask for a contact in their headquarters, generally in New York, and contact that office. Your library may also have stock analyst reports on file.

Another source of analyst reports is *Zack's Investment Database of Wall Street Estimates*, available on *Compact D/SEC*, on CD-ROM.

Other Sources of Company Information

Below are some other possibilities of sources that you might tap for company information.

Indexes, similar to *Standard & Poor's*, providing basic company data along with, in some cases, more in-depth information include:

Moody's Manuals, published by Moody's Investors Services. These are standard information sources for the business world. The manuals are issued annually, with semiweekly supplements, and information for each company usually includes a brief history, comparative income tables, products, balance sheets and record of earnings, key personnel and directors, and subsidiaries. Titles include:

Moody's Bank and Finance Manual
Moody's Industrial Manual
Moody's Municipal and Government Manual
Moody's OTC Industrial Manual
Moody's Public Utilities Manual
Moody's Transportation Manual

Thomas Register of American Manufacturers and Thomas Register Catalog File, organized by product or service, and arranged alphabetically by company.

Directory of Corporate Affiliations, published by National Register Publishing Co. It lists major American parent companies, with business lines, number of employees, and other basic information. It is cross-referenced by subsidiary, and contains a geographic index as well.

America's Corporate Families, published by Dun's Marketing Services. It lists U.S. parent companies.

Directory of American Firms Operating in Foreign Countries, published by Uniworld Business Publications. This is a directory of American companies that control subsidiaries and affiliates in foreign countries. It is arranged by company, as well as by country.

Ward's Business Directory of U.S. Private and Public Companies 1992, offered by Gale Research, with organizational, financial, and ranking information on private and public companies in the U.S.

You may also want to contact the major stock exchanges for information about their activities and their member companies. Addresses include:

New York Stock Exchange
11 Wall Street
New York, NY 10005
Telephone: (212) 656-3000

American Stock Exchange
86 Trinity Place
New York, NY 10006
Telephone: (212) 306-1610

Midwest Stock Exchange
One Financial Place
440 South LaSalle Street
Chicago, IL 60605
Telephone: (312) 663-2222

Pacific Stock Exchange
301 Pine Street
San Francisco, CA 94104
Telephone: (415) 393-4000

Caution ...

Company information, like other kinds of information, is written from a specific point of view. What a company says about itself, for example, will differ from what an outside observer might say. And financial data, like statistics, can be presented in differing lights.

The facts are in the bottom line . . . usually. If you know what to look for, a balance sheet can tell you a lot about a company's past, present, and future. Business people refer to them with regularity as a snapshot of facts needed in the decision-making process. Balance sheets often have notes attached explaining the circumstances surrounding irregularities or apparent discrepancies. To ignore them is to miss the whole picture.

Also watch out for what you read in annual reports. Annual reports serve many purposes. While reporting the company's annual progress to current investors, they are also used to describe the company to potential investors and customers and the press. While most companies are not intentionally dishonest, they do need to present themselves in the best possible light. For example, what an annual report might refer to as a misstep might be called a disaster by an industry analyst.

It always pays to look at multiple viewpoints when assessing information about a company.

In Search of Industry Facts

In addition to brokerage firms and the companies themselves, a wide range of individuals and groups have something to say about business and industry. These potential sources for industry information include industry-watch groups, research companies, trade organizations, and newsletter publishers. While these resources have been discussed previously in this chapter, they play a particularly important role when facts about industry characteristics and trends are needed.

Market Research Reports, particularly when they are reporting secondary research, are often industry-focused. For example, a study of the automobile industry might include past and future trends in buying patterns, comparisons of the relative strengths of one company versus another, and expectations about the future. Firms that specialize in transportation would conduct a study like this, as would a trade association or industry organization. Your best bet would be to look to an industry organization first for such a report.

Specialized Newsletters focused on one industry, such as utilities, or even one specific niche of an industry, such as coal or nuclear power, often include articles that discuss industry directions. These newsletters, as mentioned previously, may discuss research conducted by other groups. While newsletters may be published by industry organizations and may also be available to outsiders, others are published by small, for-profit groups. As with research reports, try the organizations first. But a telephone or written request to a publisher of a private newsletter, with a specific question, may also yield results.

When using outside sources like these, be aware that biases are also inherent. Industry groups are charged with promoting their own industries, and most research will be interpreted in a positive light. While you're asking, "Who would be interested in collecting this information?" also ask, "Why would they want to collect it?" And when opinions and interpretations are obvious in what you are reading, and make sure you obtain alternate viewpoints.

Reference books are also a good source of information for facts and figures related to specific industries. For example, you may be looking for the results of surveys of specific industries; a list of stock markets in the U.S. and abroad; or the country's top growth companies. This may all be included in a business reference book. One to look for is:

The Business One Irwin Business and Investment Almanac, edited by Sumner N. Levine, and published annually by Business One Irwin. It includes sections such as Financial Statement Ratios by Industry, Taxes, Investing in

Real Estate, and U.S. Demographics. This is a good source for industry and company statistics, and includes a Business in Review chapter chronicling major business events of the year.

Check the shelves of your library and your local bookstore for others.

Business Issues and History

The business world is a favorite topic for writers, and myriad books focusing on the history of companies, business people, and industries are available, as are books about business issues, on topics such as management, marketing, and global competitiveness. Start with the business section of your local library.

For specific business chronologies of industries and companies, you may want to begin with a reference book in this area. You may be able to look up the specific industry, and go straight to the dates and events you are seeking. Some of the major business reference books include:

Everybody's Business: A Field Guide to the 400 Leading Companies in America, edited by Milton Moskowitz, Robert Levering, and Michael Katz, and published by Doubleday (1990). This is a nontechnical guide, with business facts about each company, supplemented by a behind-the-scenes look at the company, with fragments of history, short essays, and background facts.

Hoover's Handbook: Profiles of Over 500 Major Corporations, edited by Gary Hoover, Alta Campbell, and Patrick J. Spain, and published annually by The Reference Press. *Hoover's Handbook* features large one-page profiles of major organizations that include an overview of the company, a history, leading officers and their salaries, and ten years of selected financial and stock data, as well as other key facts.

Inside U.S. Business: A Concise Encyclopedia of Leading Industries, by Philip Mattera, published by Dow Jones–Irwin (1987). This book covers a broad range of key industries, and is organized by general categories that include communications, consumer goods and services, electronics, energy, finance, and heavy industry and transportation. Each chapter provides extensive background and historical information on the individual industry.

Louis Rukeyser's Business Almanac, edited by Louis Rukeyser, and published by Simon & Schuster (1988). It includes chapters on business issues, including the role of the government and stock markets, and profiles a wide range of industries with current and historical facts.

As always, trade association and business organizations are also a good resource for historical information. Many of these groups have their own libraries, and their reference librarian may be able to answer your question over the telephone or by letter, or send you the information you need.

You may also want to use your library's online catalog to check for books on an industry, or on a company's history. Check through newspaper indexes. In the case of specific events, you'll not only get dates and times, but the viewpoint of someone who went through it. There's no more chilling account of the stock market crash of the twenties than the one you can read in the *New York Times*.

Technology Access Program

The Small Business Administration (SBA) and the National Institute of Standards and Technology cooperatively operate the Technology Access Program (TAP) to encourage individuals from small businesses to log on to the many online services available through various sources. Online resources that can be accessed through this program include the major commercial services, as well as more limited-access, government-sponsored databases. TAP is not available in every state; contact your local SBA office, listed in your telephone directory under "Federal Government."

The Business Information Business Is Booming

Here's a motto to keep in mind when you are searching for business information: Don't take no for an answer. There is so much out there that often you can consult multiple resources for the same information. When your library doesn't have one resource in stock, check around in similar sources to find the same information in another form. Maintain a focus on the facts you need, yet be open to multiple sources and viewpoints.

Tricks Librarians Use

Business Information Sources, by Lorna M. Daniells, published by University of California Press (1985), is a comprehensive guide to sources of business information, including business and economic trends, statistical sources, industry statistics, companies, and organizations. It is extremely helpful in finding a potential source for almost any type of business information.

Encyclopedia of Business Information Sources, edited by James Way and published by Gale Research

---

(1991–92), is a bibliographic guide to approximately 20,000 sources covering about 1,000 business-related subjects. It includes almanacs and yearbooks, directories, online databases, research centers and institutes, and resources.

8

Dial an Expert

While much can be gained through reading, there's nothing like going directly to the source. And sometimes that's the only way to obtain the facts. Getting in contact with individuals who have a specific expertise is the subject of this chapter.

When It's Time to Call In an Expert

Pulling information from books and other printed information and from computer-based resources has many benefits. One benefit is that the material is more likely to be there when you want it, based on your schedule. However situations often arise where your best source is *the* source: the expert. While *expert* is a fairly nebulous term—who decides what an expert is?—think of experts as people who, by virtue of their title, professional responsibilities, or extensive interest, have gained a high level of knowledge in a specific subject area. Experts might include practicing professionals, college professors, museum curators . . . or someone who has been a hobbyist for twenty years. A conversation with an expert might be the one factor that helps you make your fact-finding a success.

Suppose you are researching a topic of current interest, such as national health insurance, and you want a quote from someone directly involved in the issue. Or you are looking for business opportunities in the former Soviet Union, and most of your sources of print information are too outdated to be helpful. An expert might be able to suggest possible markets and shed light on any legal concerns. If you are searching for an obscure fact, it's possible that nothing will be available in print.

Talking to an expert can add color to your fact-finding by providing that touch of real experience that turns your results into something more than a restatement of facts. Experts are also valuable as referral sources. Just when you think you have hit a brick wall, an individual in the field can point you toward other resources and help you to put your fact-finding back on track.

When should you consider calling an expert? Here are some guidelines to consider:

1. When the information you need is very timely, and not available through an online service.
2. When you are interested in a "moving target," such as a dynamic market or political situation, and you need a solid perspective on its past, present, and future.
3. When you need highly specific information that is more in-depth than what is available in printed publications.

4. When you need an opinion, or a "war story" to add authenticity to your results.
5. When you need information beyond what has been published, information that is available only from the person who originally conducted the research, or wrote the opinions.

Keep these guidelines in mind, but do not limit yourself to them. If you have ready access to an expert, make use of this resource as you plan your research strategy. This guidance can be invaluable in helping you to target your search and to avoid the potential blind alleys. But you shouldn't assume that you don't have access to an expert—with some brainstorming, you might realize that you have one in your own community.

Experts Are Everywhere

Depending on how obscure your area of interest is, you might find someone as close as a local telephone call away. For example, someone with technology or marketing expertise will be readily available in most cities. For a published authority on a more targeted or academic subject, such as the Civil War, Soviet politics, or the Art Deco era, you might have to look to a university, or a research institute in another city. But you might also find a hobbyist in your own city who has the exact knowledge you need to tap into, as well as the time and the willingness to share it.

The key is to begin your search for an expert in your own neighborhood and, as needed, gradually move outward. By starting locally, even if you don't find the person you need directly, you may obtain a referral. And the cost may be free.

Locating an Expert

As you seek out people who can offer you the benefit of their expertise, you will find some through a direct route—by seeing a name in a publication, for example, or having the good fortune to have someone pass along a name to contact. At other times, you will have little more to go on than the name of an organization or an institute, which will require some added work to locate the right person. Depending on your need, finding an expert will most likely be a combination of direct and indirect routes, with a few blind alleys along the way.

Below are some suggestions for locating people who might offer expert advice.

Magazine and Journal Articles

Newspapers, magazines, and journals are full of experts. They write some of the articles, and are often quoted in the articles they don't write. People who write, and are quoted, are displaying their names for anyone who wants to read them. That doesn't mean they have the time or interest to be contacted, but it doesn't necessarily imply that they mind, either. You won't know until you try.

Begin with local publications. Scan through your newspaper for articles that relate to your area of interest. Suppose you live near a Civil War battlefield, and your research focus is on medical care in the Civil War. Are there feature articles in a local publication that cover Civil War events, even if the articles are not specifically related to medical care? Who is the author or reporter? If it's a reporter, he or she may have written articles on your topic, and may be able to refer you to them, or provide the names of sources for you to contact. If the article is written by an expert in a related area, he or she may have colleagues who specialize in your interest. Follow up, and you've got a start at finding an expert in your own community. Depending on your topic, a local business journal and magazines and newspapers from larger cities in your state can also be helpful.

At the national level, the sky's the limit. Not only do you have many, many publications from which to choose, but also many national periodicals either publish their own indexes, or they are included in indexes like the *Reader's Guide*. The obvious place to begin is your local library. Start with the appropriate periodical indexes (your librarian can direct you to them), and locate specific articles that touch on your area of interest. You may already have done this during the process of gathering information. Who wrote the article? Who is quoted in it? Write down names and affiliations. Suppose your topic is international business. An article in a business magazine may include quotations from leading entrepreneurs, consultants on import/export issues, or executives from companies and institutes. Look in directories for the telephone numbers and addresses of each one. Now you have a list of experts.

Trade and national magazines will include articles and quotes from practitioners and academics, whereas articles in scholarly journals will be mostly contributed by university and college faculty. Don't worry too much about making distinctions between practitioners and academics—you'll find that their interests and expertise often cross, and when they don't, they can refer you to other experts.

Another option is the classified ads in specialized magazines. People often advertise their services, products, or expertise to potential clients and customers. Some of these people may want to sell their advice, while others are happy to share what they know. Make a list; you may want to contact a few of these people as you begin gathering your expert information.

At some point in time, you might also consider placing

your own classified ad, especially in a professional or academic journal or hobby magazine, indicating your fact-finding need. You might be surprised at the responses.

National Organizations

The potential information resources offered by national organizations—trade, industry, nonprofit, political—were described in Chapter 6: Searching Off the Beaten Track. Not only are organizations a great source of printed information, but they are filled with individuals, both on staff as well as among the membership, who have expertise in specialized areas. You may want to refer to Chapter 6 to review techniques for locating organizations.

You could locate experts in an organization from one of these sources:

1. A membership directory.
2. A staff directory, or a brochure that lists key staff members.
3. A copy of a newsletter or journal, which lists the editors and the names of authors.
4. A brochure about an upcoming annual meeting, listing the names of workshop presenters.

The best way to obtain a membership list is to contact the organization and ask for member services, or the public relations/public information office. If you clearly state your purpose, they may be willing to send you a copy of the directory. However, many organizations protect the identities of their members, to keep them from being contacted indiscriminately by advertisers and recruiters, and to protect themselves from losing a source of revenue—many organizations sell their directories to advertisers and mailing list companies. Each organization has a different policy.

If you can't obtain a membership directory, you might ask for the names of the board of directors. You could then contact them by letter, stating your purpose and asking for a referral to someone who could help.

Most organizations offer a brochure that describes their purpose and services, and this brochure generally includes both a list of staff members as well as the names of the board of directors. If the telephone contact person at the organization can't refer you to someone who can help, you could then choose names from the staff list, and make individual contacts, by telephone or by letter. Organizations are often willing to allow outsiders to attend their annual meetings, or at least to read about them. By requesting a brochure of the upcoming meeting, you might gain a whole list of potential names, particularly if the brochure includes a list of workshops and the individuals who will serve as presenters. Professional societies also publish the proceedings from their conferences, which may be available at a local academic library. The papers or abstracts included in these proceedings will include the name and affiliation of the author, with whom you can subsequently make contact.

Local Organizations

National organizations often have local chapters. In any case, a number of local groups, with or without national affiliation, are operating in your community. These groups can be as diverse as the national organizations—from social workers to Republicans to stamp collectors—with a local focus. As such, you may have a much better chance of locating someone who has the time and motivation to share information with you. In fact you might even arrange for a personal meeting.

You can obtain the names of local organizations through

the membership office of a national organization, through a local resource guide, or the Yellow Pages. Keep in mind that local organizations generally do not have their own offices—you will possibly need to contact the president at his or her place of work, so the initial contact may be brief. With a local group you have a greater chance of obtaining a membership list. You might also ask to attend a meeting, where you can conduct your own networking. Again, local organizations publish newsletters that may have a variety of names for you to contact, as well as an opportunity to place your own ad.

Universities

Universities, as discussed in Chapter 6, are good sources of expert opinion and advice. While it is possible to make the right contact and gain a wealth of information, this may not be the easiest source to tap into. Universities are notoriously understaffed, with a minimum of support people to refer your calls or letters to make sure you get an answer.

At times faculty members, as well as staff members of research institutes, do enjoy talking to people in the community they serve. By catching someone on the right day, you might gain all kinds of useful information with a brief request, or at least a referral to another person or publication. It doesn't hurt to try.

Corporations

Depending on the nature of the information you are gathering, the expert you need may be employed in a corporation. For example, if you were looking for information about how prescription drugs are tested and approved, you might check with a pharmaceutical company. For information on manufacturing processes, or industrial marketing, any number of companies would have people on staff who could offer advice. The key is to get to the right person.

Corporate people often belong to trade associations, at both the national and local levels. The best place to start is locally, assuming you want to find an expert at a local company. Talk to a representative from a trade association in your community, or obtain a membership directory. A few telephone calls should get you started.

To contact an expert at a corporation in another state, call or write to the public relations department of that company. As always, include a specific description of the information you are seeking, and why. The public relations office may be willing to forward your request to the specific department or individual who could help you. But don't expect miracles. People in corporations are busy, and their responsibilities do not include providing fact-finding assistance. You may have better luck by obtaining a referral through a national trade organization.

Nonprofit Organizations

While many nonprofit organizations are focused on social service and political activities, others help to build small businesses, encourage writers and artists, and foster medical research. As such, they employ experts such as scientists, physicians, artists, and business people in their specific subject areas. Each nonprofit organization has a board of directors, comprised of professionals, as well as a referral system of people whose expertise they draw upon from time to time. Foundations also fall into the nonprofit category.

To locate nonprofit organizations, follow the guidelines from Chapter 6. Your local library, with various directories of national and international organizations, as well as local resource guides, is the best place to start. Also check your Yellow Pages, under headings such as "Social Services," "Associations," and "Organizations," and the heading that corresponds to your topic. Many local groups have their own expert resources, both on staff and on-call, and you are likely to reach a local person much more easily.

Museums and Institutes

Don't forget museums and institutes, at the national, state, and local level. Museum curators often specialize in specific subject areas, such as the history of the automobile, medical research discoveries, technology, silent movies, the art of the Renaissance, etc. Regardless of your area of interest, someone at a museum somewhere could shed light on facts that you haven't been able to find in books and articles. Locating these people will also require a trip to the library to check in a directory. Getting in contact with a specific person at a national museum will not be an easy task, and will possibly require a combination of letters and multiple telephone calls. The guidelines for contacting experts, discussed later in this chapter, should make this process easier for you. Remember to focus in on your own state and community as much as possible.

Universities often have their own museums, which are staffed by curators and graduate students with expertise in specific areas, such as Egyptology and paleontology. State governments often sponsor museums, featuring collections focused on their state's history. While community museums may have limited resources, the curators in these facilities will be the most accessible. If they can't offer assistance in your specific area of interest, local curators often consult with experts within the community, and at the state and national level. You may be able to receive assistance with a referral.

Research institutes are also staffed by experts. As with museums, you will have your best luck by starting at the local level, and moving outward from there.

Reaching an Expert

Individuals who have more than run-of-the-mill knowledge about a topic are much in demand. Getting through to them, for even a five minute telephone conversation, can be a long and arduous process. To complicate matters, associations, organizations, magazines, universities, and nonprofit institutions all are understaffed to some extent, so even support staff, who you will need to rely on to gain access to the experts, will often be unable to spend much time forwarding messages and chasing experts down. Expect to make numerous attempts.

But don't be discouraged. You'll be surprised at how willingly people will talk when you take the time to work around their hectic schedules, and then present them with well-worded, concise questions.

To place yourself in the best possible position to obtain expert advice, here are some guidelines to help you through the process.

Start with the Telephone

Once you find who and where the experts are, the next step is to make contact. Your best bet, at least initially, is the telephone. When you send someone a letter, you are asking him or her to take the time to read it, formulate and possibly type the answer, and send it back to you. That is a lot to ask, in spite of the savings on long-distance costs. With a telephone call, you can wrap this all up in a fraction of the time, and also avoid the possibility that the person you are trying to reach will either leave the letter on a "get to it later" pile, or decide that it is too much bother and throw it away.

For most settings, the first stop in a telephone call is the receptionist's desk. If possible, always ask for the person you are trying to reach by name. If you don't have a name, ask for a department. Be very specific with the receptionist, because he or she has neither the time, nor the responsibility, in most cases, to help you to decipher your needs. If it's a magazine, ask for a specific section, such as "features" or "editorial." If it's a museum, ask for the department, such as "prehistoric America," or "modern art." If the potential, unnamed expert is at an association or organization, specify his or her department, or as a last resort, ask for a general department, such as "publications," or "public relations."

You can also be specific with your first contact by having prepared a statement like "I'm looking for someone to answer a question about _____" (Egyptian history, the stock market, etc.). Make sure you provide a concise description of what you are looking for to keep from being bounced around the organization.

By the way, avoid long-distance calls as much as possible. Organizations often have toll-free numbers. If you are not sure, call toll-free operator assistance at (800) 555-1212.

Once you get through to the department, the next step is to reach the expert. Again, if you know who you are asking for, request her or him by name. Otherwise restate your need concisely to the individual who answers the telephone. You will often have to leave a message. If you do, ask for the name of the person for whom you are leaving the message. That way if you haven't heard back in a day or two, you can try again, only by a more direct route. Busy people are not always very prompt about returning calls, especially if they don't know the caller, so be prepared to keep trying.

Obtaining Your Information

It is always advisable to constantly review your research plan. This way you stay abreast of what you have gained so far, and what you still need to locate. The individual you eventually talk with will not have a lot of time to spend with you, so the better your preparation, the more direct you can be.

Start with your purpose. Are you looking for business opportunities? Completing a family history? Doing a research paper? Briefly state your reasons for selecting the information first, to help the other person formulate responses that will better meet your needs. Then ask questions.

Start the conversation by talking in relatively general terms, briefly describing your interest and what gaps you are trying to fill. "I want to find out about . . ." will not be enough, unless you are merely looking for a referral to other resources. Instead, posing specific questions will help the expert to focus his or her attention, and make you seem much more credible as a fact-finder. As you talk, ask for an explanation when the person you are talking to uses terms and jargon that you don't understand.

Always take notes, even if it means holding the phone to your ear with your shoulder as you talk. Remember that the person you are talking to will not have time to wait as you copy every word. Get the gist of each answer, and then fill in the other words from memory after you hang up.

You may also want to consider setting up a state-of-the-art system to record telephone conversations. For a relatively low price—approximately fifty dollars—you can buy an inexpensive tape recorder and a mechanism that connects the telephone to the recorder. Keep in mind that if you are recording a conversation, you need to notify the other party before the conversation gets under way. Otherwise, recording the conversation is illegal. Also, carefully check to make sure that your recorder is set up correctly; you only have one chance at this person's valuable time.

Don't Take No for an Answer

Never underestimate the value of contacts. Even if you reach individuals who don't have expertise in your particular topic, you can still ask for a suggested next step. Alternatives could include:

- A colleague within the same organization
- A colleague with another institution
- Related publications

You may be asked what resources you have tried so far. If so, have your research plan ready so you can quickly go through the list.

When you do receive leads for further investigation, follow up on them quickly—don't procrastinate and lose your motivation. This process of making contacts and asking for further leads could continue for a few more cycles, and these delays could affect your deadline.

Don't Forget to Write!

A letter could end up on a desk unnoticed and even unopened. A letter could also open doors for you. The key is not only in the writing of the letter, but also in how it is addressed.

If you can't get through to anyone on the telephone, or if lack of funds prevents you from making a call, a letter may be the next logical step. Sometimes the person you need to reach would rather respond to a brief, clearly written letter, which can be answered during non-working hours, away from daily interruptions. Or your name on a letter may serve as a reminder that she or he needs to respond to the stack of messages that you have already left.

Avoid addressing a letter to an organization without first finding a contact name. In the process of having your call passed through receptionists and secretaries, you may have obtained the name of the person you need. You may even want to address your letter to a secretary or administrative assistant, and request that he or she pass it on to the appropriate person. If you still haven't been able to obtain the name of the person you need, use the same considerations in addressing your letter as you would if you were making a telephone call. Include a department name, if possible. Otherwise address it in care of public information, public relations, or publications.

Make sure your letter is specific. State the purpose of your fact-finding, and the importance of the information sought in helping you reach your goal. List your questions one after another, keeping them as specific and brief as possible. Request additional contact names, in case the person you are writing to can't help you. And include a telephone number, in case your contact decides to reach you personally. People appreciate having their names spelled correctly, so take the time to verify spelling as you ask for contact names.

Letters are often ignored. Be prepared to make an additional call within a week to follow up on a letter you have sent. It may also be necessary to send additional letters.

Go High Tech!

The old standbys, the telephone and letter, can be the quickest route to the people you need to contact. Still, high-tech resources can streamline the process. The facsimile machine, and a computer with modem, can be particularly helpful.

Fax It

Sending your letter over a facsimile machine can save time in your schedule by eliminating the amount of time it takes to mail a letter. You can then do your follow-up telephone call the next day, instead of the next week. Additionally, if you contact someone who wants written verification of your purpose, a quick fax can take care of this for you. Generally organizations are willing to give out their facsimile numbers, so don't hesitate to ask for it when you reach a receptionist or secretary.

Reach Experts Online

A computer modem, with access to an online service like CompuServe, or a computer network like Internet, can save you hours of telephone calls and frustration. Many online services have various kinds of forums and "discussion groups," which are ongoing and chaired by experts in the subject area. Examples of forum subjects include art, astronomy, international business, consumer electronics, photography, and political issues. Forum members respond to questions and discussion topics set forth by the forum leaders, and they also respond to messages from other members.

As an information-gatherer, you can make use of a forum to gain access to an individual with expertise in your area of interest simply by sending a message to a forum. The message should briefly state the purpose of your work, and either the questions you want answered or a brief description of your topic. For example, if you want to talk with an expert about the history of the American automobile, you could express this in a few words, and send it as a general message to members of an automobile forum, with instructions for reaching you (either online or by telephone).

Your library may subscribe to online services that include forums of one type or another. University libraries, for example, may be able to send a message over Internet. Or you may have a friend who subscribes to an online service, and who might help you out.

Be Skeptical!

Each person, in her or his own right, is an expert on something. And, each person has an opinion. Often, expert advice and personal opinion can be blurred, so that the person on the receiving end doesn't understand the difference.

Through the years, people with expertise in their respective fields have also learned what does and doesn't work for them. They have formed opinions that may differ widely from other experts in the same field. When an expert passes on information, he or she is most likely also passing on opinions that may not be expressed as such. Though opinions are interesting, and even valid, they are still opinions.

As you evaluate the people you talk with, here are some things to keep in mind:

1. Were they referred by a reliable source, e.g., a reliable person or printed source?
2. Are they recognized by their peers? For example, are they published in major journals or quoted in major periodicals?
3. Do they respond clearly and directly to your questions, rather than "beating around the bush"?
4. Do they appear to be up to date on recent developments in the field?
5. Are they currently involved in the field, on a hands-on basis, or are they currently serving in an administrative, or inactive, role?

If your fact-finding consists mainly of gathering information from experts, be sure to talk to more than one individual. That way, if you are getting an opinion from one, you are at least going on to obtain a second opinion.

Tricks Librarians Use

1. Over the years, librarians often maintain files of experts with whom they have come into contact over the years. Don't hesitate to ask a librarian to brainstorm with you and to check with colleagues, especially those with interests in your specific subject area.

2. The *National Trade and Professional Associations of the United States*, published annually by Columbia Books, lists hundreds of these groups, arranged alphabetically, and indexed geographically and by subject.

3. The *Official Museum Directory*, published by Macmillan (1992), includes information on 6,800 museums, including activities, publications, and the names of key personnel.

9

Going International

As communications make the world a much smaller place, chances are that your fact-finding will carry you around the world—even if you don't leave your desk. This chapter will give you the foundation for finding international information on any topic, from sources in the United States, and worldwide. This chapter also includes a section on international business.

The World Is Your Oyster

The term *global community*, though a bit of a cliché, is certainly becoming an appropriate description of the world. Telecommunications technology can assure a clear telephone link or computer connection to the farthest reaches of the earth. Multinational corporations link the economies, and the people, of countries around the world. With the end of the Cold War, our former enemies are eager to cooperate through economic, cultural, and scientific programs. Recently, the nations of the world convened in Brazil for an international summit on environmental issues. It is difficult to conceive of an issue—from economics to ecology to culture—that does *not* have a global impact.

As a fact-finder you will most likely be quite surprised at the sheer numbers of international resources that are available to you. These include foreign magazines, newspapers, online databases, and reference books, all of which are available here in the U.S. Foreign organizations are also willing to provide information and assistance. If your interests are broadly focused, on a continent or a foreign language, or a specific country, you'll easily find resources that are similarly focused. And if your interests are more narrow, on a topic or activity, such as culture, recreation, politics, or business, you'll also be able to choose from a number of options. While some of these resources will be more complete or up to date than others, you can rest assured that when your fact-finding has an international focus, you will have a variety of resources from which to choose, both high tech and traditional.

Under most circumstances, you can begin your international search in the United States.

Locating International Resources

As with finding any other kind of information, you can begin your search for international information in your local library. While you may not find everything you need, it's the best place to at least acclimate yourself to what is readily available, as well as obtain information on specific resources, including organizations, that you can contact for further research.

Your library is likely to have many of the resources described in this section. If not, keep in mind that within each category, such as directories, similar offerings are published by various publishing companies, so if your library doesn't have the one you asked for, it might have a similar one. Additionally, if your library doesn't have a CD-ROM version, for example, it may have it in print. Also remember that copies of specific pages from reference materials can often be obtained from cooperating libraries.

Reference Books

Numerous reference books with an international focus have been published. Some are broad in focus, with the basic characteristics—including population, industries, and culture—of every country in the world. Books also exist with a similar approach but with more in-depth information focused on one particular country. Others are organized around a specific subject, such as politics, culture, religion, or economics and discuss regions of the world in this context. Reference books that are basically guides to other information sources, and list the major organizations and agencies in each country, are also published.

Using reference books can be a good way to get started. They provide a one-source approach to a country, giving you a brief overview and even some suggested sources for further investigation, so that you begin with the big picture. Some suggested international reference sources include:

> *Handbook of the Nations*, published annually by Gale Research, with up-to-date economic and governmental data for nearly 250 nations and smaller political units.

The Europa World Yearbook, published annually by Europa Publications Limited, lists a wide range of international organizations for countries around the world.

The Statesman's Yearbook, published annually by St. Martin's Press, has statistical and historical information organized by country. International organizations are also included.

The World of Learning, published annually by Europa Publications Limited, lists academies, learned societies and research institutes, libraries and archives, museums, universities and colleges, and schools of art and music. It is organized by country.

CBD Research Ltd. also publishes *Directory of European Professional and Learned Societies*, *Directory of European Industrial and Trade Associations*, and *Directory of British Associations*.

There are a wide variety of reference books available, some more complete and up to date than others. Those listed above are only suggestions; if your library does not have these, others are likely to be available.

While international reference books are a good beginning, keep in mind that, generally, they are just a beginning. To obtain detailed information, you will need to look further.

Organizations in the U.S.

The U.S. is still a melting pot of different cultures. This is evidenced by the large numbers of organizations with an international focus in large and small cities across the U.S., particularly in areas where there are pockets of people with roots in the same foreign country. These groups not only arrange social activities, but also sponsor cultural events, offer opportunities for making business contacts, and publish newsletters. Some are large enough to maintain small museums and libraries with information about the home country, and assist those who wish to trace their ancestry. In larger cities, you are likely to find these groups to be numerous and well organized.

Individuals in these organizations will not only be knowledgeable—veritable experts on various aspects of their countries—but may also be able to refer you to other groups and individuals, both in the U.S. and in the country you are interested in. For example, a business entrepreneur seeking import and export opportunities could contact a local international social group to obtain advice about products and companies, as well as to make contact with a potential business partner.

To locate an international organization, start with your local community. Most likely, your public library will have a community resource guide that lists social and cultural organizations, with contact names. You can also call your chamber of commerce.

Most international groups are clusted around large cities. For example, New York City, Chicago, and Los Angeles, with their large ethnic populations, are the home of numerous groups, some with a specific focus such as politics, culture, or business. The most expedient means of locating one of these groups is to refer to a directory that includes international organizations. The most common of these directories, which are all described in previous chapters, include:

International Organizations, published by Gale Research
World Guide to Trade Organizations, published by K. G. Sauer
Encyclopedia of Associations, published by Gale Research

Washington, DC, is the center for groups that have a political focus, as well as those that serve as a central base for associated groups around the country. You will find the groups in Washington to be especially well organized and, because they are called upon to communicate with other groups and the federal government, they will also be willing to send information and answer questions. Washington-based international groups usually have a staff who can either answer questions over the telephone or respond to letters. Many also have publications lists. These groups will also be located in the *Encyclopedia of Associations* if they are headquartered in the United States.

Many philanthropic organizations have an international focus. For example, the Lion's Club is active in countries around the world, as is Junior Chamber International. These groups can refer you to groups in other countries who might be sources of information and provide a means of making further contacts in your country of interest. To contact these groups:

Junior Chamber International
400 University Drive
Post Office Box 140577
Coral Gables, FL 33114
(305) 446-7608

Lion's Club International
300 22nd Street
Oak Brook, IL 60521
(708) 571-5466

Washington, DC, is teeming with organizations and think-tanks with an international focus, including:
The Population Institute
110 Maryland Avenue NE
Washington, DC 20002
Telephone: (202) 544-3300

The Population Institute is a nonprofit, independent, grass-roots organization specializing in global population issues, and primarily concerned with bringing the world's population into balance with its resources and environment, creating population stability, and enhancing the quality of life. In addition to a newsletter and monograph series, the Population Institute also operates an online database system on population research.

International Publications

Though some digging may be required, a surprising number of international publications are available, both in the U.S. and abroad. These include newspapers, magazines, and newsletters.

Community newspapers that serve natives from other countries or regions—Korea, Poland, and South America, for example—are published in major cities. Some of these publications are written in the native language of the country, others are written in English, while still others are written in a combination of the two. You might locate other resources through these publications, and the names of individuals whom you could contact for further assistance. While you might start with your own community, you can locate local newspapers from other cities by consulting:

Gale Directory of Publications and Broadcast Media, published by Gale Research. It is an annual guide to publications and broadcasting stations, including newspapers, magazines, journals, radio stations, television, and cable stations. The scope of this directory is the United States, Puerto Rico, and Canada.

Newspapers from other countries can also be a good resource. Though many are written in a language other than English, most major cities of the world also offer an English-language newspaper. In addition to providing an insight into daily life in that country, you can also gain much by perusing advertisements. Most larger newspapers are also indexed. To obtain the names of international newspapers, consult *Benn's Media Directory* and *Ulrich's International*, both described in Chapter 4, as well as:

Willings Press Guide, published annually by Reed Information Services Ltd. This is a guide to the press of the United Kingdom, and to the principal publications of Europe, the Americas, Australia, Asia, Africa and the Middle East.

You might also refer to one of the newspapers published for a worldwide audience. These newspapers have an international focus, with selected news and commentary from countries worldwide. These include:

International Herald Tribune
850 Third Avenue
New York, NY 10022
(800) 572-7212
International Herald Tribune, published in association with the *New York Times* and the *Washington Post*, is an international newspaper published Monday to Saturday, covering areas that include business and finance, politics, economics, arts, science, food, fashion, books, and travel.

World Times
424 World Trade Center
Boston, MA 02210
World Times is an international affairs monthly publication that draws upon a worldwide network of journalists, policymakers, and business leaders who are native to the regions on which they comment and report.

International concerns are also the focus of newsletters. These are generally political in nature and published in Washington. Newsletters are published concerning topics such as Latin American human rights issues, communism in China and other countries, and changes in Eastern Europe. While these newsletters are available only to subscribers, often at a high price, you may be able to obtain a sample copy. And the editor may be willing to talk with you. To locate a newsletter, consult the *Directory of International Newsletters*, published by Gale Research.

Organizations in other countries are also a good source of information.

International Organizations

Think of all the various types of organizations in the United States. They include cultural organizations that focus on opera, dance, and music; social/political organizations that cover political action for problems such as homelessness, fund-raising, and research; and academic organizations, with areas of interest that vary from archaeology to medicine to zoology. The numbers and variations are limitless, as are their potential as sources of information. Imagine counterparts of these same organizations in each country of the world.

While there is not necessarily a one-to-one correlation between organizations in the U.S. and those in other countries, the fact remains that people with common interests and concerns banding together for socialization and information exchange is not solely an American phenomenon. And as a fact-finder, organizations can provide you with a wealth of valuable information. Many will correspond with individuals by letter (though for some, language may be a barrier), and almost all publish newsletters and offer other publications as well. It is also possible to make contacts with individuals with expertise in your area of interest, and obtain referrals to other people and organizations.

The starting place for locating international organizations is through a directory, one of which your local library is likely to have in its holdings. These include:

International Organizations, published by Gale Research
Yearbook of International Organizations, published by Reed Reference Publishing
Encyclopedia of Associations, published by Gale Research

Another organization you might want to consider getting into contact with is:

North Atlantic Treaty Organization (NATO)
Office of Information and the Press
1110 Brussels, Belgium

NATO's Office of Information and the Press will respond to questions and provide publications.

Contacting International Organizations

The best way to contact an international organization is with a letter. With time-zone differences, language differences, and the expense of long-distance calls, telephone contact is not practical.

Letters should be brief, clearly stating your purpose and the information you need. General requests, with phrases like "seeking information about . . ." may be misunderstood, as might slang and abbreviations. If you are trying to obtain a few facts, or have information sent out to you, you may want to express this as a list, keeping in mind that the person reading the letter has a first language other than English. Also, be as polite as possible.

When contacting organizations outside of the U.S., be prepared for long lead times. Mail can take weeks in both directions, and with language barriers, the actual response to your request can also require a few days, if not weeks. An alternative is to send a letter by facsimile, assuming you have the facsimile number of the organization you are contacting. It's always a good idea to send facsimiles when the telephone rates are lowest.

If you need a quick answer, international organizations may not be your best source. And you should also be prepared to receive information, and even a written response, expressed in a foreign language. You may want to call on a friend with language ability, or hire a translator.

Embassies and Consulates

Embassies and consulates of foreign countries are other potential sources of information, supplementing and adding to the information you may have obtained through books in your local library. Some embassies are set up to offer more than others.

In general, embassies are primarily interested in helping nationals from their own country who are currently living in the United States. Services are similar to those offered Americans by the State Department, and include advice on current political conditions and travel regulations. Embassies also offer visa information to U.S. residents who want to visit the embassy's home country. Embassies are headquartered in Washington, DC, and some countries also have branches in other major U.S. cities. Consulates, on the other hand, serve to represent the interests of a foreign country in the U.S., and are staffed by personnel with expertise in areas like business or culture. Consulates are usually located in major cities outside of Washington, DC.

Embassies and consulates may overlap in terms of the kinds of information services they offer. For example, one country might have a cultural or commercial officer on staff in its Washington embassy, while other countries only offer these services through consulates.

In either case, a representative of an embassy or consulate can answer specific questions about his or her respective country. For example, you could inquire as to the major religions practiced, or the major industries, assuming you had not obtained adequate information elsewhere. More likely, however, you might call an embassy for referrals to other resources, such as major companies, cultural organizations, educational institutions, publishing companies, political groups—the kinds of specific information that you are somewhat less likely to obtain from a reference book.

Some embassies will also send you information from their countries, such as pamphlets and brochures, and samples of newspapers and magazines. However, much of the information that embassies have to mail you (if any) concerns travel conditions, visa requirements, and guides to various travel destinations—the kinds of information you would receive from a tourist office. Most embassies are simply not set up to offer more than this.

You can find a listing of embassies, with addresses and telephone numbers, in a variety of international directories, reference books, and almanacs. Additionally, if you live near a major city, you may want to start there. Your library may also have a recent copy of the *Diplomatic List*, which is also available from the United States Government Printing Office (ask for Department of State Publication 7894). The *Diplomatic List* is a comprehensive listing of embassies and consulates and their various departments, and includes the names of ambassadors and other staff people.

Contacting Embassies and Consulates

Embassy employees are barraged with questions every day. And for many staff members, English is a second language. Reaching the correct person, and enlisting his or her assistance, will often require numerous telephone calls and letters.

When calling an embassy, be prepared to give the receptionist a brief idea of what you need. For example, "I would like to speak to someone about export opportunities" (or education, culture, tourism, etc.). This will help in directing you to the correct person. If the person you should speak with is not available, ask for the name of that person (and ask the receptionist to spell it). This will make subsequent telephone calls quicker.

When you do reach someone at an embassy who can help, you will achieve the greatest results through specific, carefully phrased questions, such as "Do you have a list of major universities in your country?" or "Can you refer me to organizations in your country that promote the arts?" or "Can you tell me how to find out about employment opportunities in your country?" Sometimes you will be asked to state your purpose, and your questions, in a letter. If this is requested, make sure you know who to send it to, and follow it up with a telephone call. Avoid addressing letters to an embassy without also indicating the name of the person who should receive it, or at least the department (culture, business, etc.). This will streamline the process of routing the letter once it reaches the embassy, and help prevent it from being ignored.

Politeness will take you far when contacting an embassy—they deal with demanding people all day long. If the person you talk to can't help, ask where else you may try. The staff may have suggestions regarding consulates, other people, or agencies, for you to call.

U.S. Embassies and Consulates in Other Countries

For additional assistance in international fact-finding, you may want to consider making contact with a U.S. embassy in your country of interest. Each U.S. embassy is staffed by foreign service officers with areas of responsibility that include cultural affairs, agriculture, and import–export, depending on the size of the embassy. Due to the time required in mailing letters to foreign countries, as well as the hectic schedules at U.S. embassies, your search could be a time-consuming process, and should be considered after other resources have been exhausted.

An exception to this advice is the area of international business, discussed later in this chapter. Most U.S. embassies in other countries are staffed by commercial officers who are empowered to assist U.S. businesses through arranging appointments with local business and government officials; providing counsel on local trade regulations, laws, and customs; identifying importers, buyers, agents, distributors, and joint venture partners for U.S. firms; and other business assistance.

To locate the names and addresses of U.S. embassies worldwide, refer to *Key Officers of Foreign Service Posts* (Department of State Publication 7877), available at your library or from the U.S. Government Printing Office.

What Your Library Might Have

Your library is the logical starting place in locating the resources discussed so far in this chapter. You might also discover that your library has compiled its own international resources. An enterprising librarian may have organized clipping files, arranged by country, with articles and brochures that have been collected and stored through the years. Also check for special databases, compiled by the library, or available through an online service. And don't forget to look for reference books and directories. Talk to a librarian about what your library has available in this area.

International Information from the U.S. Government

Many agencies and departments of the U.S. government are directly, and indirectly, concerned with issues of an international nature. These agencies and departments publish useful materials, as well as provide telephone consultation.

Department of State

Through the Bureau of Consular Affairs, the Department of State offers various passport, visa, and emergency services for U.S. citizens traveling abroad, and for foreign nationals in the United States. The Bureau also offers travel advisories through its Citizens Emergency Center. Travel advisories generally warn prospective tourists about physical dangers, unexpected arrests or detentions, serious health hazards, and other conditions. The Citizens Emergency Center can be reached in Washington, DC, at (202) 647-5225.

Two online services are also available for travel advisories. The Official Airlines Guide (OAG) provides the full text of travel advisories on many computer services. To obtain information on accessing travel advisories through the OAG Electronic Edition, call (800) 323-4000.

The Overseas Security Electronic Bulletin Board provides State Department travel advisories as a free service for American firms doing business overseas. This service is available by addressing: Executive Director, Overseas Security Advisory Council (DS/OSAC), Department of State, Washington, DC 20522-1003.

The Department of State also offers a variety of relevant publications. Check your library first, especially if you're in a hurry. In any case, Department of State publications can be obtained through the U.S. Government Printing Office at (202) 783-3238. These include:

Background Notes, which include brief, factual pamphlets describing the countries of the world. They contain the most current information on each country's people, culture, geography, history, government, economy, and political conditions.

Your Trip Abroad, with tips on obtaining a passport, considerations in preparing for the trip and traveling, other resources for travel, and customs information.

Tips for Americans Residing Abroad, with information on dual citizenship, including tax regulations, voting, and other overseas consular services, for U.S. citizens living abroad.

This is only a sampling of the rich international information resources available through the Department of State.

Department of Commerce

The International Trade Administration of the U.S. Department of Commerce provides services to U.S. businesses interested or involved in exporting. These include international trade shows and trade missions; matchmaker trade delegations; the foreign buyer program; catalog and video/catalog exhibitions; an agent/distributor service; an export contact list service; a trade opportunities program; foreign market research and trade statistics; comparison shopping service; world traders data reports; and individual counseling programs.

A variety of publications are also available. These include *Foreign Economic Trends*, a series presenting business and economic developments and the latest economic indicators for almost all countries, prepared by the U.S. Foreign Service. The Department of Commerce also publishes *Overseas Business Reports*, with current and detailed marketing information, trade outlooks, statistics, regulations, and marketing profiles. Single copies can be obtained by writing or calling the Department of Commerce.

The International Trade Administration has also established country "desks"—a Rumania desk, for example—each staffed by an individual who can answer trade-related questions and make referrals. The general telephone number for country desks is (202) 377-2000.

District offices of the Department of Commerce are located in most cities around the U.S.

International Business

The numbers of international information resources that fall under the category of international business are truly phenomenal. Books, publications, online databases . . . not only are the resources readily available, but in many cases, you can pick and choose among mediums. Thus, if your library doesn't have a specific reference book, it probably has one with a similar focus. And if your library's online resources are limited, alternatives, both in print and CD-ROM, are probably available.

Even if your interest is not international business, don't automatically assume that the business resources will not be relevant to your needs. When companies make decisions about doing business outside of the U.S., they take into account factors that include culture, religion, weather, education, political situation, and other noneconomic concerns. Much of this kind of information can be accessed in various forms. Also, art and culture are major import and export items. And another reason to make use of international business resources is that organizational and personal contacts made through business can lead to more referrals and expert advice.

As you consider the options among international business resources, keep an open mind. The alternatives are numerous, and they can lead you to the ends of the earth.

Business Organizations

Business organizations, both in the U.S. and abroad, offer publications, expert consultation, referrals, and online databases. You may want to start with those located in the U.S., and expand from there. Types of business organization include trade promotion organizations, chambers of commerce, and those that are organized around a specific industry.

Trade Promotion Organizations

Many countries have set up their own trade promotion organizations, based locally, but with offices in the major countries of the world, including the U.S. These organizations are usually located in New York, and some have offices in cities such as Los Angeles, Chicago, and Dallas. Examples of trade promotion organizations are JETRO (Japan External Trade Organization) and AUSTRADE (Australia Trade Organization). Trade organizations offer pamphlets and brochures, as well as information and referral services, by telephone or letter. Some also have libraries and online databases of companies and products. Generally, these services are provided at little or no cost.

You can locate a trade organization by contacting the embassy or consulate of the country you are interested in. Trade organizations may be staffed by commercial counselors and be directly associated with the embassy, while others are more loosely associated, and instead sponsored by the equivalent of the U.S. Department of Commerce. You will find that trade organizations are eager to answer questions regarding import/export regulations and issues, and may also be able to give you ideas about resources for related information-gathering.

As discussed previously, commercial counselors are also on staff at embassies and consulates. In the absence of a formal trade organization, these individuals can also answer business-related questions.

Chambers of Commerce

Chambers of commerce are the best way to make individual business contacts within a foreign country, as well as to find answers to related business questions. Amazingly, almost every major, and not so major, city in the world has a chamber of commerce. And even more amazing is that the services offered by each tend to be similar. Chambers of commerce basically offer opportunities for making business contacts through activities and services that promote the products and services of their members. These activities include meetings, special interest and industry workshops, and trade fairs. Most also maintain a library of business information resources, publish a newsletter with local business news, and offer telephone consultation services to members.

As a nonmember, you can also take advantage of chamber of commerce services. For example, you might place an ad in the newsletter, describing your interests, and ask members to respond. For a small fee, most chambers will send you a membership directory, which is full of potential local business experts with whom you can converse directly. Also, the individual in charge of a chamber of commerce library may be willing to correspond by letter. Most will correspond in English. Online services may be available to nonmembers, but connecting to these services will require making a long-distance international telephone call.

Locating chambers of commerce in other countries is relatively easy. Here is one possible source:

World Wide Chamber of Commerce Directory, published by Johnson Publishing Company, Inc. It lists chambers of commerce all over the world, with addresses and phone numbers, along with foreign embassies and consulates in the U.S., and U.S. embassies and consulates in foreign countries.

You may also want to contact:

U.S. Chamber of Commerce
1615 H Street NW
Washington, DC 20062
Telephone: (202) 659-6000

The U.S. Chamber of Commerce maintains information on chambers of commerce worldwide. Addresses for specific countries can be obtained by calling the office in Washington. Additionally, the U.S. Chamber of Commerce has extensive international business interests, and employs staff members who specialize in the business affairs of countries and regions of the world. Also, the U.S. Chamber sponsors business committees that promote understanding between the U.S. and other countries. Additional information can be obtained by calling or writing to the U.S. Chamber of Commerce in Washington, DC, or one of the regional offices in New York, Chicago (Oak Brook), Dallas, or San Francisco (Burlingame).

International Chamber of Commerce
38, Cours Albert 1
75008 Paris, France

Founded in 1919, the International Chamber of Commerce (ICC) comprises more than 7,500 companies and business associations in 110 countries. ICC National Committees in 59 countries in Europe, North and South America, the Middle East, Asia, and Africa represent ICC views to their governments, and alert the Paris headquarters to local business concerns. A main goal of the ICC is to support an open world economy in order to maximize trade and investment across borders. The ICC has an extensive publications list, with guides and corporate handbooks on topics ranging from banking practice and arbitration, to advertising, commercial terms, and telecommunications.

Industry-Specific Trade Organizations

Numerous business organizations exist to promote specific industries, such as petroleum or forestry, on either an international basis, or within a specific country. Others exist to promote entrepreneurs or small companies. The sky is the limit in terms of the sheer numbers of these organizations, and the focus of each. Contacting an organization in this category can be a good source of materials, expert advice, or referrals. Many offer newsletters and publications lists. Some also maintain online databases.

A good source for locating the names of these organizations is *World Guide to Trade Organizations*, published by

K. G. Sauer. *International Organizations*, offered by Gale Research, is another good source. Your library will have one of these books, or something similar.

You can also obtain the names of trade organizations through a representative from the chamber of commerce in your country of interest. Major trade organizations include:

World Assembly of Small and Medium Enterprises
27 Nehru Place
New Delhi 110 019
India
Telephone: 11 6414058
The World Assembly of Small and Medium Enterprises is an international, nongovernmental organization engaged in the promotion of small- and medium-size enterprises, with a focus on newly industrialized and developing nations.

International Association of Crafts
   and Small- and Medium-Sized Enterprises
Case Postale 1471
CH-1001 Lausanne
Switzerland
Telephone: 31 247785
The International Association of Crafts and Small- and Medium-Sized Enterprises has a worldwide membership, and promotes the interests of its members through a variety of activities and publications.

International Executive Service Corps
Eight Stamford Forum
Stamford, CT 06904
Telephone: (203) 967-6000
The International Executive Service Corps is a nonprofit organization that recruits retired, highly skilled U.S. executives and technical advisors to share their experience with

businesses in the developing nations and countries entering into free market economies. Services include American Business Linkage Enterprise, an in-depth information service designed to give overseas clients access to sources of technology and other business information.

Institute of International Bankers
299 Park Avenue, 38th Floor
New York, NY 10171
Telephone: (212) 421-1611

The Institute of International Bankers is an association of banking organizations operating in the United States with headquarters in more than 55 countries. Services include publications and a newsletter.

International Bureau of Fiscal Documentation
Post Office Box 20237
1000 HE Amsterdam
The Netherlands
Telephone: 20 626-7726

The International Bureau of Fiscal Documentation is an independent, nonprofit foundation engaged in impartial research in the field of comparative and international taxation law. The bureau publishes a wide range of specialized journals, looseleaf services, and books. It also operates an electronic database service.

International Federation of Stock Exchanges
22, boulevard de Courcelles
FR-75017 Paris, France
Telephone: 1 40547800

The International Federation of Stock Exchanges promotes closer collaboration between the member stock exchanges and associations of stock exchanges. Publications include an annual report, with a list of stock exchanges worldwide, and an annual compilation of economic statistics.

GATT—General Agreement on Tariffs
and Trade Information
Centre William Rappard
Rue de Lausanne 154
1211 Geneva 21, Switzerland
Telephone: 22 395111

The GATT Secretariat in Switzerland oversees the activities related to the General Agreement on Tariffs and Trade, a multilateral treaty to which 96 governments subscribe, together accounting for nearly 90 percent of world trade. Numerous publications and newsletters are available by writing to GATT.

International Advertising Association
342 Madison Avenue, Suite 2000
New York, NY 10017
Telephone: (212) 557-1133

The International Advertising Association is the only global tripartite organization that represents the common interests of advertisers, advertising, and the media. Members are from countries around the world. The association publishes a newsletter and booklets on international business topics.

International Organization for Standardization
1, rue de Varembe
Case Postale 56
CH-1211 Geneva 20, Switzerland
Telephone: 22 749-0111

The International Organization for Standardization (ISO) is a worldwide federation of national standards bodies with 89 members, each representing a member country. The goal of ISO is to promote the development of standardization and related activities in the world with a view to facilitating international exchange of goods and services. ISO publishes a newsletter and other publications.

The organizations listed above are only a sampling. Refer to a directory for organizations in your area of interest.

International Business Reference Books and Directories

The reference-book market is flooded with books that focus on international business. Similar to international reference books in general, the business books run the gamut from those that focus on doing business with a certain country, to those that are focused on a region of the world, the whole world, or a specific industry, like technology. Some offer detailed information, while others list resources that can be consulted for further information.

Your library will most likely have one or more reference books related to the area of international business you are interested in. These sources can be useful in helping you get started, by offering you a thumbnail sketch of your subject with ideas about where you can look next. Bear in mind that reference books are quickly outdated, which is the reason many of them are updated often. Statistics, even governments, can change quickly. Thus, it's a good idea to be mindful of when the reference book was published—don't quote economic statistics or population numbers from a book that is ten years old. Remember that even reference book writers have their own biases and sources of information. It's a good idea to look at more than one book, to make sure your view is as balanced and complete as possible. Reference books are basically secondary sources in that the writer has gleaned a variety of sources, summarized them, and then organized all the materials to make your job easier. Again, this is a nice way to get started, but also do your own fact-finding. Follow up on what you read with some investigation of your own, by contacting organizations, perusing online databases, and reading journal articles.

The following are samples of the many international business reference books in print:

The Arthur Anderson European Community Sourcebook, published by Triumph Books, Inc. It includes indepth profiles of countries in the European Community, as well as topics of special interest, including policy and regulations.

Dun & Bradstreet Principal International Businesses, published by Dun & Bradstreet. It lists leading companies around the world, along with their line of business, approximate sales, number of employees, and other key information.

Who Owns Whom: Continental Europe, also published by Dun & Bradstreet (London). It lists parent companies, arranged by European country, and provides a list of foreign parent companies.

Kompass Worldwide Business Directories, published by Reed Business Publishing Group. This is an extensive series of business directories, each of which is focused on a specific country. Each directory lists companies of international interest, with products and services cross-referenced to the companies that manufacture, distribute, or provide them.

Disclosure Worldscope, available from Disclosure, Inc., but also in business libraries. This is a series of industry studies, based on industries such as automotive, energy, chemical, and others. Financial performances of companies around the world are evaluated.

Exporters' Encyclopedia, published annually by Dun's Marketing Services. It compiles essential importing, exporting, travel, communications and research information for over 170 worldwide markets. Updates are issued twice per month.

Directory of Foreign Investment in the U.S., published by Gale Research (1991). It identifies more than 11,000 foreign-owned real estate properties and businesses.

While reference books and directories can be helpful, the international business situation changes daily. Don't forget to investigate high tech resources.

Computer Links and Databases

As the early adapters of online database technology, business people now have a wide range of online databases available to them, including databases oriented toward international business resources. Some of these services will be easier to access than others. Your library may subscribe to services that offer international business databases—check there first. However, you may also be able to connect to an online service from your own computer and modem at home, either directly or through services like CompuServe. This option will be described in Chapters 11 and 14.

Online databases will also be listed in:

Trade Directories of the World. It lists trade, industrial and professional directories, as well as data banks, and is organized into more than 800 categories. It is available from Croner Publications, 34 Jericho Turnpike, Jericho, New York 11753. Your library may also have a copy.

Online databases potentially available from your library include:

Disclosure/Worldscope, previously described under International Business Reference Books. It is also available through an online database and CD-ROM.

Also try *PTS Newsletter Database*, offered by Predicasts, which includes the full text of more than 500 business and industry newsletters published in the United States, Europe, Latin America, the Middle East, and Asia. The newsletters in the database are from a wide array of industries and subjects, including biotechnology, computers, manufacturing, international trade and telecommunications, as well as many others.

Major international online databases also include the following:

BUSINESS Datenbanken GmbH
Postrasse 42
D-6900 Heidelberg
Germany

BUSINESS is an online service for the storage, dissemination, and matching of business opportunities. It is a venture undertaken by leading European financial institutions and information specialists. Advertisements are listed for more than seventy countries and include company profiles, lists of products, and new developments. Users can run advertisements for goods and services wanted or offered, or express interest in licensing, representations, joint ventures, or mergers and acquisitions.

BUSINESS permits selection by product, sectors, institutions, countries, and types of business, offering quick access to up-to-date business contacts covering a comprehensive range of sectors and countries.

While your library may be able to help you contact BUSINESS, you can also write for information.

Infomat International Business
Predicasts
11001 Cedar Avenue
Cleveland, OH 44106
Telephone: (216) 795-3000

Infomat International Business, produced by Predicasts, offers extended coverage of business events and conditions in all areas of the world, with a focus on Europe. Infomat contains abstracts of more than 600 business newspapers and trade and business press resources, many of which are published in Europe, and provides access to publications covering market information, technology, industry trends, regulatory activities, and the economic environment.

While your library may have access to this database, you may also want to contact Predicasts directly.

Also try CD-ROM-based international business resources. This includes:

European Corporations CD, from SilverPlatter. It contains the full and unedited text of the annual reports and financial statements for 3,000 companies throughout Europe that are listed on the International Stock Exchange in London. It is updated monthly.

Other CD-ROM resources are described in Chapter 13.

Other International Resources

While you're hunting for international resources, don't forget to look around your own community and state. Here are some other options to consider:

Travel/Tourism Offices

Tourism is a big business for many foreign countries. To promote it, they issue pamphlets and brochures, showing travel destinations, describing folklore and history, and outlining tips for travelers. These materials can be helpful in gaining further insight into the culture of the country you're interested in, and in giving you a feel for what it might be like to visit.

You can obtain tourism information from numerous sources. Many countries operate their own tourism promotion offices, usually in major cities. In addition to providing you with literature, these offices are often staffed by natives of the country who can answer questions and possibly provide you with ideas about where you can call or write for nontourist information.

To locate tourism offices, check your telephone directory under the country name. If you don't see anything, you may be able to obtain it from a local travel agency. You can also call the country's embassy.

Universities

Universities, as discussed in Chapter 7, are excellent sources of information about foreign countries. Many universities have institutes for the study of foreign languages, culture, and politics, and they can be useful for the information they provide, as well as a means of obtaining other contacts.

Colleges and universities located in foreign countries can also provide information on diverse topics, from culture to business to history. Consult *World of Learning*, discussed in this chapter under "Reference Books," for a listing of these foreign institutions.

The United Nations

The United Nations is a wealth of information on a vast range of topics. The key is to reach the right agency—some are located at the headquarters in New York, while others are located in other countries. Go directly to the agency that best suits your needs, if you have the name and address. If not, the Public Inquiries Unit in New York City can help you get started. Contact them through a written inquiry or telephone call, and clearly, but briefly, outline your area of interest.

The United Nations
Public Inquiries Unit
Public Services Section
New York, NY 10017
Telephone: (212) 963-4475

The United Nations publishes many pamphlets, booklets and books. These include:

Statistical Yearbook, with data provided for 150 countries on such topics as population, labor, agriculture, industry, consumption, wages and prices, national accounts, finance, education, and mass communications. An index by country is included. Your library may have a copy—keep in mind that it runs two to three years behind.

UNESCO Statistical Yearbook, which concentrates on educational and cultural data. It contains statistics on population, illiteracy, educational attainment and fields of study, foreign students by country of origin, human and financial resources for research and development, generation of historical data, film production, book production, radio and television broadcasting, and cultural events.

Below are examples of some agencies and committees of the United Nations, and their services.

The World Health Organization (WHO) is an intergovernmental organization within the United Nations system. Its objective is the attainment by all peoples of the best possible level of health. WHO acts as the directing and coordinating authority on international health work and encourages technical cooperation with member states for health. Areas of intervention include tropical diseases, AIDS, mental health, and nutrition. WHO publishes books and journals on topics in public health, and also publishes *World Health*, a magazine, and *World Health Forum*, a quarterly journal. You can contact them at:

World Health Organization
Liaison Office with the United Nations
Two United Nations Plaza Building
Rooms 0956 to 0976
New York, NY 10017
(212) 963-6005

The International Women's Tribune Centre is a nonprofit, nongovernmental women's organization, which is part of a worldwide women's movement given impetus by the United Nations Decade for Women, from 1976 to 1985. The center provides a communications link for individuals and groups working on behalf of women in 160 countries in Latin America, Africa, Asia, the Caribbean, the South Pacific, and the Middle East. It is a source of information and technical assistance in the areas of appropriate technology, community economic development, and low-cost media. You can contact them at:

International Women's Tribune Center
777 United Nations Plaza
New York, NY 10017

The Center for Science and Technology for Development was created in 1979 to aid in strengthening and restructuring the science and technology decision-making capacity of developing countries. Activities include sponsorship of training and development programs, and information gathering and dissemination. Publications include a newsletter and a technology journal, which are available by contacting:

Center for Science and Technology for Development
One United Nations Plaza
New York, NY 10017

From an international business perspective, the United Nations has much to offer. The International Trade Centre (ITC) is the focal point in the United Nations systems for technical cooperation with developing countries in trade promotion. The center was created by the General Agreement on Tariffs and Trade, and is operated jointly by GATT and the United Nations. ITC works with developing countries to set up national trade promotion programs for expanding their exports and improving their import operations. ITC can be reached by writing:

International Trade Centre
Palais des Nations
54–56, rue de Montbrillant
CH-1211 Geneva 10, Switzerland

ITC technical cooperation projects are carried out in all developing areas and administered from ITC headquarters in Geneva. ITC headquarters also conducts research and development on trade promotion and international marketing. Several market information and statistical services operate from the Geneva office, including the import tabulation system, a series of tables on microfiche. Numerous market studies, handbooks, directories, bibliographies, and a magazine, *International Trade Forum*, are published by ITC.

Another agency of the United Nations is United Nations Conference on Trade and Development. Its role is to promote international trade, particularly that of developing countries, with a view to accelerating their economic development. Activities include research and policy analysis. Information about services and publications can be obtained by contacting:

United Nations Conference on Trade and Development
New York Office
United Nations
New York, NY 10017

In addition, many countries have established ministries to the United Nations, generally located in New York City at the U.N. Plaza. Ministries to the U.N. are created to coordinate the U.N.-related activities of their country, and usually have staff members that can answer general questions about their home country, offer referrals to other organizations, and may even publish a newsletter and other brochures. Ministries to the U.N. differ in terms of the services they offer to the general public. The ministry may simply refer you to the nearest consulate or embassy. Locate the addresses of ministries to the U.N. through international directories, from the Public Inquiry office of the U.N. (address listed above), or from an embassy of your country of interest.

Going International Begins at Home

The international information market is flooded with resources—not only printed publications, but also CD-ROM and online services. Before you start making telephone calls to embassies, or writing letters to the four corners of the world, check out what's available right in your own community, beginning with a visit to your local library.

Tricks Librarians Use

1. When using online or CD-ROM resources to locate information on international organizations or companies, use the browse mode as you perform an alphabetical search. This way, you are more likely to pick up any variations in spelling that you might otherwise miss.

---

2. *Countries Encyclopedia* from Bureau Development is a CD-ROM-based resource for international information, drawn from 106 *U.S. Army Country Handbooks*, the *CIA World Factbook*, and information provided by 151 embassies. *Countries Encyclopedia* covers more than 190 countries and territories in more than 5,000 pictures, illustrations, and tables. It can be searched by word, author, title, or subject, and is both Apple Macintosh and IBM compatible.

10

Information Brokers and Services

Somewhere along the way, during the process of information gathering, you may want to consider hiring the services of an information broker. The services offered by information brokers, and how to best make use of them, are described in Chapter 10.

Calling In an Information Broker

Information brokers prepare and conduct research for a fee, often from their own home offices. This field has grown rapidly in the past few decades, stimulated in part by the advent of online databases and then CD-ROM. When online services were first introduced they were command driven, and using them was considered too daunting for the average, occasional user. Also, home users did not have ready access to online services, nor did public libraries. Unless you worked in a corporate setting, or were a student, chances are you would not have been able to avail yourself of computerized media.

As a result, the role of information broker increased in importance, as individuals with their own research expertise and computer modems began offering their services. Because of the continually expanding need for information services in all areas of our society, the information broker has continued to provide an important service, even as online databases have become more readily available and affordable. Knowing what information resources are available and how to locate them can still be a challenge, particularly when time limitations are involved. Often, the information broker can step in and get the research process on track quickly.

Information brokers can continue the work that you have already done, by finding facts that still remain elusive, and by tapping into databases or other sources that are unavailable to you. They may simply step in to do some of the leg work when your own time is limited. Or, you can hire a broker to handle the whole fact-finding process, start to finish. Practitioners in this field generally have finely honed research skills, as well as their own tricks and contacts and, subsequently, have the potential of streamlining your efforts. What may take you weeks, especially if you only have limited computer-based resources at hand, can be accomplished by an information broker in a matter of hours.

But keep in mind that you will be paying for every one of those hours, as well as for any additional costs that come up in the search. Be informed and prudent as you make use of an information broker to ensure that the process is mutually rewarding for you and the person you hire.

Consider the following points before you begin contacting information brokers.

Why Use a Broker?

Unless your budget is unlimited, do some careful planning before you initiate contact with an information broker. This planning should begin with questioning why you are contacting a broker in the first place. Below are some of the reasons why you might initiate this process.

Your Time Is Limited

Time is usually an important element in research. You may be on a deadline, and need the facts to make a decision, or complete a project, by a certain date. If time is an issue, you may need someone to ferret out a few last details. Or you may not have time to contract the research at all.

The Information You Need Is Too Specialized

There is an inverse relationship between the narrowness of your subject and availability of information; the more specialized your need, the less likely the facts will be readily available. If you are searching for facts in a subject outside of your expertise, or for facts related to current events, you will have difficulty getting answers in a library. An information broker, particularly with a background in the specialization you need, can save a multitude of steps.

Your Own Resources Are Limited

If the town you live in has limited library facilities, and you don't have ready access to corporate or university resources, an information broker can be the deciding factor between a low- and high-tech search.

If you have one or more of these limitations, you may want to consider an information broker. But not necessarily. Before you decide, let's take a closer look at information brokers and the services performed by professionals in this field.

Who Are Information Brokers?

The term *Information Broker* can be used to refer to individuals who work out of their homes, as well as larger companies. The range of services that an individual can offer will generally be much more limited, and specialized, while a company might offer comprehensive research and consulting services, including many of those listed later in this chapter.

Often, information brokers who work on their own are former librarians, or individuals who are simply adept at locating information. Or they may also be individuals with extensive work experience in areas such as business intelligence, who limit their practices accordingly. These types of individuals might also work for a company that offers information services as well.

Generally, companies that offer information services are hired by other companies, on a retainer or project basis. As such, their costs will most likely be higher than those charged by someone working on their own. The section "Where to Find Information Brokers" will help you to decide on the kinds of information broker services that will be best suited to your needs.

What Information Brokers Do

Services offered range from conducting your research from start to finish for you, to jumping in at some point during the process, even if only for an hour. This includes helping you to define the questions you want to ask, identify the information you need, choose the most likely resources to access, ask the research question, analyze the information, and recommend decisions based on the information.

A market researcher with a computer software company might use an information broker to conduct research on its competition, including their strengths and weaknesses, major products, and strategic plans. On the other hand, parents whose child was diagnosed with a serious illness might hire a broker to obtain facts that will help them make treatment decisions. An individual looking for export opportunities might also use an information broker to help locate specialized markets.

Here are some of the services that you might obtain from an information broker:

Abstracting
Information analysis
Background for grant preparation
Cataloging documents or other materials
Specialized information
Locating directories
Editing
Identification of experts
Indexing information
Industry overviews
Competitive analysis
Literature searches, online or manual, on any topic
Market research
Online searching
Locating and purchasing reports
Locating training seminars
Subject updates
Verification of facts

These are only a few of the general kinds of services that you might expect from an information broker. However, as in any field, information brokers differ in practice from each other in terms of specialty subject areas as well as services performed.

Specialties

Information brokers come from a variety of backgrounds. Some are experts in a specific subject area, such as international business or biotechnology, for example. Individuals who specialize by subject often have professional experience in that area. Information brokers also specialize in terms of the types of services they offer, limiting themselves to literature searching, or fact verification, for example, while others offer a range of research services. Often, the latter type have a background in library science.

Tools

Most information brokers have a wide range of tools at hand, and for those tools that aren't immediately available, the brokers probably know how to quickly obtain them. Information brokers make extensive use of online databases, which is why many make their living from a personal computer and modem in their own homes. They also use CD-ROM and microform, call subject experts, and even, when necessary, make a trip to the local library. Individuals in this field are valuable not only because they can access various information resources but because they can make decisions about which medium is best, and because they also know what to do with the information.

Costs

Information brokers generally charge by the hour. And rates vary from one broker to another, depending on variables such as specialty, experience, and type of search required. An information broker with a specific subject specialization, such as medicine, will charge more than a generalist. One with years of experience will charge more than a less-experienced broker. And a search that requires the broker to seek out nontraditional resources, like rare books, will also increase the costs, because of the time involved. Additionally, if you hire an information broker from a company or firm, the fee will most likely be higher than for an independent broker, due to overhead and associated costs.

Also keep in mind that information brokers will also pass on additional costs to their clients. Online service connection charges, as well as charges for printouts and access to certain databases, will be billed to the client, usually at cost. Long distance telephone calls, which may be lengthy if experts are being consulted, will be itemized and charged. Other costs, such as mileage for any type of travel, may also be added, as well as Federal Express or delivery charges.

Where to Find Information Brokers

Information brokers are everywhere. Now that we are living in the information age, and the wonders of telecommunications have made it possible to access the information resources of the world from a home office, information brokers have the freedom to set up their practices in the geographical areas of their choice. Again, the decision of who to work with should be based on your need.

An information broker in your own town might be helpful in performing specific services, especially if your subject is not specialized. But you might also consider a broker with expertise in a specific topic or technique, who is based in another state.

As with any other information resource, it is advisable to begin in your own geographical area. Generalists are located throughout the country, and most likely advertise in the Yellow Pages under "Information Brokers," but also "Information Services and Bureaus," or "Information Bureaus." The costs of locally based information services may be lower, especially since you avoid initial lengthy long-distance conversations. Also, you'll probably feel more comfortable if you can meet with your broker personally.

In addition to the Yellow Pages, also check community resource guides for information broker services. You can also ask a librarian. He or she may know someone who has gone into the field.

Many information brokers belong to the Association of Independent Information Professionals, which sponsors professional events and publishes a newsletter. The association can also be a source for obtaining the names of professionals in the field. To contact them:

Association of Independent Information Professionals
c/o Cooper Heller Research
622 S. 42nd Street
Philadelphia, PA 19104

The Burwell Directory of Information Brokers, edited by Helen Burwell and published by Burwell Enterprises, Inc., lists information brokers by state, and includes a description of their services, the subjects they specialize in, and how they can be reached. It also includes indexes by city, company name, contact, subject, and service. Your library may have a copy of the *Burwell Directory*, or you can purchase a copy by contacting the publisher:

Burwell Enterprises, Inc.
3724 FM 1960 West, Suite 214
Houston, TX 77058
Telephone: (713) 537-9051

Burwell Enterprises also publishes a newsletter, *Information Broker*, for professionals in fee-based information services.

During your search for information brokers, it is a good idea to obtain the names of a few potential candidates. This way, you'll have options to draw upon as you decide which broker to work with.

Selecting the Information Broker

The best information broker for you to work with is the one who can offer the most expertise at the most reasonable cost, and who can deliver within your time frame. Selecting this person is not an easy process. However, by conducting a short interview with each candidate, you should be able to feel that you are making the right decision by choosing the candidate that best matches your needs.

If you have found one or more locally based information brokers, you may be able to meet with each of them in person to talk about your needs and their services. If not, a local telephone call may be sufficient for learning enough about the candidates to make your decision. And if, as discussed earlier, your subject is specialized, or the services you need are specific, you may have fewer choices in your locality.

As you talk to potential information brokers, some of the questions you might want to ask are outlined below.

1. What is your specialization?

Specialization will be an important consideration as you go about choosing an information broker. Keep in mind your original reason for seeking the services of a broker. If your information needs are highly specialized, you will want someone who has an expertise in that, or a related, area. Don't hire someone with a science background to help you look for art investment opportunities. By the same token, if you need someone who is basically a generalist, with a strong background in online searching, an understanding of your subject may be less important than the ability to access a wide range of databases.

2. What tools do you use?

When you make decisions about information brokers, you will want to ask specific questions about the kinds of tools they use. Make sure they can indeed extend your searching capabilities by using the major resources in your field, but also resources that are less available to you. For example, if you have already exhausted the shelves of your local library, you will want someone who can take your search to the next step. Also, in the absence of online and CD-ROM resources, make sure the potential information brokers are willing to do manual searches. Get specific names of resources; if they are ones you have already exhausted, the broker will just be wasting time. Ensure that the broker will be helping you by trying *new* sources.

3. What is the final product?

While you are hiring the information broker to conduct fact-finding for you, the actual end result, or the product, still needs to be spelled out clearly. Will it be a specific fact, or set of facts? A list of citations? Research reports or articles? The form of the final product should also be agreed upon in advance—summarized and bound as a report, or simply jotted on a sheet of paper and faxed to you. With an agreed-upon end product, you will be neither disappointed nor overwhelmed. The end product will also affect cost. You may be able to keep the costs lower by not requiring a polished final product, especially if you plan to take the results and incorporate them into some other form.

As added security, agree upon an intermediate checkpoint to verify that the research is going in the direction you want, and also to make sure that the information broker understands what you are communicating about your expectations.

4. Can *you* handle the job?

While there are no more guarantees in fact-finding than in any other profession, a reputable information broker will be honest about his or her confidence in locating the information you need. Ability to conduct your research may also require formal training and work experience, if not in a related field, certainly in library science or research. Asking for references, and checking them before you make a decision, is not a bad idea, either.

5. Is the research confidential?

If your fact-finding is for some reason confidential, as in the case of research about business competitors, or research for a new product you are developing, make sure your information broker understands, and is willing to comply with, this confidentiality. You may want to ask her or him to sign an agreement to this effect.

And ask yourself:

Is this a person I can work with?

Even if you never meet the information broker, you are placing a large amount of trust, not to mention money, in his or her hands. Make sure you work with someone who listens to what your needs are, and is willing to act as a consultant. In fact, a good information broker will ask you questions to draw out, and help you express, your specific need. If you don't feel comfortable expressing your needs, you may find yourself settling for less than you expected simply to avoid a confrontation. Under those conditions, neither of you can do your best work.

Many information brokers want to spend some time with you, either in person or over the telephone, to conduct a presearch interview. If you have agreed to work with the information broker, you will most likely be charged for this time. This is an important step in the process, and another positive sign that the broker is dedicated to performing a good, thorough search.

6. What are the costs?

Ask the information broker specific questions about the potential costs. The hourly rate is only the beginning. Online database searching, as discussed previously, includes connect charges, with additional charges for search requests, citations, abstracts, and full-text articles. When you ask for an estimate of the job, specify the inclusion of these additional costs. If the information broker is in another geographical area, you will most likely be charged for calls that she or he makes to you, as well as calls made in the process of completing your project. And if he or she has to "go to the information," travel costs will also be added. Discuss the question of payment if the broker is unable to provide you with the information you need.

Research can be expensive. The only way to avoid unpleasant surprises is to tackle the cost specifics with your information broker before the fact(s).

Agreeing on Cost

Don't undertake a relationship with an information broker until the two of you have agreed on cost. If your budget is open, and you are willing to pay whatever is necessary for the results, then this may not be a concern. Most likely, however, you will want to gain as clear a picture as possible before the work begins.

Ask the information broker for a written estimate of the number of hours required to complete the project, and for an estimate of the additional costs for the use of information media like online services. Keep in mind that, although most information is readily available, and even free of charge, the kinds of specialized facts you will be hiring an information broker to ferret out for you may not be so readily available. Therefore, these facts will probably not be free of charge either. Specialized facts, by virtue of the limited market for this information, are the most costly to obtain.

Once you have a clear picture, you have a few options for staying within your budget guidelines. One way is to ask the information broker to agree to a set fee for the completion of the project. This way, you know the final cost in advance. While this protects your budget, you run the risk of short-changing yourself in the end if the information broker en-counters unexpected problems in the process of conducting your search. At that point, you would have to renegotiate the agreement.

Another cost option is to place a cap on the number of hours the information broker spends on your project. For example, if the estimate is ten hours of time, you can indi-cate to the broker that this is your limit. Once ten hours have been accumulated, the two of you evaluate what has been accomplished so far, and then negotiate the next step. With these margins, you can control the costs while oversee-ing progress. Also, let the broker know if you are willing to have him or her adjust the search in terms of additional cost, or if you want to be notified first.

As you discuss costs with the information broker, don't hesitate to ask about alternatives. Can the online search be limited to lower cost services? Can you place a limit on the number of citations retrieved? Don't cut corners that will lower the quality of the final product—you can end up paying more further down the road if your cost consciousness results in information gaps.

Conducting the Search

While the information broker is handling the fact-finding process for you, keep in mind that you are ultimately responsible for the results. As the client, it is up to you to be specific about the research questions you want answered, and what you expect from the information broker.

At the onset of the relationship, you and the broker you choose should talk about exactly what facts you need and how the search will be conducted. A good information broker will help you to refine your research questions so that the required conclusions are clear. These questions will guide the pricing, and serve as a basis for you to evaluate the results. And, you should be forthcoming about any research you have conducted so far. Reinventing the wheel will delay your answers and result in higher costs.

The relationship with the information broker is a business relationship and, as such, the individual you hire is essentially working for you, at least for the duration of the project. While the broker is responsible for providing the designated data, you also have a responsibility in this process. Begin by communicating what you need, clearly and specifically, not only at the onset but periodically during the process.

A formal business relationship may entail signing a contract, or a letter of agreement. Most information brokers will probably request a letter of agreement. If so, watch for liability in regards to the accuracy of the information the broker actually delivers.

Depending on the depth of the search, you may want to

establish a formal agreement between you and the information broker that not only includes a final product, but deliverables along the way. For example, if you are asking for abstracts of articles for background information, followed by specific facts, with a report at the end, you may want to turn each of these into deliverables. Once a deliverable is completed, you and the information broker can then have a conversation in which you evaluate what has been completed thus far, and redefine the next step.

Keep in mind that though you are the "boss" in the relationship, information brokers have professional skills and resources from which you will gain. Be willing to listen to suggestions from the information broker, even if it means revising your original expectations about how the research should be conducted. The broker may also suggest alternate research questions to add depth to your fact-finding.

Information Brokers—Your Temporary Staff

Information brokers can leverage your efforts, just as your own research staff would. The key to gaining the most from this resource is communication. Take the time to convey exactly what you expect from the relationship, while also listening to the professional advice from the person you hire. And make sure you choose someone who understands your needs and has access to the required resources.

Assistance in writing this chapter was provided by Melena Henzel, an independent information broker in Ballston Spa, New York.

11

What You'll Need to Set Up at Home

As high tech research options become increasingly available, and prices decline dramatically, it is now feasible to set up your own home-based research center. The options for setting up your system are described in this chapter.

Why Do I Want My Own Resources?

As you've read in the preceding chapters, the computer is the key to state-of-the-art fact-finding. Virtually every aspect of our daily lives has been influenced by the computer and with this exposure has also come an increasing comfort level. Banking can be conducted through an automatic teller machine so that it is rarely necessary to step foot in a bank.

Train and airline tickets can be purchased through a machine with the use of a credit card. Through online services it is possible to conduct a variety of business activities, including purchasing products and making stock transactions. Most of us are getting savvy about how to use a computer in conducting our day-to-day business activities, and even prefer its convenience.

The benefits and ease of use of computer-based information has become more widely recognized, and not only are new resources being developed, but more and more print resources are being issued in computer-based format. In fact, many reference works are being released in both printed and CD-ROM or online versions, so you are not limited to one medium.

Your fact-finding is not necessarily constricted without the use of computer-based information, but having it available can certainly make for a streamlined search. Computer-based information is available in three major forms—CD-ROM, online databases, and through software. As you'll see in this chapter, although each form is fundamentally different, the overriding benefits are the same. With the computer, you have quicker access to information. Sitting in front of a terminal and "thumbing" through volumes of information with the click of a key on a keyboard is infinitely faster than manually thumbing through the same material in print.

And you can do more targeted searching—combining search criteria, such as subject, author, and date, so that you get to your destination in a more direct manner. Also, because it is much easier to make a change, or an addition, to a computer database, CD-ROM disc, or a software diskette, the computer-based information is often more up to date than the information in books.

With the rapid growth in the Information Age, prices are

declining to the point that many computer-based resources are now affordable for your own home-based system. Some of this information, and its purposes, are obvious. If you are a student, a researcher, or a business person, you are constantly relying on facts and figures as you make decisions and handle other responsibilities. The convenience of accessing information from your own desk, by plugging into a modem or popping in a CD-ROM, can revolutionize your workday, saving you the time and, in many cases, the money involved in seeking out traditional resources.

A wide range of consumer-oriented resources are also available. Through an online service you can check weather reports, read movie reviews, and make flight reservations. You can replace your shelf of encyclopedias with a CD-ROM version. And there's a software package that helps you plan a cross-country driving route. These types of resources will be described in more detail in Chapters 13, 14, and 15.

To take advantage of these resources in all areas of your life, consider setting up your own system. As you'll see, it is not only feasible, but it makes a lot of sense.

Your Home-Based Research Center

The possibilities for the kinds of research you can conduct from your own home are absolutely endless. Personal computers, modems, CD-ROM players . . . these are all readily available in computer stores and by mail-order. Most of the online databases can be accessed by ordering a subscription. CD-ROM discs and software can be bought in a computer software store or through mail order directly from the publisher. As an example, think about information brokers and their services as described in Chapter 12. While individuals in this profession have specific experience and expertise, the tools they use, for the most part, are available to anyone who wants to take the time to assemble a home-based research center.

There is one limit to the lengths that you can go in setting up your research center—the limit of your budget. Some of these resources can become very expensive, so much so that public libraries limit access to keep costs in line. Still, the home-based researcher can assemble a relatively sophisticated system, and access a wide range of computer-based information, and still stay within a budget.

The information presented in this chapter is based on an important premise—the assumption that you are not independently wealthy, and that cost is a concern. It is also assumed that you are conducting research as an adjunct to your other responsibilities, rather than as a career. Options for keeping costs to a minimum, while maximizing your fact-finding potential, will be described.

The Components of Your Research Center

While you will most likely want to add options and capabilities to your research center over time, you can get started with a minimal amount of equipment. A personal computer and modem will get you started in style. From there, you can add a CD-ROM player and continue building your storehouse of resources.

The Foundation: A Personal Computer

The foundation of your research center is a personal computer. While at first glance a personal computer seems like a straightforward consideration, you may find the options, features, and prices, to be confusing. With today's technology, you can purchase a personal computer with enough power to run the software packages that allow you to perform basic functions like word processing and spreadsheet, or you can get one with enough additional power to run the software required to manage the operations of a small factory. Yet even though these two examples are at the extremes of the power spectrum, either computer would fit on your desktop. And the price difference between them might be less than you would expect.

The best place to start in choosing the features you need in a personal computer is to make a list of the kinds of functions you want it to perform. These might include the obvious ones, like word processing and spreadsheet, as well as database management, communications, graphics, and desktop publishing. Once you have these functions in mind, you can make decisions about features like color, as well as the amount of storage and memory you will need. It will help even more to look at potential software packages, so you can be assured before the fact that you will have the required hardware features and power to do the kinds of things you want to do.

If you already own a personal computer, the good news is that much of the equipment needed to set up your own system can be added to even the most basic of systems. Even if your personal computer is a few years old, you can still most likely use it as foundation for your home research center. For example, your computer can be upgraded with a hard disk drive, if necessary, and modems can be added either externally or internally. And, with the declining prices of personal computers, you can upgrade your system for less money than you might expect.

If you do not currently own a personal computer, or if you want to take the plunge and buy a new system, the sky is the limit as to what you can purchase. However, remember that you are making a decision that you will live with for a few years. And the more thought-out your decision is, the more likely you will want to live with the system you buy.

While choosing a computer is an individual decision, what follows are some recommendations based on the kinds of capabilities you will need to conduct your own fact-finding expeditions from home.

What Manufacturer?

It never hurts to ask around when you're looking for a computer manufacturer to purchase from. If you notice some consistency among rave reviews, or horror stories, you'll know you're onto something. Keep in mind that everyone you talk to about personal computers will give you different advice about manufacturers, whether or not these "experts" actually own a computer themselves. Somewhere early on in your search, you're going to have to make a decision among the major manufacturers, including IBM, Apple and Compaq, and the IBM-clones (also referred to as IBM-compatibles).

IBM and Apple, the leaders in the market, often conjure up all kinds of images, from navy blue suits and wing tips to nuts and granola. There are many manufacturers out there, and you may not want, or need, to purchase systems from either of these companies. Yet the fact remains that each is associated with an established personal computer operating system—IBM and IBM-clones use the DOS operating system (actually MS/DOS from the Microsoft Corporation) while IBM's PS/2 line of computers make use of IBM's OS/2 operating system. And Apple has designed its own operating system for the Macintosh. These operating systems are upgraded periodically with new features and capabilities. Each new upgrade, also referred to as a release, is identified by a number. For example, DOS 5.0 refers to the fifth release of DOS.

Companies who develop personal computer software products, for word processing or spreadsheet, for example, will develop their products to be used with one of the major operating systems, or other different versions of the same product for each of the different operating systems. So while the options are many, IBM and Apple are associated with two different operating systems. If you buy an IBM PS/2 machine, and decide to use IBM's OS/2 operating system, a third operating system is also among your options. Before you can shop for your computer, you've got to make a decision about manufacturers.

IBM personal computers are known as high-quality, general-purpose business computers, with large numbers of software packages designed to work within this framework (IBM PCs and IBM-compatibles have also made major inroads into the home market). IBM machines originally used the DOS operating system, created by Microsoft Corporation. DOS quickly became an industry standard in the sense that it became an established favorite among both software developers and users. Though IBM recently introduced an additional operating system, OS/2, chances are that MS/DOS will continue to be the market leader for the foreseeable future, based on the strength of the numbers of applications available, as well as the popularity of Microsoft's Windows program. Windows is a software program that allows you to perform a wide range of functions by manipulating small symbols, or icons, with a mouse (a small device that allows you to move the cursor around on the computer screen, and initiate commands). Microsoft also periodically offers new releases of Windows with additional features.

Originally, Apple Computer's products were associated with the home market, as well as with schools. This has changed. Apple Computer's Macintosh is known for its graphical user interface—functions and capabilities that are identified by icons—and for its excellence as a desktop-publishing tool. The Macintosh is also gaining an increasingly strong presence in the business community, in both small and large corporations, for electronic mail, spreadsheet, database, and many other applications. Many of the software application packages originally associated with the IBM market have also been released for the Macintosh market.

With the wide range of software applications available for either MS/DOS-based or Macintosh machines, you can choose either computer and still have most of the capabilities of both machines. A consideration is price. IBM products have been generally considered to be higher priced than compatible machines; and, because Apple Computer has traditionally had no direct competitors, the Macintosh has been considered high priced as well. However, both companies have recently introduced lower-priced options.

You can also consider an IBM-compatible personal computer. These machines use Microsoft's MS/DOS operating system, and will run the same software as IBM machines, in many cases with a high performance level at a much lower cost. These computers can be purchased from computer stores or through mail order. Again, it helps to talk to other computer users as you make decisions about IBM compatibles, because quality and service differ among companies. However, don't hesitate to purchase an IBM compatible, either in a retail store or through the mail, if it meets your needs.

When making personal computer decisions, word of mouth is only one of your potential sources of information. You can also consult one of the many magazines that offer product comparisons. These are available at newsstands, and include: *PC World*, published by PC World Communications, Inc.; *PC Computing*, published by Ziff Communications Company; *Home Office Computing*, published by Scholastic.

An excellent book is also available: *Que's Computer Buyer's Guide*, edited by Joseph Desposito and published annually by Que Corporation. It offers extensive background information for the nontechnical reader, with listings and comparisons of products in categories that include personal computers, monitors, printers, and peripherals.

Processor Size

If you make the decision to go with an IBM or IBM-compatible personal computer, you are going to have to make a decision about microprocessor size. The microprocessor, also referred to as the central processing unit, is where the calculations take place that allow the personal computer to do its work. Based on a silicon chip, the microprocessor is the "brains" of the computer. IBM computers are based on microprocessors manufactured by Intel, while Apple uses microprocessors from Motorola. Think of the microprocessor in terms of the power and speed it offers you, with sizes ranging from the Intel Model 8088 to the Model 80486 (and even a 80586). This is one of those decisions you will want to make carefully, based on your needs today, as well as what you anticipate your needs to be in the near future.

Early IBM computers were based on the 8088 microprocessor and, for a few years, it was the fastest microprocessor available. It was great for spreadsheets, for example, and word processing. By the mid-1980s, Intel, who also manufactured the 8088, introduced the 80286, which was more powerful and much faster than the 8088. Many of the newer software packages, particularly in the graphics area, require at least a 286-based personal computer. In fact, very few computer companies even manufacture 8088-based machines anymore.

Yet you have even more choices. Personal computers based on a 80386 microprocessor provide you with even more speed. Additionally, with the 386 you can run multiple programs at one time (referred to as multitasking). For this reason, Microsoft's Windows program (a graphical user interface, which uses icons, for IBM and IBM compatible personal computers), as well as sophisticated applications such as computer-aided design and desktop publishing, are designed to work with 386-based machines.

Microprocessor size is one of those areas that everybody has an opinion about. However, consider how the microprocessors have evolved since 1981, and the fact that more and more software vendors are focusing their development efforts on 286 and, increasingly, 386-based machines and larger. Also consider that the prices of these more powerful machines have dropped to the point that they are lower in cost than the basic 8088 machine was a few years ago. Manufacturers of IBM compatibles have had a major impact on the personal computer industry by making 386 machines available at lower costs.

Most experts recommend the 386- or 386SX-based machine. It should run practically any application you need for the foreseeable future.

Hard Disk Drive and Memory Size

When making decisions about hard disk and memory size, it is important to understand the concepts of main memory and mass storage. Data that is stored in memory is being stored on chips. Generally, the program you are currently using (such as word processing) and the data you are currently using (such as the letter you are creating) are stored in main memory. Main memory is also referred to as random access memory (RAM). This data is quickly accessible, but if a power outage occurs, you will lose any information that has not been saved.

Mass storage refers to the use of media such as diskettes and a hard disk. Generally, much more data can be stored in mass storage than in main memory. Additionally, mass storage is more permanent than main memory; in the event of a power outage, stored data will still be reusable.

If you purchase a personal computer with a 286 or larger microprocessor, mass storage through a hard disk with at least 40 megabytes of storage will most likely be a standard feature. This is enough space to store a word processing program, a communications program for your modem, a spreadsheet, and a few games. As long as you do not allow word processing documents to pile up on your hard disk, 40 megabytes is enough mass storage space.

However, if you add programs, particularly applications such as graphics, computer-aided design and desktop publishing, you will find that the 40 megabyte hard disk quickly becomes overloaded. Again, it all comes down to planning for the future. If 80 or 100 megabytes is a consideration, and within your price range, it's a good idea to take the plunge. It won't cost you much money and will save you headaches, as well as future installation fees if you decide to upgrade later.

The same applies to main memory, or RAM. Most standard spreadsheet and word processing programs require only 640 kilobytes (1 megabyte equals 1000 kilobytes) of main memory, while sophisticated programs like Windows and graphics packages require two megabytes or more. Memory can always be added later, but again, you are better off staying a step ahead of your needs by having additional computer memory. Go for at least two megabytes—it won't cost much more.

Choosing a Monitor

When you purchase a computer system you may or may not have a choice of monitors. Pricing strategies are often such that the monitor is included as part of the package, though you may have additional options at incremental prices. A wide range of monitor types and styles exist on the market, from numerous manufacturers. However, for our purposes the essential question is monochrome or color. Monochrome implies "black and white," though most likely your monitor will show data in amber, on a black background. Color, on most monitors, is associated with VGA (Video Graphics Array), currently the most technically advanced color technology. While there is a monochrome version of VGA, which shows varying intensities of grey tones, VGA offers 16 colors.

As a fact-finder, the majority of the applications you use will not require color. While color can enhance word processing, database, and spreadsheet applications, you can perform these functions fine without it. Online database services generally do not make use of color, and many CD-ROM discs do not require a color monitor, even if it is an option. Also, many experts argue that if you spend hours in front of a monitor, an amber monitor may actually be easier on your eyes.

However, some exceptions to the rules do exist. If you are using a graphical user interface, such as Windows on an IBM or compatible, or if you have a Macintosh, color makes the icons more interesting to use. Also, purchasable software packages, like maps, are less effective without color, even with monochrome VGA.

Again, it all comes down to personal preference. However, if you're in a position to choose, you can often obtain a color monitor for an additional fee. Keep in mind that having color is more than a matter of simply hooking up a color monitor. You will also need a video adaptor, often referred to as a card, installed in your computer. If you are purchasing a complete personal system, the necessary card will most likely be installed by the manufacturer. Otherwise, you can purchase a card from a computer store, or through mail order, and easily install it in your computer.

Keyboard and Mouse

Like the monitor, the keyboard is likely to be a standard offering with the personal computer you choose; in most cases, it will be a 101-key keyboard. If you do a lot of word processing, the touch of the keyboard will also be important. Some people like a firm touch, while others don't. Try the keyboard, if possible, before making your purchase. In any case, keyboards are relatively inexpensive, and you can always buy a different one later.

The mouse is becoming a standard accessory with personal computers, fueled in part by the popularity of graphical user interfaces in which icons are used as symbols of functions and operations. The mouse is also used in graphics programs and, increasingly, with other applications like spreadsheet and word processing.

Some communications software programs, which assist you in going online with your modem, also make use of the mouse, especially if they have been developed for use with Microsoft Windows or the Macintosh. For example, the Crosstalk for Windows communications software package is designed so that the user can "click" on an icon to initiate dialing the number of an online service. This can save time and prevent potential errors from misdialing.

While a Macintosh always comes with a mouse, if possible supplement your IBM or compatible with one as well—you'll increase your usage over time.

Completing the Foundation

As the foundation for your home-based research center, your personal computer is your vehicle for accessing information, as well as storing and modifying it. With the multitudes of information available, don't be surprised if over time you find yourself using much more than you expected—adding games and interesting software packages, and subscribing to more services—until your PC is much more an integral part of your daily life.

Make sure you prepare for this eventuality by asking some very direct questions to the salespeople you deal with, concerning issues such as service, warranties, and expandabilty. The personal computer market is highly competitive, and many of the IBM compatible vendors, in particular, are competing not only on price but on service. And so are the market leaders.

Look for service contracts that include service lines that you can call free of charge, as well as service contracts. And if you are offered a service contract, make sure you understand whether you will have to bring your computer to a service center for repair, or if a repair person will come to your home. Make sure that the manufacturer also offers warranties on parts. And to ensure your system will grow with you, ask about expandability. Are there adequate ports to add a printer, modem, mouse, joy stick, CD-ROM player, and other peripherals that may be of interest further down the road? Can the memory or storage be upgraded?

Again, a good personal computer magazine will include

articles that compare the features and prices of different manufacturers' products. Pick up a copy of one of the many books that explain the basics of the personal computer, and describe terms such as *serial/parallel ports*, *expansion slots*, and *motherboard*. This way, you can make some decisions about what you need, and then ask informed questions as you evaluate the many products on the market.

Computer magazines periodically list and rate personal computer vendors by product quality and service. Check a magazine store, or a local library, for a recent copy.

Even with declining prices, a personal computer is an important investment. Make sure you take the time to choose one that will continue to meet your needs in the future, as those needs expand.

Choosing a Modem

With the growing availability of online database services, and the lowering cost of carriers, there's no reason why access to online services shouldn't be one of your fundamental capabilities. And to get started, all you need to do is attach a modem to your computer.

A modem connects you to the outside world, allowing you to receive (download), as well as send (upload), information. By connecting to an online bulletin board, for example, you can hold conversations with experts all over the country, simply by typing on your keyboard. And by accessing up-to-the-second data, such as stock quotes and company information, you can be as informed as if you were on Wall Street.

Modem technology has developed rapidly over the last few years and, though the options have increased, the basic technology remains the same. Still, you have some decisions to make.

External versus Modem Cards

In the early days of personal computers, the modem was a small box, referred to as an external modem, that connected to the computer through a port. While external modems are still available, you can also add an internal modem, which is inserted in a slot inside of your computer.

Internal modems do not necessarily have advantages over external modems, though there are a couple of points in favor of choosing an internal modem. First, because they reside inside your computer, they don't take up space on your desk. If space is a consideration, you would do well to go with an internal modem.

With an internal modem, you have the option of including facsimile capabilities as well. With a fax/modem board, your computer is set up to send and receive facsimile messages. You are spared the added expense of a facsimile machine, as well as the space and paper it would require. As messages are received you simply read them from your computer monitor, with the option to print, save, or delete.

Depending on the way your computer is set up, with a communications port for an external modem, or with an expansion slot to place the modem internally, installing your modem may be a relatively easy task. If you are not technically experienced, you may not want to install an internal modem on your own. Consultants are discussed later in this chapter.

Baud Rates

Baud rate, which counts the number of data bits per second, refers to the speed at which a modem can send or receive messages. The baud rate of the earlier modems went as low as 300, now baud rates of 9600 are fairly standard. Modems for home use tend to have baud rates of 1200, 2400, 4800, and 9600. As implied, a 2400-baud modem will be twice as fast as one that has a 1200-baud rate.

For using online services, a 2400- or 9600-baud rate will be adequate. Many services base their charges on baud rate, so you will pay higher online rates for a 9600 baud rate than the 2400 rate, but, of course, you will receive the information faster with the former. Check with the specific services you are interested in using as you make this decision, but if cost is a concern, you will definitely want to stay with a lower rate.

If you are communicating with other modem users, or with your job, baud rate becomes a more critical concern because to communicate with another modem, *both* modems must use the same baud rate. For example, if you have a friend in another state with a 2400 baud modem, you will need to have the same rate on your modem in order to communicate. Also, if you are installing a modem with a fax option, you will need to consider a 9600 baud rate because that is what most facsimile machines use. This will impact your online connect rates.

Also consider adding features like data compression and error correction. Data compression speeds up the sending process, while error correction ensures that the information you send is actually the same information that the other party receives. But again, these features add cost and the modem to which you send information must make use of these same features, or you will not be able to communicate.

Separate Telephone Line?

If you are using your modem often, particularly if you have also chosen the facsimile option, you may want to consider installing a separate telephone line. With one line, you obviously can't talk on the telephone and use your modem at the same time; if your use of the modem is relatively limited, this may not be a concern. However, you cannot have your facsimile receiving capabilities at the ready when your telephone line is not connected to your modem. This will limit your ability to receive facsimile messages, and will force your senders to call you first and wait while you switch lines. You can avoid this problem by purchasing a piece of equipment that senses the nature of incoming calls and automatically switches them to the facsimile or telephone. But this adds further costs and complexity.

While even with current rates a separate telephone line is not expensive, you will be charged for connect and installation charges. It's all a matter of weighing your overall modem usage against the inconvenience of one telephone line.

Purchasing Your Modem

As you approach purchasing your computer modem, begin by making a list of your own needs. What services will you use it to access? Will you be sending messages? Once you have determined your usage plans, follow up with a few calls to the services, and individuals, with whom you want to make contact. Make sure your modem will place you in a position to communicate as you choose.

The standard for personal computer modems was set years ago by Hayes Microcomputer Products. If you choose not to purchase a Hayes modem, make sure that it is Hayes compatible. Modems can be purchased through computer retail stores, as well as through mail-order.

Adding CD-ROM

CD-ROM technology is rapidly gaining in popularity, but it is still relatively new compared to other technology such as the personal computer and modem. As a result, prices are also comparatively high. However CD-ROM prices are beginning to decline, now that its usage has become more widespread.

With CD-ROM, the hardware decision is similar to that of modems. You can purchase an external CD-ROM drive or you can have one installed internally. External drives are connected to one of the ports on the back of the computer. Internal CD-ROM drives are installed in a manner similar to that of, and even adjacent to, the disk drive. Regardless of whether you choose an internal or external CD-ROM drive, you will also need to add a board to one of the expansion slots inside your computer. This may be easier in some computers than others, depending on the design of your PC.

In an internal drive, the CD-ROM disc is inserted into the appropriate slot, just as a standard diskette is. With an external drive, the design varies among products. You may need to open up the top of the device to insert the CD-ROM, or you may be able to slide it in the front. These are important considerations, depending on where the CD-ROM drive will be located—on, under, or next to your desk.

Keep in mind that while CD-ROM drives are designed to work with your personal computer and display data on your screen, they will also play music from the compact discs that you buy in a music store. Most CD-ROM drives include a jack that will accommodate earphones so that you can listen to the audio included on some CD-ROM discs, or to compact disc music while you do your other work.

Access time will differ among CD-ROM drives—some are faster than others. If time is a concern, you will want to consider a higher speed (and more expensive) model.

Finding a CD-ROM Drive

Make your CD-ROM decision based on your current personal computer hardware capabilities. Do you have an available port for an external drive? Do you have space for an internal drive? Do you have the expansion slot? PCs vary in terms of the number of expansion slots provided. You may be able to answer these questions for yourself, or by reading the manual that accompanied your computer. If you have access to a technical service line, through your vendor, you can also consult with them.

Choosing a Printer

If you don't have a printer attached to your personal computer, it is something you will most likely want to think about. For example, you usually have the option to print from an online database, though there may be an additional charge for doing so. This way, you have a copy for future reference. CD-ROM information can also be printed. And while researching, at some point you'll want to write up results with a word processor and print them out.

A dot-matrix printer is adequate for most of the work you will be doing at home. Most dot-matrix printers offer you the option of printing in a faster, yet lower print resolution, draft mode, as well as in a slower, high resolution letter-quality mode. The draft mode is fine for printing information from your screen to be referenced or edited later. And it's fast. In letter-quality mode, the print is hardly distinguishable from a typewriter. The prices of dot-matrix printers have declined to the point that they are less expensive than many word processing software packages.

Choosing Software

If you haven't explored the mind-boggling multitudes of exciting software packages available, a visit to a computer software retail store, or a look through a software catalog, will open up all kinds of possibilities. While the sky is the limit, let's start with some of the packages you will want to consider as you set up your research center.

Communications

If you have a modem, you have half of what you need to be able to communicate. The other half is the software to help you make the connection. Communications software, as mentioned earlier, is a vehicle for using your modem to send and receive data over telephone lines. Communication software has come a long way in the past few years. It now offers menus that walk you through the process of making a modem connection, and helps you to code the numbers you dial most frequently, allowing you to speed dial just as you would with a telephone.

A variety of communications packages are on the market. The two most common ones are PROCOMM PLUS and Crosstalk. These packages are easy to install and use. Whichever package you choose, make sure it is also compatible with the modem you have chosen, as well as with your computer's operating system.

If you are limiting your modem use to one or two online database services, you may not need to purchase a communications software package. For example, CompuServe provides users with software that provides a means of connecting to CompuServe. It can't be used to initiate communication with other services or individuals, but if you are only using CompuServe, that may not be of concern. You can always add a communications package at a later time, as your needs expand.

Word Processing

Even if you are not a proficient typist, and have no need to create formal reports and letters with your computer, a word processing package is always useful. For example, you may want to make lists, type notes, or put together an outline. While you can always write things out the old-fashioned way, a word-processing package enables you to whip your document into shape, and make it presentable, with a minimum of effort. And if you want to write letters to ask for advice or information, a professional looking letter can make the difference between getting a response or being ignored.

Database

Once you start making contacts with individuals and organizations, and accumulating various facts and figures, you may find that storing scraps of paper in file folders is not an efficient method of recordkeeping, and besides, it wastes space. A good database package provides you with a means of designing your own file system, with a file—database—for contact names and addresses, another for statistics, and yet another for historical facts. You can also create databases based on specific subjects—or for anything you want. With some initial planning, you can create a sophisticated system for storing and retrieving information so it is not only available at a glance, but easy to update.

Other Purchasable Software

As time goes on, you will want to add other software packages that will aid you in conducting research. These include maps, thesauri, and other disc-based data. This will all be discussed in Chapter 14. Also, consider software that will be useful in other areas of your life, including home finance, games, desktop publishing, and computer-aided design. Once you get rolling with a personal computer, there are no limits.

And if you need some help getting started, you can always call in an expert.

Finding a Consultant

You can gain a lot of valuable information about what products to buy from reading the many available computer magazines and buyer's guides. Also coworkers and computer-literate friends will have ideas, and especially experiences, that they can share with you. However, when it comes to setting up your system, and adding options like internal modems, you may not feel comfortable with your current knowledge level. And you may not trust your friends. Calling in an expert to act as a consultant is an option to consider.

The most obvious place to find a personal computer consultant is in the Yellow Pages, under "Computers." This is not necessarily the only place to look. You may only find large companies listed here, with services oriented to the business, rather than home, market. This may be overkill for what you need, as well as expensive. It can't hurt to call and check on rates, but you don't have to limit yourself to these companies.

The best place to find experts is through the companies that hire them, or the organizations to which they belong. For home computer specialists, the place to start is a local, retail computer store. Many of the individuals who work in computer retail stores, particularly on the repair side, either perform consulting on the side, or know people who do. Additionally, local computer societies often have consultants as members, or again, members will know of consultants. Ask the manager of your computer store for names of both individuals and societies, and go from there.

Before you hire a consultant, even for a minor task, make sure you are working with someone who is fully qualified. Don't hesitate to ask if he or she can supply you with references for the specific task you need performed.

Going Mail Order

A few years ago, buying computer equipment through the mail was almost an impossibility, especially for the home-user. Because of the rapid growth of small companies who manufacture high quality IBM-compatible personal computers, with high quality, superior service, and low prices, and offer them only through the mail, going this route is now a viable option. Even if you are not technically proficient, you should not hesitate to consider purchasing your system through a mail-order based company.

Before you make a decision about what company to purchase your system from, you need to cover a few bases. First, have a very clear picture of what you are looking for, including processor size, the amount of hard disk storage and memory you need, the number and size of the disk drives, and the kind of monitor you want. While the sales person you talk with will most likely be helpful, she or he is trained to take orders, not offer consultation.

Also, do your homework before you decide which companies to contact. Publications such as *PC Magazine* and *Home Office Computing* periodically rate the mail-order companies, as do the various buyer's guides. Check these ratings carefully to make sure you are doing business with a quality, well-rated company. Feel free to contact a few companies to find the best deals. However, don't make your decision on price alone. Ask about warranties, technical service lines, and on-site service. Protect yourself in advance from faulty equipment or set-up problems by making sure that the mail-order company will not only stand by its products, but also offer you assistance without additional cost.

Ten Tips for Buying Direct

The May 1992 issue of *PC World*, a major personal computer magazine, listed the following guidelines for buying personal computers and other equipment through mail-order vendors.

1. Buy from companies with a proven track record.
   Whenever possible, go with companies from whom friends and associates have purchased goods.
2. Investigate unfamiliar companies.
   Call the local Better Business Bureau and the regional U.S. postal inspector's office to determine whether a company has a history of complaints.
3. Evaluate products at your local computer store.
   Do this before you even place an order.
4. Investigate service options and return policies.
   Look for a 30-day money-back guarantee and after-sale support.
5. Be wary of incredible deals.
   If prices seem too good to be true, they generally are.
6. Keep detailed records.
   Note whom you spoke with (first and last name), as well as promises made about price and delivery.
7. Confirm phone orders.
   Do this with a letter or a fax to your salesperson.
8. Don't send checks.
   Credit card and COD purchases offer protection against nondelivery of goods.
9. Don't assume the validity of advertisements.
   Even the most reputable of magazines, newspapers, and other periodicals do not routinely verify the claims made in advertisements.
10. Know your rights and exercise them.
    If a company fails to ship your order on time, you can cancel the order and obtain a full refund.

(Excerpted from "Consumer Watch: SCAM!" by Roberta Furger and Mike Hogan, *PC World*, May 1992, page 153. Reprinted with permission.)

"Ten Tips for Buying Direct" reprinted with permission of *PC World*, excerpted from "Consumer Watch: SCAM!" by Roberta Furger and Mike Hogan, May 1992.

Where to Locate
Your Home Research Center

When thinking about where to locate your home research center there are a couple of major considerations to keep in mind—your comfort, and the security of your equipment. If you have a spare bedroom that can be converted to a research center, you are already ahead. However, if your options are less flexible—say you live in a small studio apartment—you can still work within your limitations.

Fact-finding can be an intense process and uninterrupted periods of time are essential in order to devote concentration and energy to your task. If you are using computer-based techniques, time is also money. An interruption can result in increased online connect costs. Locating your research center in a prethought space—even a corner of a room—will help to facilitate your concentration. If it is an area in which you can separate yourself from noise, so much the better.

Also think about ergonomics. Place your monitor at eye level so that you don't have to strain your neck to look at it. Use a comfortable chair with adequate back support. Make sure there is sufficient lighting. All of these factors combine to keep you at your best so that you can think clearly and work at your peak, while avoiding fatigue and physical strain.

Although computer equipment is surprisingly durable, it will not survive being dropped or banged around. By keeping your computer equipment in an area that is somewhat separate from the rest of your living area, you will minimize the chances of accidental damage.

If your space is really limited, so that you do not even have a corner for your research area, you might want to consider portable equipment. You can purchase a portable or notebook computer with a built-in modem, small (or even portable) printer, and even a portable CD-ROM drive, for similar prices as desktop equipment. This way, you can store your research center in a closet, assemble it on your kitchen table, as well as take it on trips with you.

What's in the Future?

Industry experts are saying that by the year 2000, we'll be using the computer as we now use telephones and automatic teller machines. It will be second nature to manage many aspects of our daily lives with the aid of a computer, and that means the computer will meet many more of our information needs.

When you set up your own home research center, you are getting a jump on the twentieth century. With advances in online, CD-ROM, and multimedia technologies on the horizon, we are just seeing the beginning of what the computer industry has in store for us. And as new services and products become available, you'll be ready to integrate them into your lifestyle.

Tricks Librarians Use

Think about checking a source such as *Consumer Reports* at your local library before buying a computer, modem, printer, or other equipment. You may save yourself a lot of hassles by choosing a well-rated piece of equipment. Ask your local librarian what other product rating sources your library carries.

12

Information
From a Compact Disc

Compact disc technology, as you have read in previous chapters, offers benefits not only for the music listener, but also for the state-of-the-art fact-finder. CD-ROM resources are outlined in this chapter, with examples of how to conduct a CD-ROM search.

Why CD-ROM?

CD-ROM opens a new realm of possibilities for information searching, allowing you to perform creative and streamlined searches (some examples are included later in the chapter), without either the physical constraints of paging through stacks of periodical indexes and books, or the potentially costly connect time associated with online searching. With CD-ROM, you can do a word search through whole volumes of encyclopedias, for example, just as you would an online database, without taking your eyes off your computer screen, and without the pressure of online searching time constraints.

CD-ROM is a great storage method for "static" kinds of information, like encyclopedias, journal indexes, and newspapers—information that does not have to be updated daily. But for searches where timeliness is crucial, the online database will still be the leader.

The kinds of information you are most likely to find on a compact disc can be categorized as follows:

Full Text	Complete text of encyclopedias, journals, books
Numeric	Statistics and census data
Graphic	Maps and charts
Bibliographic	Periodical indexes with citations and, in some cases, abstracts

CD-ROM offerings are growing rapidly. Not only are new sources becoming available, but resources previously attainable in print form and online are increasingly being offered in CD-ROM format as well.

How CD-ROM Works

In virtually any CD-ROM product, it is possible to enter a few terms and retrieve a multitude of citations or other desired information. However, to use CD-ROM products effectively requires an understanding of how the CD-ROM data is structured and organized, as well as your options for searching. For example, can you search the contents of each entry (or "record") on the disc, or can you only search as far as the title of each entry? Most likely, your search will include every word in every entry on the disc, but it's a good idea to be aware of any limitations. Otherwise, you risk missing information that could have been retrieved if your search had been worded in a slightly different manner.

The best way to begin a CD-ROM search is to check to see if there is a thesaurus for the CD-ROM database you are using. The thesaurus is the list of descriptors or index terms that are associated with the information contained in the CD-ROM database. Without this list of terms, it is easy to miss important data simply because you didn't have the correct terms in your search. For example, you might use "Movie" instead of "Motion Picture," and come up empty handed. Or worse, you may come up with some records, but you won't realize there are lots more you are missing.

The thesaurus may actually be part of the CD-ROM disc, or it may be provided in printed form, and included with the accompanying product documentation. You can find this out by asking a librarian (if you are in a library), by reading the product documentation, or by calling a technical support line.

Also keep in mind that you can be searching for a concept that is so new that the vendor has not yet included it in the thesaurus. You are not limited to searching terms from the thesaurus. Again, CD-ROM information may not be as up-to-date as that included in an online database. If the term you are using is not included in the thesaurus, you can also do a free-text search, using your own terms. While this will take more time, and require that you also identify any possible synonyms and variant spellings, it may be the only way for your search to be successful.

While a well-thought-out search strategy is essential, always beware of the differences between search software among CD-ROM publishers. Some software is more powerful, and allows for more flexibility when you conduct searches. The options and functions, and associated commands, will vary among products. If you are using multiple products, you may also have to learn different systems for conducting searches.

CD-ROM vs. Online Databases

As you make use of CD-ROM, it's important to be aware of how it differs from its online counterparts. CD-ROM is a newer technology than online databases, and the market is dynamic. While many of the indexes and abstracts available online are available in CD-ROM, as are many of those in printed form, this is not true in all cases. Thus, you will not always be able to take advantage of CD-ROM searches of the resources of your choice.

The period of time covered by a particular CD-ROM database will not always correspond exactly to the online version of the same information. Furthermore, even more disparities may exist between the CD-ROM and printed versions of the same information. Some CD-ROM databases extend back as far as the online version, while others may only include the most recent three or five years. Many CD-ROM databases are updated quarterly, while online databases may be updated monthly or even more frequently.

As you make choices about CD-ROM and online searching, these differences can become important. In a library, CD-ROM searches are generally free of charge and you can probably conduct the search yourself, whereas online searches are often conducted by librarians and can be expensive. As a result, you have more flexibility in CD-ROM to consider alternative searches as you go along. If you are completing an online search request form and passing it on to a librarian, you may not have this flexibility.

Considering the possible differences in timeliness of information, you may want to combine your CD-ROM and online database searches. For example, if you have available both CD-ROM and online indexes of the same title, you may want to use CD-ROM to search for articles that were published in the past, and then conduct an online search for more articles from issues that are too recent to be indexed on the CD-ROM.

It's all a matter of taking the time to make sure that the information you need is actually included in the resources you choose to use, and then making decisions about the most efficient, and cost-effective, way to retrieve it.

CD-ROM Cautions

Whether you install your own research center at home, or use CD-ROM resources at your local library, you will find this medium to be both efficient and fun to use. However, while CD-ROM-based information is rapidly becoming available, it's important to be aware of its limitations.

CD-ROM searches are conducted with software designed for this purpose. Because CD-ROM is still an emerging technology in many ways, there are no real standards, and the software changes often. Thus, the rules and techniques that work with one CD-ROM product will not necessarily work with another. While a veteran user will quickly adapt to differences among products, this can be vexing for a new user.

Major CD-ROM Offerings

Here are some of the major CD-ROM offerings—arranged by category—that are most likely to be available in your library.

Bibliographic Indexes

PsycLIT, from the American Psychological Association, contains citations and abstracts of international journal articles in psychology and related disciplines.

Business Periodicals Index, from H. W. Wilson Company, consists of citations to articles and book reviews in over 300 business periodicals. It includes citations of feature articles, interviews, biographical sketches, book reviews, research developments, new product reviews, and reports of associations, societies, and conferences.

Academic Index on InfoTrac, from Information Access Company, indexes scholarly and general interest journals, in areas that include art, history, literature, psychology, science, and cultural studies.

ABI/INFORM ONDISC, from University Microfilms International, contains the most recent years of the ABI/INFORM database, with full bibliographic citations plus abstracts from over 800 business journals.

Full-Text

Business Periodicals on Disc, from University Microfilms International, provides digitally scanned, full-text images of complete articles from business and management periodicals.

Consumers Reference Disc, from National Information Services Corporation, includes product evaluations, recalls, alerts, and warnings, articles on travel and transportation, finances, jobs, computers, food, and health issues.

Electronic Whole Earth Catalog, from Broderbund Software, Inc., contains entries from a wide array of subjects, illustrated with digitized images and recordings. Each entry includes a review by an expert, informative excerpts, and information on where to obtain the product or service.

Encyclopedia of World Crime on CD-ROM, from Crime-Books, Inc., contains the full-text from the *Encyclopedia of World Crime*, with biographical and historical entries, and dictionary terms from crime-related subject areas.

USA Wars: Vietnam, from Quanta Press, covers U.S. involvement in the Vietnam conflict, and includes biographies, equipment, missions, bibliography, chronologies, and battle images.

Facts on File News Digest CD-ROM, from Facts on File, Inc., contains the full text of the Facts on File News Digest, 1980 to the present.

New Grolier Electronic Encyclopedia, from Grolier, Inc., consists of the full text and pictures of the Academic American Encyclopedia.

Health Encyclopedia, from Artificial Intelligence Publishing, is composed of books of data and images of medical subjects.

USA Factbook, from Quanta Press, is an electronic almanac of the U.S. and its territories, covering state geography, vital statistics, government/politics, economies, icons, traditions, maps, state seals, and other state and territory specific information.

Statistical

Business Indicators, provided by U.S. Department of Commerce and published by Slater Hall Information Products, contains U.S. economic data, including Gross National Product, production, prices, finance, employment, foreign trade, and other information.

County and City Statistics Compendium, provided by the U.S. Bureau of the Census and published by Slater Hall Information Products, contains census data for all U.S. counties, states, and metropolitan areas, and for larger cities.

Lotus One Source: CD/Banking, provided by Shesunoff Information Services and published by Lotus Development Corporation, has complete financial performance information on bank holding companies, federally insured commercial banks, savings and loans, and savings banks.

Miscellaneous

Jane's Military Logistics, from Jane's Information Group, is the only unclassified analysis of military vehicles and support equipment in the world.

Image Gallery, from NEC Home Electronics, contains clip art and graphics in categories that include business, fitness, travel, fashion, food, sports, and people.

Languages of the World, provided by NTC's *Comprehensive Dictionary of American Idioms* and 18 bilingual dictionaries, consists of definitions, translations, synonyms, and antonyms in a variety of languages.

General Motors Electronic Parts Catalog, from Bell & Howell Company, is a complete General Motors Parts Catalog with both full text and illustrations.

Obtaining CD-ROM Information

CD-ROM databases are generally obtained through subscriptions, with updates issued periodically. These subscriptions can be quite expensive.

If you use CD-ROMs in a library, you will probably not be charged for use, though you may have to pay a small charge for printing. Still, libraries that have invested in CD-ROM technology may invest in a limited number of CD-ROM databases. The ones they choose will depend on the needs of their clientele. If you are interested in a relatively obscure database, it may not be available at your library.

If you are building a CD-ROM library, you will definitely want to be selective. While your budget may dictate just how far you can go in establishing a collection, use your own interests as a guiding principle. Begin purchasing CD-ROM information that you will use most often. For example, if business is your interest, you will most likely want to look in this area first.

Start slowly. It's easy to become excited about a technology and to invest heavily, only to discover that your day-to-day needs are really more limited than you expected. Acquire what you are sure you will use and expand as your needs grow.

Where to Look

As CD-ROM grows in popularity, more and more options are becoming available. You'll find CD-ROM resources described in various types of publications. One that is CD-ROM specific is, *CD-ROMs in Print*, compiled by Norman Desmarais and published by Meckler. It is a comprehensive listing of CD-ROMs, organized alphabetically.

Magazines are also a good source of information on available CD-ROM products. General computer magazines will include articles on CD-ROM technology and advertisements for products. Don't forget to consult magazines focused on your specific area of interest, including business and hobby magazines, and specialized journals.

Professional associations and organizations also offer CD-ROM-based information, generally for purchase. These offerings might include past issues of publications, or bibliographies and indexes oriented toward their area of interest or service. These may be worth the investment if you need extensive resources in a specific area of interest.

Computer user groups are another source of CD-ROM information. You are likely to locate people with an interest in CD-ROM who may in turn provide you with leads for low-cost, high-quality products. And, with the growing demand for CD-ROM information, user groups may form their own CD-ROM disc lending libraries.

CD-ROMs can be compared to software during the earlier days of the computer. As the demand grew, the options increased and the prices declined. Most likely, many new avenues for building your collection will materialize.

When to Go CD-ROM, When Not To

CD-ROM isn't always the best route. When preparing to do a literature search, consider how electronic databases, both online and in CD-ROM format, fit your needs. Investigate whether the best indexes or abstracts are available electronically, or only in print format. Find out what years of the index a database covers, and decide if you will need to search additional years. If your search topic is very complex and you are new to CD-ROM searching, you might feel more comfortable if an experienced searcher does an online search for you. While searches of electronic databases can provide excellent results, the databases don't contain the answers to all questions. Many indexes, handbooks, encyclopedias, and other reference tools are still only in print format and, depending on your research, will need to be consulted for the information they provide.

Example of a CD-ROM Search

While substantial differences exist between the various CD-ROM packages on the market, the principles on which search strategies are based are all similar. The following pages are examples of CD-ROM searches conducted with three products, *Business Periodicals Index*, *Expanded Academic Index*, and *Magazine Article Summaries*.

The Movie Search: Continued
In Chapter 2, you were introduced to a search for information about movies, with the goal of predicting the hot movies for the future. Let's assume that during your search you want to access information on CD-ROM to get ideas about what kinds of articles have been written about the movie industry.

Because you are using this information to make a business decision about potential blockbuster movies as investment opportunities, *Business Periodicals Index* is a logical place to begin.

We'll start the search by using the words *movie* and *industry*. Notice that these words yield 155 potential entries; some are directly on target, while others aren't (Figure

Figure 12-1

Business Periodicals Index

Data Coverage: 7/82 thru 01/30/9
READY

ILSEARCH PRINT MODE

5 of 155 Entries

#5
Petersen, Laurie
From the streets to our living rooms (TV movie Crazy from the heart
carries debate over targeting alcohol and tobacco ads at
minorities into America's living rooms)
AdWeek's Marketing Week v32   p9 August 26 '91

SUBJECTS COVERED:
Outdoor advertising
Television broadcasting/Motion pictures
Advertising/Appeal to minorities
Cigarette industry/Advertising
Alcoholic beverages/Advertising

for Next Entry or ESC to STOP DISPLAY

F1 = HELP   F4 = PRINT Entry   F5 = Go to an Entry   F6 = Print from HERE to limit

Reprinted with permission from the publisher, H. W. Wilson Company.

12-1). The reason is that the search was based on both of these words, but not in relation to each other. Thus, you were provided with entries that include "movie" and "industry," but not "movie industry." Depending on the CD-ROM software you are using, it might be possible to specify that these words should be linked, eliminating a "false hit" as in Figure 12-1. Also notice that this system automatically searches for both the singular and the plural of your search words.

By the way, when you see that your search criteria yielded so many potential citations, that's a sure sign that your search is too broad. You may want to narrow your search by including more keywords.

One of the citations, shown in Figure 12-2, also includes the additional keyword: marketing. Since this specific citation is on target, it suggests that the search could be narrowed to obtain more focused results.

This time, we search using the words "movie" and "industry" in conjunction with the word "marketing." The result is narrowed from 155 to 47 items, which is more manageable. There are limits to how many terms you can combine—eventually, the resulting set will become too small or nonexistent. For example, if you add the word "women" to this search, there are no matching citations.

Just as a check for numbers of potentially relevant articles—or "hits"—in the database, here's the result of a count based on three keywords: "motion," "picture" and "industry" (Figure 12-3). Notice that *Business Periodicals Index* provides you with the total number of entries that result from the three key words—638—as well as the potential number of citations for each of the keywords separately.

Figure 12-2

Business Periodicals Index   Data Coverage: 7/82 thru 01/30/92
                                                                    READY

WILSEARCH PRINT MODE   12 of 155 Entries

   #12
   Independent movies find their niches in blockbuster summer
   Marketing News v25 p6 June 24 '91

   SUBJECTS COVERED:
   Motion picture industry/Marketing

   for Next Entry or ESC to STOP DISPLAY

F1 = HELP   F4 = PRINT Entry   F5 = Go to an Entry   F6 = Print from HERE to limit

Reprinted with permission from the publisher, H. W. Wilson Company.

Figure 12-3

Business Periodicals Index   Data Coverage: 7/82 thru 01/30/92
                                                              READY

SEARCH SET	WILSEARCH COMMAND		NUMBER of ENTRIES
1	FIND MOTION (BI) AND PICTURE (BI) AND INDUSTRY (BI)		638
	(BI) MOTION	1534 Entries	
	(BI) PICTURE	1653 Entries	
	(BI) INDUSTRY	89002 Entries	

```
┌─────────────────────────────────────────────────┐
│        638 ENTRIES FOUND                         │
│   HIT — ENTER                                    │
└─────────────────────────────────────────────────┘
```

                                              Thu Apr 09 08:09:36 1992
F1 = HELP   F2 = END

Reprinted with permission from the publisher, H. W. Wilson Company.

Because the term "motion picture" is a subject heading used by this particular index, it yields even more results than the word "movie." Keep this in mind as you conduct CD-ROM searches—sometimes a shift in terminology can result in a more comprehensive search.

Now, let's move on to *Expanded Academic Index*, with a search based on the keywords "movies" and "industry." Using these two keywords, we have a count of 75 citations (the first five are shown in Figure 12-4). *Expanded Academic Index* first provides you with a list of brief records, enough to give you an idea of what is covered in the articles.

After you have skimmed the list, you can then choose to look at a more detailed description of specific entries, as shown in Figure 12-5.

As with *Business Periodicals Index*, when you use the keywords "motion picture industry" in *Expanded Academic*

Figure 12-4

InfoTrac EF	Expanded Academic Index	Brief Citations

R3 movies and industry

-- 1 of 75 --

1   5 from Sandollar. (movies by Sandollar Productions)
Lawrence Van Gelder. The New York Times, Jan 10, 1992
v141 pC10(L) 10 col in.

2   Computer brings cheap tricks to screen. (use of computers to
make motion picture special effects) Barry Fox. New Scientist,
Dec 14, 1991 v132 n1799 p23(1).

3   The year in movies. Peters Travers. Rolling Stone, Dec 12, 1991
n619-20 p191(3).
-- Abstract Available --

4   Rights! Author! Action! (children's books that tie-in with
movies and TV shows) (includes related information on books based
on the 'Beverly Hills 90210' TV series) Sally Lodge.
Publishers Weekly, Dec 6, 1991 v238 n53 p48(3).
IAC Coll. 62V1182   -- Abstract Available --

5   Reality comes with the popcorn: through death and violence,
movies are keeping pace with children. Should parents be

Display	Review	Search	Browse	F1	Help	F3	Print
				F2	Start over	F4	Mark

Display full record

Index, you are provided with an extensive list of entries (Figure 12-6). For all practical purposes, 787 entries is many more than you will want to skim through. So, it is important to narrow your search.

To narrow the search, we added the keyword "marketing" to the search criteria. And as you can see in Figure 12-7, the result is a more manageable 77 entries. That's still a lot, but it is more focused on our interest in investment opportunities.

Also, by doing some research before we started searching, we realized that the *Business Periodicals Index* is

Figure 12-5

Database: Expanded Academic Index
Key words: movies and industry
Library: university at albany

The year in movies.

Rolling Stone, Dec 12, 1991 n619-20 p191(3).

Author: Peters Travers

Abstract: Most movies in 1991 were awful. Formula action films like 'Terminator 2' and 'Robin Hood: Prince of Thieves' dominated box office earnings, and dysfunctional relationships were the theme in most romances.

Subjects: Motion picture industry -- 1991
Motion pictures -- Criticism, interpretation, etc.

Features: illustration; photograph

Reference Number: 11657407

Copyright © 1992 Information Access Company, ACADEMIC INDEX™

focused on different magazines and journals than those included in *Expanded Academic Index*. Thus, the searches complement each other.

Going on a hunch that films featuring women, as directors or leading characters, will be big winners, let's find some information to support our hunch. This time, we focus our "motion picture industry" search with an additional keyword: "women." As you can see in Figure 12-8, this narrowed the list of entries down to a highly manageable 12.

When we tried finding information on women in *Business Periodicals Index*, we struck out. That was because we were combining three concepts: movie industry, marketing, and women. Here we are just using two.

And a sample item (Figure 12-9) looks as if it will be on target in supporting our interest in women in films.

Information From a Compact Disc

Figure 12-6

InfoTrac EF	Expanded Academic Index	Brief Citations

R4 motion picture industry

--- 1 of 787 ---

1 Studios and the critics: how near is too near?
   (relationship between motion picture industry and film critics)
   (Living Arts Pages) Bernard Weinraub. The New York Times,
   March 11, 1992 v141 pB1(N) p817(L) 25 col in.

2 Streisand. (Barbra Streisand) (Hollywood Is Talking)
   (motion picture industry) Jack Kroll. Newsweek, March 2, 1992
   v119 n9 p60(1).
   IAC Coll. 63Y1985   -- Abstract Available --

3 'The Player.' (director Robert Altman's new film)
   (Hollywood Is Talking) (motion picture industry) David Ansen.
   Newsweek, March 2, 1992 v119 n9 p61(2).
   IAC Coll. 63Y1986   -- Abstract Available --

4 'Wayne's World.' (Hollywood Is Talking) (motion picture
   industry) (Brief Article) John Leland. Newsweek, March 2, 1992
   v119 n9 p62(1).
   IAC Coll. 63Y1987

Display	Review	Search	Browse	F1	Help	F3	Print
				F2	Start over	F4	Mark

Display full record

Now let's check yet another CD-ROM database, *Magazine Article Summaries*, which includes over 300 magazines and the *New York Times*. We started out with "movie industry" as the keywords, and yielded 143 summaries of articles. Several are shown in Figure 12-10.

Next we searched with "motion picture industry" as the keywords. As previously, this term yields even more entries—267 of them. Some of these are shown in Figure 12-11. We also used "motion picture industry" and "marketing" with a result of 11 entries, while "motion picture industry" and "women" yielded 9 entries.

Figure 12-7

InfoTrac EF	Expanded Academic Index	Brief Citations

R5 r4 and marketing

-- 1 of 77 --

1   Syndies eye primetime bigtime; will antsy affils zap their webs
        for slick studio fare? John Dempsey and J. Max Robins, Variety,
        Jan 27, 1992 v346 n2 p1(3).
        -- Abstract Available --

2   Conspiracy over 'JFK' buttons? (at theaters) (Brief Article)
        Charles Fleming. Variety, Jan 27, 1992 v346 n2 p10(1).

3   What Hollywood got for Christmas. (how the movie studios
        marketed various new films for the holidays) Bernard Weinraub.
        The New York Times, Jan 19, 1992 v141 pH1(N) pH1(L) 83 col in.

4   Thirty years later. Hollywood is unleashing five new films that
        deal with the Kennedy assassination. Andrew Kopkind. Vogue
        Jan 1992 v182 n1 p64(4).
        IAC Coll. 62L5962.   -- Abstract Available --

5   Bankrupt but best-renting. (list of bankrupt Orion Home
        Video's popular video rentals) The New York Times, Dec 26, 1991
        v141 pD18(L) 1 col in.

Display	Review	Search	Browse	F1	Help	F3	Print
				F2	Start over	F4	Mark

Display full record

But here's an example of the importance of choosing the best keywords. A search consisting of "motion picture or movies" combined with "women or woman" yielded 175 entries.

This also illustrates the importance of taking the time to try different keywords, and combinations of keywords, to see what you come up with. CD-ROM searching is an *iterative* process—your search is like an experiment, based on different hypotheses, that close in a result. The more willing you are to be creative, and diligent, the better your results will be.

Figure 12-8

InfoTrac EF	Expanded Academic Index	Brief Citations

R2 motion picture industry and women
-- 1 of 12 --

1   Female leads. (Cinenova women's film cooperative, feminism and women film makers) Lizzie Francke. New Statesman & Society, Oct 18, 1991 v4 n173 p33(1).
-- Abstract Available --

2   Killer women. (actresses in roles of professional killers) Julie Baumgold. New York, July 29, 1991 v24 n29 p24(6).
IAC Coll. 60M3433.

3   Why are Black actresses having such a hard time in Hollywood? Racism and the film industry's limited vision contribute to the scarcity of roles for Black women. Robin Givens. Ebony, June 1991 v46 n8 p36(4).
IAC Coll. 60C1443.

4   Women on the verge of a nervy breakthrough: bucking Hollywood's musclemania. Jodie Foster and a clutch of fine young actresses snag some serious roles. Richard Corliss. Time, Feb 18, 1991 v137 n7 p58(3).

Display	Review	Search	Browse	F1	Help	F3	Print
				F2	Start over	F4	Mark

Display full record

Copyright © 1992 Information Access Company, ACADEMIC INDEX™

Here's a citation of the search conducted with the keywords "motion picture industry" and "women," with a result of nine entries. Some are shown in Figure 12-12.

And here are the results of searching on the keywords "motion picture or movie" and "women or woman"—175 entries! Some are shown in Figure 12-13.

Rules for Efficient Searches

As you expand your use of CD-ROM, here are some rules to keep in mind.

Figure 12-9

Database: Expanded Academic Index
R4   rl and women

Women on the verge of a nervy breakthrough: bucking Hollywood's
musclemania, Jodie Foster and a clutch of fine young actresses snag
some serious roles.

Time, Feb 18, 1991 v137 n7 p58(3).

Author: Richard Corliss

Subjects: Actresses -- Employment
Motion picture industry -- Economic aspects

People: Foster, Jodie -- Performances

Features: illustration; portrait

Reference Number: 09867087
Mag. Collection: 58J0B63
Bus. Collection: 56T1754

1. Don't jump in without preparation. Instruction is important. You may be able to obtain this through your library—individually or in a class.
2. Read the instructions. Most CD-ROM databases provide help screens, online tutorials, and printed guidance. Save time and avoid frustration by taking a moment to make sure you're on the right track before you get started.
3. Make the right choice. When you're preparing to do a literature search, consider the CD-ROM indexes that are available to you. Some will be better than others in answering your need.
4. Check the dates. If you are looking for articles within a specific time period, you can waste a lot of time by

Figure 12-10

1. MOTION picture industry
   How Hollywood sliced the pie.

   Offers a chart detailing the decline in US movie ticket sales from more
   than $5 billion in 1990, to $4.7 billion in 1991. By H. Collingwood
   (Business Week, 1/20/92, Issue 3238-568, 1 chart, p40, 1/8p)
   (0007-7135)
   (The library has this magazine)

   -- Local Notes --

   Microfilm 1949-1979. Non circ.

2. MOTION picture industry
   What Hollywood got for Christmas.

   Discusses how well the Hollywood movie industry did with the 12 films
   it released for the Thanksgiving through New Year's holiday season
   and what marketing strategies worked and which ones did not. Big
   budget flops like 'Billy Bathgate' and 'Hudson Hawk'; Multimillion-
   dollar investments in holiday films at risk; Assessments done of the
   successes and failures of the films: 'Bugsy,' 'Beauty and the Beast,'
   'Cape Fear,' and 'The Addams Family'; More. By B. Weinraub
   (New York Times, 1/19/92, Vol. 141 Issue 48850, Section 2 p1)
   (0362-4331)
   (The library has this magazine)

   -- Local Notes --

   8 weeks with newspapers. Microfilm 1964-present. Non circ.

3. MASS media industry -- Performance
   Movie companies. TV networks and publishers have been forced to
   audition the same act: cost-cutting

   Discusses how the free-spending media and entertainment companies
   of the 1980s spent much of 1991 tightening their belts. Layoffs and
   asset sales; Of the three major networks, only ABC was profitable in
   1991; Network viewership continues to erode; Pay-TV subscriptions
   declined; Box office irony. INSET: Television is king (profiles King
   World Productions), by K. H. By K. Harris
   (Forbes, 1/6/92, Vol. 149 Issue 1, 1c, 1 chart, p140, 2p)
   (0015-6914)
   (The library has this magazine)

   -- Local Notes --

   Non circ.

4. MOTION picture industry
   Heavenly gate.

   Presents a list of movies that are North American box office champs
   based on theatrical rental fees and how 'Home Alone' a seemingly
   successful movie, did not even come close to making the list. 'Star
   Wars'; 'E.T.'; 'The Sound of Music'; More. By A. Schaffer
   (Premiere, Jan92, Vol. 5 Issue 5, p19, 1/4p) (0894-9263)

EBSCO Publishing, P.O. Box 2250, Peabody, MA 01960

Figure 12-11

1. MOTION picture industry
    Payback time.

    Reports that despite a smashing holiday season, there's real fear in
    Hollywood as a cost-cutting frenzy abounds. Unusual confluence of
    events that have contributed to new austerity; Decreasing number of
    bankable stars; How the 1980s were a boom time in Hollywood;
    Reduced star salaries; Recent hits and flops. By J. Kasindorf
    (New York, 1/27/92, Vol. 25 Issue 4, 27c, 1 illustration, p34, 7p)
    (0028-7369)
    (The library has this magazine)

2. MOTION picture industry
    How Hollywood sliced the pie.

    Offers a chart detailing the decline in US movie ticket sales from more
    than $5 billion in 1990, to $4.7 billion in 1991. By H. Collingwood
    (Business Week, 1/20/92, Issue 3238-568, 1 chart, p40, 1/8p)
    (0007-7135)
    (The library has this magazine)

    --- Local Notes ---
    Microfilm 1949-1979. Non circ.

3. MOTION picture industry
    What Hollywood got for Christmas.

    Discusses how well the Hollywood movie industry did with the 12 films
    it released for the Thanksgiving through New Year's holiday season
    and what marketing strategies worked and which ones did not. Big
    budget flops like 'Billy Bathgate' and 'Hudson Hawk'; Multimillion-
    dollar investments in holiday films at risk; Assessments done of the
    successes and failures of the films; 'Bugsy,' 'Beauty and the Beast,'
    'Cape Fear,' and 'The Addams Family'; More. By B. Weinraub
    (New York Times, 1/19/92, Vol. 141 Issue 48850, Section 2 p1)
    (0362-4331)
    (The library has this magazine)

    --- Local Notes ---
    8 weeks with newspapers. Microfilm 1964-present. Non circ.

4. MOTION picture industry
    Maybe the recession was a wakeup call.

    Discusses how movies have cut back, networks have laid off hundreds,
    and Hollywood is newly austere. Networks should pick up with Olympic
    coverage; Growth in video sales; Presidential election will boost
    networks; Box office revenues down. By R. Grover
    (Business Week, 1/13/92, Issue 3247, 1 illustration, 1 graph, p92, 1p)
    (0007-7135)
    (The library has this magazine)

    --- Local Notes ---
    Microfilm 1949-1979. Non circ.

Figure 12-12

1. MOTION picture industry
    F.Y.I.

    Presents a list of statistics concerning gender and film. Money in the
    actors guild; Women in film and screenwriting; Averages for male and
    female directors; Percentage of feature-film roles that went to men;
    Percentage increase of women with guns. By C. Wass
    (Premiere, Jan92, Vol. 5 Issue 5, 3 illustrations, p17, 1/3p)
    (0894-9263)

2. MOTION picture producers & directors
    Hollywood's new directions.

    Discusses some of the women directors currently working in the
    motion picture industry and considers their films. Martha Coolidge:
    'Rambling Rose,' her eighth film and a well-deserved hit; Kathryn
    Bigelow's sleek thriller 'Point Break'; Mary Agnes Donoghue's 'Paradise,'
    confronting basic, down-and-goofy human horniness; Penny Marshall's
    'A League of Their Own'; 'The Prince of Tides,' directed by Barbara
    Streisand; Other films; Women fighting history. By R. Schickel,
    E. L. Bland, et al
    (Time, 10/14/91, Vol. 138 Issue 15, 6c, p75, 2p) (0040-781X)
    (The library has this magazine)

    ------------------------------------- Local Notes -------------------------------------

    Microfilm 1940-present. Non circ.

3. FOSTER, Jodie
    A screen gem turns director.

    Profiles Jodie Foster, 28, talented actress turned director, whose latest
    movie is 'Little Man Tate,' a small budget film, an audacious winner.
    Outline of the film; Films Foster starred in; Growing pains; Foster's
    comments on women in the motion picture industry; Her work with
    Adam Hann-Byrd, 9, who plays Fred Tate in the film. By R. Corliss,
    M. Smilgis, et al
    (Time, 10/14/91, Vol. 138 Issue 15, 8c, p68, 5p) (0040-781X)
    (The library has this magazine)

    ------------------------------------- Local Notes -------------------------------------

    Microfilm 1940-present. Non circ.

4. MOTION picture industry
    Pretty worthless.

    Argues that the past few years have seen a dramatic narrowing of the
    issues and themes addressed in the movies. Cinematic legacy of the
    Reagan era; Confuse niceness with morality; Purpose of women and
    blacks is to help white males 'find out more about themselves'; Perfect
    family is warm, well-heeled and intact. By B. Austin
    (Washington Monthly, May91, Vol. 23 Issue 5, 5bw, p30, 7p)
    (0043-0633)
    (The library has this magazine)

Information From a Compact Disc

Figure 12-13

MAGAZINE ARTICLE SUMMARIES MAR 92   M. A. S. Bibliography

1. WHORE (Motion picture)
    'Whore.'

    Highlights scenes from Ken Russell's movie 'Whore.' Movie's three
    principal messages; Why Theresa Russell isn't convincing; How women
    and men are portrayed in the movie. By X. Hollander
    (Premiere, Feb92, Vol. 5 Issue 6, 2c, p97, 2/3p) (0894-9263)

2. DOWNTOWN (Book)
    DOWNTOWN

    When Florida orange-grower, Michael Barnes came to New York City on
    business, he did not expect to be framed for a series of bloody murders.
    (Magill Book Reviews) (0890-7722)

3. HAND That Rocks the Cradle. The (Motion picture)
    The ultimate other woman.

    Reviews the motion picture 'The Hand That Rocks the Cradle,' directed
    by Curtis Hanson, screenplay by Amanda Silver, and starring Annabella
    Sciorra, Matt McCoy, Ernie Hudson and Rebecca De Mornay. By
    R. Schickel
    (Time, 1/20/92, Vol. 139 Issue 3, 1c, p58, 5/8p) (0040-781X)

4. FIELD, Virginia
    Virginia Field, 74, the 'other woman' in movies of the 30's.

    Presents an obituary of Virginia Field, who played secondary roles in
    dozens of films. She died of cancer on January 2. She was 74 years old
    and lived in Palm Desert, Calif.
    (New York Times, 1/9/92, Vol. 141 Issue 48840, pD23) (0362-4331)
    (The library has this magazine)

    -- Local Notes --

    8 weeks with newspapers. Microfilm 1964-present. Non circ.

5. MOTION pictures -- Reviews
    Movies.

    Reviews several recently released movies, including: 'The Prince of
    Tides,' 'Rush,' and 'Rambling Rose.' All are directed by women. By
    B. Hersey
    (Glamour, Jan92, Vol. 90 Issue 1, 6c, p68, 2p) (0017-0747)
    (The library has this magazine)

popping in the wrong CD-ROM disc. Check—and double check—the dates.

5. Remember to use synonyms and other alternate terms to your topic for best search results. If you are getting too many items, try to narrow your search by adding another concept. Don't waste your time looking through hundreds of citations. This defeats the entire of purpose of the CD-ROM. Remember, the strengths of CD-ROM are speed and search flexibility.

6. Keep a record of which terms you've searched on which databases. If you run across an alternative term for your topic, you can check to see if you've already tried it.

7. Don't be afraid to ask a librarian for assistance if the results you are getting aren't what you need. He or she may be able to suggest different search terms or ways to link the terms, or another CD-ROM or printed index more specific to your interest.

8. Print your results, or download them onto a disc. It's easy to miss key information when you quickly jot citations down on a sheet of paper. Don't risk having to backtrack due to your own recording errors.

Tricks Librarians Use

As with any new technology, companies that produce CD-ROM information are established, and then merge with other companies or otherwise fade from view, all in the blink of an eye. When you see a product advertised, or read about it in a publication, take a moment to verify that it is still being made before you assume up-to-date availability and buy it. The advertised copy may be the last one produced.

13

Boot It Up: Finding Purchasable Information Software

As you build your software library, you'll find a massive array of software products to choose from, many of which will be useful in your research work. Discover some of the options and potential benefits of purchasable software in this chapter.

Boot It Up!

CD-ROM and online resources are relatively quick and accessible sources of information. But you can also gain an edge—or numerous edges—from software. These products include diskette-based data, maps, graphics packages, and other offerings ranging from almanacs to thesauri. And the good news is that software products are relatively low in cost and, in some cases, free of charge.

Why would you want to purchase a software product? In some cases, you won't. For example, if you want to look at a map to find a specific location, you may not find it necessary to purchase software when you could simply refer to an atlas. Or if you need a piece of information such as the name of an organization, and don't anticipate needing it again in the future, then you may not be able to justify the cost of purchasing this information on a diskette. Of course, if diskette-based information is the most economic alternative, and this is increasingly becoming the case, you may reconsider.

Many of your information needs are ongoing. After using an almanac for the first time, for example, you may begin to find it indispensable. And being able to boot it up on your computer will really revolutionize your use. Along the same lines, a software-based world map, with the ability to zoom in on specific countries and cities, as well as access the population statistics that often accompany these packages, could easily become one of your most often-used resources. And while you are composing your reports, a thesaurus accessed through your word processor will streamline your writing.

Another benefit of purchasable software is updates. Most packages are supplemented periodically by new releases, and these are usually offered at a much lower rate to current users. As a result, you can easily, and economically, stay up to date.

Space is another benefit. If you have a shortage of shelf space and don't want to load the space you do have with dusty volumes, you have the option of loading your computer instead. With the compact size of diskettes, as well as the storage space on your computer's hard drive, you can store information much more efficiently and still have it available at your fingertips. And that's what having an electronic home office is all about.

There are a lot of other benefits associated with purchasable software; these will be discussed in relation to specific categories of software products.

Data on a Disc

Increasingly, information that was traditionally printed on paper is being optionally offered on diskette. Information that you can expect to find in diskette format includes lists of organizations and associations, and membership lists, as well as statistical data. A diskette is much lower in cost than a stack of paper, particularly when binding costs are added, and a diskette is much less expensive to mail.

If you contact a professional association and request a list of local chapters, or a membership list, it is likely that a diskette version will be an option. If you have a computer, this is a viable option. You can pop the diskette in your disk drive, and you're ready to go. If it's a list that you use often, you may even want to install it on your hard disk so that in the future you don't have to go through the steps of inserting the diskette every time you want to access the information.

Statistical information from professional or research organizations may also be offered on diskette to save on printing and mailing costs. As you scan through this information on your personal computer, you can usually print the information that interests you on your own printer.

More and more, other types of documents are also being offered on diskette. For example, user manuals for products or services are often available on diskette. Once you have read through the information on your computer screen, you have the option of printing whatever interests you.

In addition to printing, diskette-based information can often be updated. For example, if you obtain an organizational membership list, you may be able to keep your own version updated, or add to it along the way. And statistical data can be "pulled" into your own report if the data is stored in such a way that it is compatible with your own word-processing package.

Building Buildings to Building Wealth

The software market is flooded with products that offer reference information on specific topics, as well as products that can simplify your worklife. Much of this software is well under $100. For example, if you are interested in genealogy, there are programs available that can facilitate the process of building your family tree. Others can help you do the work of an architect, or locate and use financial investment information. And still others, like thesauri, can help you write better.

As you make choices about the software products in this category, you will find that there are many competing products in every niche. As you make decisions, it's important to read a review. Personal computer magazines are constantly evaluating these products, and they are also rated in buyer's guides. And, you can ask friends for a recommendation.

Prices are also competitive. Check around for software stores that sell the latest products at a discount, and for sales. And, once you have made your decision, buying through mail-order is also a viable alternative.

The list below is but a brief sampling of the kinds of products available. In many cases, both DOS and Macintosh, as well as Windows, versions are available.

Design Your Own Home: Architecture, Design Your Own Home: Landscapes, and *Design Your Own Home: Interiors,* all from Abracadata, include sample plans, and guide you into creating designs that meet your personal needs.

CalenDAr, from Psybron Systems, Inc., allows you to keep track of future activities and helps you to schedule yourself while avoiding time conflicts. You can even set reminder alarms.

Grammatik 5, from Reference Software International, assists you in writing by pointing out grammatical errors, such as tense shifts and incorrect verb forms. It also has a spell checker.

The Random House Webster's Electronic Dictionary & Thesaurus College Edition, provides synonyms, definitions, idioms, example usage sentences, and other capabilities. The product works within your own word processor.

Bodyworks, from Software Marketing, allows you to study all the structures, functions, and systems of the human body. It includes detailed information on sports injuries, advice on illnesses, and first aid and physical fitness information.

Reunion: The Family Tree Software, from Leister Productions, is genealogy software. It automatically creates detailed multigenerational, pedigree, and descendant charts, and includes a log feature that helps you keep track of your research.

WealthBuilder by *Money Magazine,* and published by Reality Technologies, is an investment planning package, which includes a subscription database of stocks and bonds, and mutual funds.

Maps

Once you've used a map software product, you may never want to go back to a printed version again. First of all, after you use it you don't have to struggle trying to fold it back up. You simply insert the diskette in your drive, or install it on your hard disk, and you've got the whole world in your hands.

Map software ranges from world atlases to road maps of the United States. You can use map software to find where countries are in relation to each other, locate major (and minor) cities, and even plan a trip. Furthermore, map software is often accompanied by population and weather statistics, socioeconomic and cultural information, time zones, currency rates, and other facts.

Here are some examples of the major packages:

PC Globe 3.0, from PC Globe, Inc., has world, continent and individual country maps showing city locations and major world organizations. The country maps display elevations, lakes, rivers, mountains and other important geographical features. Also included are population data, age distribution, ethnic and religious groups, national leaders and political parties, tourist attractions, and other information. With PC Globe, you can also produce custom charts that can be "pulled," or exported into your word processor, for use in your reports.

PC USA, also from PC Globe, Inc., has maps of the U.S. and the 50 individual states, as well as information on major cities, including population, income, tax rates, and area and zip codes.

MacGlobe, from PC Globe, Inc., for the Macintosh, includes maps of countries around the world, as well as demographics. It allows you to display national flags and hear national anthems.

Graphics

Graphics packages can give you an edge when you compile the results of your research. A good chart or graph can add much to the overall clarity of your report, and illustrate your results more clearly than text alone.

Graphics software products run the gamut from the very easy to use, with fewer capabilities, to those that are used primarily by professionals. All can perform basic functions, like pie charts and bar graphs; others offer more sophisticated design, with shading and even color. As you decide what packages you want to buy, make sure you have your needs in mind. For basic reports, you will not need a sophisticated, expensive, and more-difficult-to-use product. Most graphics packages can be used with standard word-processing programs, so that you can create graphics, and then pull, or import, them into your document. Check on word processing product compatibility as you make product choices.

Also in the graphics category are products that help you to "spiff up" your reports and presentations with images and logos. Some of these products guide you in designing your own logos, while others are essentially libraries of images and logos that you can choose from and then use for your own purposes. Again be careful about buying capabilities that you may not need, and that add to the overall complexity of using the package.

Hardware compatibility is another concern to be aware of as you make decisions about graphics packages. Make sure you have enough computer power to make use of the product of your choice. For example, many require a Macintosh or at least a 286 IBM-compatible machine. Also make sure you have enough RAM (Random Access Memory). Some products require 2 megabytes or more. Another consideration is your method of printing. The sophisticated graphs that many packages produce deserve a laser printer; to print them with a dot-matrix printer does not do them justice, and may even be impossible.

A few of the major products in this software category are:

Freelance Graphics, from Lotus, is a graphics package with features such as automatic composition of data charts, a library of full-color clip art images, and other ease-of-use features.

GraphMaster, from Visual Business Systems, is a charting and graphing package, with numerous types of charts, the ability to draw your own illustrations, and other features.

allCLEAR, from Clear Software, Inc., allows you to automatically create diagrams and flowcharts, based on your text.

Draw!, from Micrografx, is an easy-to-use graphics product that can be accessed through a variety of word processing packages.

Presentation Task Force, from New Vision Technologies, Inc., includes an extensive library of clip art and various images that can be added to presentations to help illustrate the material.

Harvard Graphics, from Software Publishing Corporation, is a presentation graphics package with extensive capabilities for creating a wide range of charts and graphs, all of which can work with word processing and spreadsheet products.

Using Software in Research

Software products have also been developed to support the process of fact-finding. A limited number of products are specifically research software products, while others offer supporting functions, including project management, idea organizers, and statistics. Depending on the level of sophistication at which you are working, you may find some of these products helpful.

Research Software

Research software assists you in the process of conducting online research, performing functions such as dialing telephone numbers for online services and helping you formulate your search criteria. It acts like a research assistant, doing some of the more time-consuming and error-prone tasks for you, so that you can concentrate on locating the information you need. With research software, you can conduct more efficient, and cost-effective, searches because the software helps you to avoid making costly mistakes that can result in retrieving extraneous information.

Examples of advanced feature research software include *Biblio-Links*, *Pro-Search*, and *Pro-Cite*, all from Personal Bibliographic Software:

> *Pro-Cite* is a database system designed specifically for organizing bibliographic references and formatting bibliographies. Each database can hold up to 32,000 references from books, journals, dissertations, or any other source. Workforms, or record types, are predefined for 20 different media sources and users can define their own workforms for specialized information management. References can be searched, sorted, indexed, and formatted into bibliographies based on any bibliographic style.

Biblio-Links are companion programs to *Pro-Cite*. Each program transfers records downloaded from online services, automated library systems, CD-ROM services, and diskette data products directly into Pro-Cite.

Pro-Search is a specialized user interface, or "front-end" software program that simplifies the searching of databases available through the BRS and DIALOG information retrieval services. It also acts as a general communications package for other online systems.

Some online services, like CompuServe and DIALOG, provide their members with search software. These products will be discussed in Chapter 14. Products like *Pro-Search* are designed for use by researchers whose work requires extensive use of online services.

Project Management

Project management software does just what it sounds like: it helps you to manage large projects. For example, you can use it to plan exactly what you need to do, at each step in your project, until you finish. As you complete each step, the product keeps you aware of what else needs to be done. If you miss a step, or are late, the product helps you to recalculate your timeframe. Within each project step, the software helps you keep track of needed supplies, noting when those supplies should be ordered. It also outlines how costs are eating into your budget. With project management software, you have an up-to-the-second perspective on how close you are to meeting your own schedule, what else you need to do, and how much it's costing you.

A few of the available project management software products include:

CA-SuperProject, from Computer Associates. This software is designed to help you manage a project from start to finish, including specifying resources, linking multiple projects, and creating schedules.

Microsoft Project, from Microsoft. This project management package has features that include options for how you view your data. For example, you can choose among various tables and graphs.

Project management software is especially helpful if you are handling multiple projects, even if they are small. The software is designed to keep track of all of the elements of a project, and shows you logical links between multiple projects. If your life seems like a series of projects, with yet another starting before the last one is finished, project management software is worth thinking about.

Idea Organizers

Idea organizers are computerized filing systems for all the scraps of information and details in your life. Idea organizers help you see connections that you may not be aware of, and because of the computer's ability to deal with hundreds of scraps of information more or less simultaneously, it can come up with connections between long-forgotten ideas. For example, you can use idea organizer software to connect facts and ideas with topics or names—it stores whatever you enter, and you direct how the ideas should be organized. As a result, you could enter a name, or a topic, and your idea organizer would show you any associated fact or thought.

Here are some of the major idea organizer products:

IdeaFisher 1.1, from Fisher Idea Systems, assists you in being creative by helping you to uncover your ideas. It is an aid in brainstorming and solving problems, as well as implementing ideas.

Info Select, from Micro Logic, is an information manager software product. Functions include storing bits and pieces of random information, and helping you make logical associations. It also helps you to prioritize information, and organize it in such a way that it can be stored, retrieved, and used in logical groups. Using *Info Select* is like having someone come in and make organizational sense of the scraps of paper, clippings, and other notes you might have scattered around your desk.

If you are constantly thinking of ideas or concepts that you don't want to lose track of, idea organizer software might be just what you need.

Statistical Analysis

Statistical analysis is a mystery to many of us, while for others it is second nature. Statistical analysis software helps to level the playing field, offering features that help the user in choosing which methodology to use, entering the data, and coming up with reliable, and understandable, results. Many statistical analysis products also have graphics capabilities for organizing the results into professional-looking graphs and charts. Some statistical analysis products have been developed for professionals, while others offer fewer capabilities, but enough ease-of-use features for the layperson to produce credible results.

Statistical analysis software products include:

Kaleidagraph, from Synergy, a data analysis and presentation tool. The product allows you to enter your own data or import it from other sources, run sophisticated data analysis, and create scientific or business graphics.

Statistical Package for the Social Sciences (Stat-Pak), from SPSS, one of the best known statistical software packages in the industry. It runs on the personal computer, as well as on workstations and midrange and mainframe machines. You can use it to analyze your data with a variety of statistical techniques, and it includes complete data and file management, along with the ability to create charts and tables.

If you want to support your findings with well-presented and reliable numbers, a statistical analysis software product can be a good investment.

Building Your Software Library

While the software options are plentiful, you don't have to mortgage your house and have everything you want at once. The key is to take your time, and build your library slowly. Start with the products you are sure you will need, based on your specific interests and activities. Most likely, you will want a good word-processing package. After that, take your time about buying maps, project management, and other products. Once you have integrated the computer into your fact-finding, the priorities will make themselves known. Let the need drive the decision. And then with a purpose in mind, go shopping.

Exploring the Purchasable Software Options

Since the personal computer has become ubiquitous, software packages have turned into commodity products. You can find them everywhere—computer stores, department stores, retail software stores, and even your corner store. If you have taken the time to do your homework, and know exactly what you want and why, you are ready to scout around for the product options. Here are some of the best places to find out about the different types of available software.

Computer Retail Stores

Visiting computer software stores is a good way to get started. There you can see what software packages are available, observe them in action, and even try them out. This way, you can assess the look and feel of the product before you consider buying it. Also, store personnel generally know something (though not everything) about the software they sell, and may be able to recommend a product to suit your needs. Store personnel are also a good source of experience and advice.

Magazines

Computer magazines are another helpful resource for discovering what kinds of software products are available. Some feature so much advertising that the ads far outnumber the text. This isn't so great for regular subscribers, but as a shopper, it can be ideal. Most ads include a toll-free number, or a mail-in card. If you have enough time in your comparison shopping to wait for your requests for information to be filled, take advantage of these options. Many advertisements offer a demonstration diskette, which is another way of finding out what the software product might provide.

Associations

As discussed previously, trade associations and other organizations may offer various software products for purchase by members, and often nonmembers. These include indexes (to their own journals), facts and other information, and membership lists. Check on availability by perusing membership literature, or calling the association's publications department.

After you've viewed the options among software products, you'll be ready to make a purchase. There are a few points to bear in mind in that department, also.

Buyer Beware

While you are likely to find the best value for your money by ordering your computer equipment from a mail-order vendor, this is not necessarily true when buying software. With periodic sales at the retail stores, as well as an increasing number of discount software stores, you may find exactly what you want, at the lowest price, in your own community.

Start with a Software Store

Stores want to please their customers, and since they are dealing with you face to face, and you are a member of their community (and one who might tell others if for some reason you are dissatisfied with the store), they have a stake in making sure you are happy with them. And, you might have better luck with a local store if you decide you are unhappy with a product and want to exchange or return it.

Check on Return Policy

If you haven't had an opportunity to test a software product before you purchase it, check on return policies. You may find that, to run efficiently, a product requires more RAM than your system has available, or needs a higher level of resolution on the screen. Or, you may purchase a product that is too hard to use, or that doesn't do what the sales literature said it would. Many software companies offer a trial period, and stores often have their own return policies as well.

Verify the Release Date

Another concern with software products is the release date. Software products are updated from time to time, with "bugs" worked out, and new features added. Some products are updated every year or so, while others are updated less often, but with more new features. Each update of a software product is referred to as a release, and each release is identified by a number. The release numbers get higher with each new release. For example, release 5.0 of a product is an older release than 5.1, or 6.0.

Check the release number, and be aware of whether the product is the newest release or not. You can find this out by asking the salesperson, if you visit a software store. You can also check in buyers' guides, or in computer magazines. Unless your needs are urgent, don't buy a release of a product that is just about to be updated; your release will be out-of-date before you get it home, and by not waiting, you may be missing out on new features.

Make Sure It's Compatible

Before you order or purchase software, you need to check on compatibility with your own equipment, and ask about any other required software.

Compatibility begins with your brand of computer. If you are using a Macintosh, DOS-based (IBM or IBM-compatible) data will not be usable with your system, and the reverse is true if you are a DOS user. But that's only the beginning.

The size of your diskette drives should also be considered. If your drives handle 5¼-inch diskettes, and information is shipped on a 3½-inch diskette, it will be unusable. And there's yet a third consideration—the density of the diskette. Older models of IBM and compatible computers (8088 and 8086) may handle only low-density diskettes, while newer models (286, 396) also handle higher-density diskettes, which can store more information. Additionally, be certain that you have the correct monitor. For example, a software package that requires color may not be usable in a monochrome system. Avoid another trip to the store, or to the post office, and make sure you will be able to make use of the software you purchase.

Check to see if any additional software is required. For example, diskette-based information may require the use of a word-processing software product. If you don't have one, the data could be worthless to you. A software product may also require that you be a certain release level of DOS, for example.

Shareware

Want to get loads of software without breaking your bank? Shareware is an option you'll want to explore. Over the past few years, shareware has grown into a viable form of software distribution, both nationally and internationally. Shareware software products are developed by independent software developers, who offer their products to users at a reasonable price. Shareware is sold on an "honors system." You order the product for a small fee—generally a few dollars—through a shareware service, and if you like it, you can send the developer a fee, usually less than $50, which makes you a registered user. You will then receive information on further releases and, in some cases, additional documentation.

Shareware products are offered in many areas including database, accounting, games, reference, spreadsheet, and word processing. It's a great way to try out some new software areas without spending a lot of money.

Major sources of shareware include:

PC-SIG
1030 D East Duane Avenue
Sunnyvale, CA 94086
Telephone: (800) 245-6717

Accusoft Shareware
14761 Pearl Road, Suite 309, Dept. 12
Strongsville, OH 44136
Telephone: (800) 487-2148

Reasonable Solutions
2101 West Main Street
Medford, OR 97501

Truis, Inc.
231 Sutton Street, Suite 2D-3
North Andover, MA 01845
Telephone: (800) 468-7487

PC-SIG, Accusoft, and Reasonable Solutions offer a wide variety of products, while Truis specializes in spreadsheet and computer-aided drafting.

For more information on shareware, also try:
Shareware Magazine, published by PC-SIG, with articles on the shareware industry, product listings, and tips for users. It is available through PC-SIG.

Don't Be a Software Thief

Have you ever had a friend offer you a copy of a major word processing or spreadsheet package, or maybe a game or two? While avoiding the expense of a software package is an attractive idea, there are a few reasons why you should refuse such an offer. Most importantly, when you commit software piracy you are breaking copyright laws, and that's a crime. But as a user, copying software affects you in other ways.

Software companies are profit-making businesses. When their software products are copied, they don't make money. This affects not only the profit margin, but also affects the ability to put money into research and development, the activities that lead to better products. When products aren't improved, the user loses.

Secondly, the purchase price of most software products also includes use of customer support. When companies don't make money from their products, they also don't have funds to offer quick response, and longer hours, on the customer support line. The user loses again.

Most software companies will ask you to provide your product registration number when you request assistance— if you have a pirated copy, you probably won't get assistance. And with a pirated copy, you won't have the documentation. That places you further behind. And when low-cost upgrades are offered to current users, you can't take advantage of that benefit either.

Cough up the cash for your software products—you'll be further ahead in the end (and think of how much better you'll sleep at night).

Seven Questions a Wise Person Should Ask Before Buying Software

Here are some guidelines for buying a software product, from *The Urgently Needed Parent's Guide to Computers*.

1. Is the software compatible with my equipment?
2. Is the software content suitable for me and my kids?
3. Does it perform satisfactorily?
4. Is it reliable under hard [frequent] usage?
5. Is it easy enough to use?
6. Is the documentation well-written?
7. Is it attractive?

From Brian Williams and Richard Tingey, *The Urgently Needed Parent's Guide to Computers*. Reading, Mass.: Addison-Wesley, 1984, p. 88.

Unlimited Potential

Software is referred to by many of the industry experts as one of the next untapped frontiers in technology. Even with the advances in product design, and the many products available, the potential is far from exhausted. Icons have revolutionized ease of use. Better design has streamlined the process of establishing relationships between different kinds of information. And in conjunction with hardware advances, like color and sound, using software has become an exciting, entertaining experience as well.

Be open to experimentation. As the advances in software design yield new products, you'll be a step ahead in reaping the benefits.

Tricks Librarians Use

1. While your local newsstand will have an array of computer magazines full of software reviews, the magazines may not have included your specific area of in-

terest that month. Check with your local library for back issues of computer magazines as well as for annual buyer's guides. This step can save you a lot of money.

2. To gain a *really* comprehensive view of what's available in personal computer software, take a look at *Microcomputer Software Sources: A Guide for Buyers, Librarians, Programmers, Businesspeople, and Educators*, published by Libraries Unlimited, Inc. The book describes published guides (books, journals, and newsletters) to the software industry, business software, educational computing, library applications, machine-specific software, free and inexpensive software, and publishing and marketing guides. *Microcomputer Software Sources* may be available in your library.

14

Going Online: Using Online Databases and Information Services

Online resources are becoming more and more plentiful, not only for library and business users, but also for your own home resource center. In this chapter, the options for online fact-finding are described, with an example of a search and guidelines for doing your own searching.

Online Terminology: Services and Databases

In Chapter 12, as well as in previous chapters, the benefits of online information were discussed. These benefits include more targeted searching with a variety of search criteria and more up-to-date information without waiting for the availability of a book or other publication. And by going online, you not only have access to a world of information, but you can also go shopping, make stock transactions, and conduct other daily business. Before taking a closer look at what's available online, and how to find it, let's start by clarifying a couple of terms:

Online Information Services

Online information services are services like Compu-Serve, which are usually available by paying a monthly subscription fee. Through an online information service, you can access a range of online databases, depending on the service, from movie reviews to business news. Online information services may also offer opportunities to conduct other kinds of business online, like travel reservations, and may even allow you to communicate with other users. By subscribing to an online information service, you have access to all databases and other services available to members, though charges may be higher for some databases.

Online Databases

An online database refers to a specific collection of information sources available to online users, such as an online database of business news. This online database might be available to subscribers of an online information service, or users might need to access it directly. Additionally, the major online databases are available through more than one service. In most cases, the fee structure and access method would be specific to the online service that you are using.

Because a specific online database may be available through multiple online information services, here is your first guideline in choosing an online service—make sure the databases you are interested in using will be available to you. And to avoid paying multiple subscription fees, you may want to make some choices among services, and choose the one that has the most relevant databases available, even if it means making a few compromises.

Major Online Offerings

While online services have been discussed throughout this book, the focus has been on those available through your local library. A number of online resources are available to the home and business user as well, which may or may not be available through your library. However, the options of services from which to choose has decreased, due to the volatility of the online information market. In parallel with the computer industry itself, many companies in this industry have either merged or gone out of business. As a result, fewer, yet larger, companies remain.

Major Online Information Services
for Home Users

Information services that are oriented to the home user will be less expensive than those that cater to the business community. The services also differ. The three major online information services for consumers are CompuServe, Prodigy, and America Online. All three are described below:

CompuServe
5000 Arlington Centre Blvd.
P.O. Box 20212
Columbus, OH 43220
Telephone: (614) 457-8650
Toll Free: (800) 848-8990

CompuServe offers a wide range of options, including shopping (you can make purchases online); news, sports and weather; reference; finance; games and entertainment; communications; and travel and leisure. Databases available through CompuServe include Associated Press Online, *Grolier's Academic American Encyclopedia*, Roger Ebert's Movie Reviews, *Consumer Reports*, *Disclosure Financial Statements*, U.S. Government Publications, Rare Disease Database, and *Peterson's College Database*. A unique feature of CompuServe are forums, or discussion groups, related to specific personal computer hardware and software products, including Commodore, Apple, Atari, Adobe, Lotus, and WordPerfect, to name but a few. You can also join a discussion group, organized around many diverse interests such as astronomy, crafts, disabilities, genealogy, photography, and religion.

Prodigy
P.O. Box 191486
Dallas, TX 75219-1486
Toll Free: (800) 776-3552

Prodigy offers many services of special interest to the home user, in areas that include travel, financial services, education, entertainment, and general information. Highlights include in-home banking, *Sports Illustrated* online, *USA Today* online classified advertising, employment advertising, extensive online shopping, as well as *Consumer Reports* and *Grolier's Encyclopedia*. You can also send messages to other users, and make use of public bulletin boards on a range of topics like food, travel, and money. Prodigy offers full-color graphics.

America Online
8619 Westwood Center Drive
Vienna, VA 22182-2285
Telephone: (703) 448-8700

America Online began as an online information service for Macintosh and Apple II users, and perhaps because of this early association, it has maintained a superior graphics interface. Services include communications and interactivity, with electronic mail and a wide range of bulletin boards and online discussion groups. A wide range of public domain software programs are available for downloading. Educational services include interactive classes for both academic and general interest, and adult education, supplemented by an online Compton's encyclo-pedia and features from *National Geographic*. Addition-ally, games with color and sound can be accessed. America Online also offers transaction services, including airline, hotel and rental car booking, a discount shopping service, and brokerage services.

Which One Is Best?

Each of the major online services has its strengths. Compu-Serve is generally associated with "power users," mainly because its range of information services is oriented to the business community. While CompuServe offers many so-phisticated information databases, additional charges are associated with many of these databases, while most of the basic, consumer-oriented services are included in the small monthly fee.

Prodigy has a consumer orientation, with a focus on family interests and concerns. America Online, with its extensive education services, offers yet another alternative.

While the costs associated with online services change often as providers shift their pricing strategies in line with market demand, these three services are all available for a few dollars per month, with additional charges based on factors such as hour of day and services being used.

Online services generally offers some type of inexpensive,

trial membership. This gives you an opportunity to go online for a while, test out the databases and services offered, and make a decision based on your own needs and interests. When making your decision, think about what you would use now, as well as what you might need in the future. Don't go overboard with services that you won't need, but don't limit yourself either. Also look for ease of use. If you have trouble maneuvering your way around an online service, or find the user interface to be easy, yet slow, then consider trying another service.

Other Online Information Services

In addition to the ones described above, an amazing number of online services, each with a wide variety of databases, is available. Some are likely to be found in academic settings, or libraries, while others are oriented toward the business community. Other major online services and databases are described below.

GEnie
c/o GE Information Services
P.O. Box 6403
Rockville, MD 20850-1785
Toll Free: (800) 638-9636

GEnie is an online service for both the home and business user, offering lower rates for non-prime-time users. Services include computer support, online learning, investment management, games, discussion groups, and roundtables on personal computer products and services.

BRS/Search Service
8000 Westpark Drive
McLean, VA 22102
Telephone: (703) 442-0900
Toll Free: (800) 955-0906

BRS/Search Service is a complete electronic library with databases covering every major discipline, including health, medicine, pharmacology, the biosciences, science and technology, education, business and finance, the social sciences, and the humanities. Databases include indexes to current and historical information from journal articles, books, dissertations, and government reports, as well, in some cases, the full text of this information. BRS also offers BRS After Dark, offering lower-cost, off-hours online search services.

DataTimes
14000 Quail Springs Parkway
Suite 450
Oklahoma City, OK 73134
Telephone: (405) 751-6400

DataTimes is a business-oriented online information service providing access to over 800 worldwide sources, including newspapers, industry journals, magazines, and wire services. Information categories include marketing, planning and development, communications, legal, and finance.

DIALOG Information Retrieval Service
3460 Hillview Avenue
Palo Alto, CA 94304
Telephone: (415) 858-3785
Toll Free: (800) 3-DIALOG

DIALOG Information Retrieval Service provides approximately 400 databases representing a wide variety of subjects, including science, business, technology, chemistry, law, medicine, engineering, social sciences, economics, current events, and more. The databases provide indexes to book reviews and biographies; directories of companies, people, and associations; and access to the complete text of articles from many newspapers, journals, and other original sources. Information from current sources is available, as well as entries from the past decade or more.

Dow Jones News/Retrieval
Information Services Group
Post Office Box 300
Princeton, NJ 08543
Telephone: (609) 520-4649

Dow Jones News/Retrieval offers a wide range of company and business information, including full text searching of major business publications including the *Wall Street Journal* and *Business Week*, stock quotations, and current business news releases. Special Dow Jones databases include the *National Business Employment Weekly*, with weekly job openings nationwide.

EasyNet
Telebase Systems, Inc.
435 Devon Park Drive
Wayne, PA 19087
Telephone: (215) 293-4700

EasyNet, the Knowledge Gateway, is essentially a gateway to other online services, including DIALOG, NewsNet, and BRS, offering simplified, menu-driven searching and online help.

NewsNet
945 Haverford Road
Bryn Mawr, PA 19010
Telephone: (215) 527-8030

NewsNet online information service contains over 560 business and industry publications, as well as 20 worldwide newswires. NewsNet also offers a special service, called NewsFlash, which is an electronic clipping service that targets articles on topics specified by the subscriber.

ORBIT Search Service
8000 Westpark Drive
McLean, VA 22102
Telephone: (703) 442-0900
Toll Free: (800) 955-0906

ORBIT Search Service specializes in technical information, and offers access to more than 100 databases with information in areas such as patent information; chemistry; materials science; energy and earth sciences; engineering and electronics; and health, safety and the environment. ORBIT includes well-known databases as well as databases not resident on other online services. Databases available only through ORBIT include *Who's Who in Technology*, with biographies of leaders in technology, and *Accountants*, with accounting literature.

WILSONLINE
950 University Avenue
Bronx, NY 10452
Telephone: (212) 588-8400

WILSONLINE, from the H. W. Wilson Company, provides online access to 20-plus bibliographic indexes, most of which are in print form. This service is designed to be used by libraries, but may also be helpful to the at-home fact finder. WilsonLine includes often-used indexes such as *Readers' Guide to Periodical Literature*, *Biography Index*, *Business Periodicals Index*, and *Social Sciences Index*.

LEXIS/NEXIS

Mead Data Central, Inc.
9443 Springboro Pike
P.O. Box 933
Dayton, OH 45401-9964
Telephone: (513) 865-6800
Toll Free: (800) 227-4908

NEXIS is an online information service focused on the business user, offering access to databases in areas that include trade/technology, news/business, international news, company/industry, and legislative/regulatory. These databases include full text major business and news publications. NEXIS is useful for tasks such as monitoring business situations, locating hard-to-find facts, gaining specialized business knowledge, developing comprehensive company profiles, cultivating international business, and following political and legal changes.

LEXIS is an online information service offering comprehensive, computer-assisted legal research information, including state, federal, and foreign case law; comprehensive specialized libraries for research in tax, securities and other areas; full-text law reviews; corporation information; U.S. and state attorneys general opinions; and other legal information.

While LEXIS and NEXIS are generally used by businesses and law firms rather than the home user, Mead Data Central offers an additional service, NEXIS EXPRESS, for occasional research needs. The NEXIS EXPRESS service is staffed by professional information specialists who act as your personal research staff, providing you with targeted research based on your topic of interest. The service is priced per half hour of time, with additional costs for printed information, rush service, diskettes, and other services.

And Now . . . Internet

Internet is an international information network that offers access to an extensive array of discussion groups, reference materials, databases, indexes, journals, newsletters, software, and more. Internet is based on a sophisticated computer network that links users from organizations around the world. It traditionally has been limited to users associated with universities, libraries, and research organizations. Internet users can join online discussion groups on topics such as folklore, politics and visual arts. They can also access reference materials such as census information, book reviews, and historical speeches, or read the electronic form of a journal such as *China News Digest* or *Biosphere Newsletter*. Databases available through Internet include Minority Online Information Service and NASA Spacelink. Additionally, Internet users may communicate with each other through electronic mail.

When you are looking for expert advice and hard-to-find information, and have exhausted other resources, Internet can add another high tech edge to your fact-finding. Since Internet users tend to be members of the academic community and other professional groups, they are likely to provide both information and referrals to other resources.

There are costs associated with the use of Internet, and the general home user has had difficulty obtaining it. However, network service providers, which operate similarly to long distance telephone companies, will provide access to Internet. This is expensive and probably affordable only for larger groups. CompuServe is now offering access to the electronic mail portion of Internet. While this does not allow you to obtain specific databases and other information services, you could connect with other Internet users and possibly receive further assistance from them.

For more information on Internet, take a look at:

The Whole Internet: User's Guide and Catalog, by Ed Krol, published by O'Reilly & Associates, Inc., 1992. This book provides an in-depth description of Internet and how to use it, as well as options for making an Internet connection.

Online Databases

An online service is only as good as the databases available to users. Online databases are organized around hundreds of topics and disciplines. Below are a brief selection, all of which are available through various online information services, including those described above. Notice that the descriptions of these databases indicate whether they contain full text information, or are indexes to publications.

Art and Humanities

Wilson Art Index, from the H. W. Wilson Company, is an index to international art publications, with topics that include antiques, architecture, art and art history, motion pictures, folk art and related areas.

Wilson Humanities Index, from the H. W. Wilson Company, is an index to periodicals in disciplines that include dance, drama, film, folklore, history, journalism and communications, language and literature, music, performing arts, philosophy, religion and theology.

Business

ABI/INFORM, produced by UMI/Data Courier, indexes periodicals in the areas of business, management, and industry. Specific areas covered include accounting, advertising, data processing, economics, finance, international trade, marketing, social conditions, and taxes.

Disclosure Database, from Disclosure Incorporated, is a full-text database and includes financial and text data that public companies have filed with the Securities and Exchange Commission.

Harvard Business Review/Online, produced by John Wiley & Sons, Inc., has the complete text of articles from *Harvard Business Review*.

PAIS International, from PAIS–Public Affairs Information Service, Inc., offers international coverage of public policy concerns. It is an index to disciplines that include business, economics, government, law, international relations, and demography.

Reuters Textline, from Reuter's, contains the full text of news and comments from international publications, including magazines, trade journals, and newspapers.

Social Sciences

AgeLine, produced by American Association of Retired Persons and the National Gerontology Resource Center, is an index covering the economic, socio-psychological, health, and political aspects of aging, and includes citations and abstracts.

Family Resources Database, from the National Council on Family Relations, includes citations to articles, documents, books, and other materials, with a focus on marriage and the family.

LABORDOC, from the International Labour Office, indexes literature in labor and related areas, such as industrial relations, management, project evaluation, the implications of technological change, and others.

PsycINFO, from the American Psychological Association, indexes and abstracts articles, reports and dissertations from around the world, on psychology and related disciplines.

Sociological Abstracts, from Sociological Abstracts, Inc., indexes and abstracts articles, books, papers and other publications in topics related to sociology.

Science and Technology

American Men and Women of Science, produced by Bowker Electronic Publishing, is an active register of U.S. and Canadian scientists in the physical and biological sciences. Biographical profiles are included, with current affiliations and contact information.

CLAIMS, produced by IFI/Plenum Data Corporation, is a series of related databases that provide information about U.S. patents issued by the U.S. Patent and Trademark Office.

CorpTech, from Corporate Technology Information Services, is a directory of company information on manufacturers and developers of high technology products, including computer hardware and software, environmental, robotics, and biotechnology.

ENERGYLINE, from Bowker Electronic Publishing, serves as an index to energy information found in journals, reports, surveys, monographs, newspapers, conference proceedings, and other sources.

Food Science and Technology Abstracts, produced by International Food Information Service, covers food science and technology, indexing articles on food safety, engineering, packaging, processing, and related areas.

GEOREF, from The American Geological Institute, covers geosciences literature on subjects that include economic geology, geochemistry, geomorphology, solid earth physics, and related topics, indexing information from journals, books, conference proceedings, government documents, and others.

Japan Technology, from Scan C2C, Inc., includes abstracts of Japanese journal articles and special reports, covering the business, technology, and science of Japan.

MICROSEARCH, from Information, Inc., focuses on microcomputer products such as hardware, software, peripherals, accessories and services. It contains product descriptions, reviews, and related information, from trade journals and product literature.

NTIS, produced by National Technical Information Service of the U.S. Department of Commerce, is an index to U.S. government-sponsored research from federal government agencies, their contractors and grantees. The scope is multidisciplinary, and includes administration and management, agriculture, business and economics, energy, health, biomedical science, and other areas of science and technology.

SAE Global Mobility Database, produced by the Society of Automotive Engineers, Inc., indexes technical papers presented at the Society of Automotive Engineers meetings and conferences.

Scientific & Technical Books & Serials in Print, from Bowker Electronic Publishing, offers a comprehensive subject selection of books and serials in scientific and technological fields.

SciSearch, from Institute for Scientific Information, has a multidisciplinary index to international science and technology journals.

SuperTech, from Bowker Electronic Publishing, is an index to areas that include artificial intelligence, computer-aided design/Computer-aided manufacturing, and robotics.

Health
Birth Defects Information System, from the Center for Birth Defects Information Services, Inc., is a database with the full text of articles on specific birth defects, organized by names and terms.

CISDOC, produced by the International Occupational Safety & Health Information Center of the International Labour Office, has international coverage of topics related to general safety, health and conditions at work.

Health News Daily, from F-D-C Reports, Inc., records the full text of the company's newsletter by the same name, covering health policy, biomedical and regulation news.

Pharmaceutical News Index, produced by UMI/Data Courier, serves as an index to publications covering news about pharmaceuticals and related health care industries, including cosmetics and medical devices.

Physician Data Query Cancer Information File, produced by the National Cancer Institute, contains information of different types of cancer. It is a full-text database, with references to relevant medical literature.

SPORT Database, from the Sport Information Resource Centre, contains abstracts of articles from journals, books, and other publications, on topics related to sports medicine, sports psychology, physical education, fitness, and other subjects.

Literature and Reference
Books in Print, from R. R. Bowker, is a comprehensive directory of all books published in the U.S.

Bowker's International Serials Database (Ulrich's), has information on an assortment of periodicals and serials published in the U.S. and throughout the world.

Cuadra Directory of Databases, produced by Cuadra/Elsevier, lists online databases offered through online services.

Magill Book Reviews, from Salem Press, features the full text of reviews from different sources of current works of fiction and non-fiction published since 1985, with additional synopses of classic books.

Popular Magazine Review Online, from EBSCO Industries, Inc., contains descriptions of articles found in popular magazines.

Wilson Readers' Guide Abstracts, from The H. W. Wilson Company, is an index to articles (with abstracts of the articles) on a broad range of topics.

Education

Grolier's Academic American Encyclopedia, from Grolier Electronic Publishing, contains the complete text of articles providing current information in a wide range of subject areas.

Dissertation Abstracts Online, from University Microfilms International, lists citations to doctoral dissertations accepted at universities in North America.

Education Resources Information Center (ERIC) is an education database produced by the U.S. Department of Education, with citations to articles in education journals and other education-related literature.

Peterson's College Database, from Peterson's, is the electronic version of the directory to colleges and universities in the U.S. and Canada, with detailed profiles on each institution.

Some online databases are easier to gain access to than others. Some are restricted to members of certain professional groups, such as physicians, while others can be accessed only through specific online database services. And, of course, cost can be prohibitive. However, bear in mind that in many cases a database can be accessed by more than one service, so you do not necessarily have to subscribe to multiple services to obtain access to the databases you are most interested in. Also, many similar databases exist, so if the service you are using doesn't access a database you are interested in using, such as current business news, your service may have access to one that is quite similar.

The key to making decisions about online information services and databases is to do some shopping, just as you would do for any other product or service, and evaluate the alternatives. And that starts with knowing where to look.

Where to Locate Online Information

While online information is available in abundance, finding an affordable resource that meets your needs can be a difficult task. The good news, as you can see, is that there are a wide range of alternatives, both among online services and among categories of databases. By doing some digging around, you are sure to locate the resources you need. Like any other aspect of fact-finding, the key is to target your search. And, as always, talk with your librarian first.

Start with Your Library

As you saw in the description of the "state-of-the-art library" in Chapter 3, easier accessibility, increasing demand by users, and lower costs have all contributed to greater availability of computer-based information resources, in both large and small libraries. Unless you have your own personal computer and a modem or CD-ROM disc drive at home, the library is the best place to start using computer-based information. Much of what you need will be there, and librarians will be available to help you use the equipment (as noted previously, self-searching through online databases is only available in a limited number of libraries).

Computerized resources are also plentiful outside of the library. Many organizations and businesses are making them available to their employees. For example, a corporate legal department could subscribe to LEXIS, an online legal information service, while the marketing departments could access an online database with up-to-the-second business news, as well as a CD-ROM index to professional and technical journals. Organizations and associations participate in forums over online database services, where individuals with similar professional interests discuss issues by messages that they send each other through computer lines.

Still, you can obtain these resources on your own, and have them available whenever the need arises. One way to find out more about online resources is through a reference book, such as:

Computer-Readable Databases, published by Gale Research Inc., and edited by Kathleen Young Marcaccio, which lists thousands of databases, arranged alphabetically. Both CD-ROM and online databases are included, supplemented by a subject index.

Alternate sources for online databases and services include computer and other specialized publications.

Computer Magazines

Online information services are often advertised in computer magazines, and articles, reviews, and comparisons are written about these products and services. Thumb through a computer magazine for ads and articles, and also check the annual index, which your library may have. *Home Office Computing*, from Scholastic, is one of the best magazines to read about online services because it is aimed at home-based workers who may depend on these services in conducting business.

Another magazine to consult:

Database Searcher
Meckler Corporation
11 Ferry Lane West
Westport, CT 06880
Telephone: (203) 226-6967
Database Searcher is a monthly magazine for online database users, with feature articles and product news.

Specialized Magazines

Because of the specialized nature of many online databases, they may not be discussed in computer magazines offered for a general readership. The best place to find out more may be in magazines for specialized markets, like trade magazines. For example, you might find out about a historical database in a history magazine, or a scientific database in a science journal, or a genealogy database in a genealogy newsletter.

Associations and Organizations

Industry specific organizations offer online databases, as do trade associations. When you are contacting these groups to receive publications, also check to see if they have online databases that you can access.

Online Information: How Does It Work?

Each online information service is accessed a bit differently. Generally, the online service provides their subscribers with a simple software diskette that contains a communications program designed to work only with that specific online information service. It will not be usable to access other online services. Once installed on the hard drive, you enter a simple command or make a choice from a menu to access the online service. The software program then does the dialing. In many cases, the service can also be accessed by choosing an icon. Additionally, if you have purchased a communications software product, such as one of those described in Chapter 14, the telephone access numbers of any online database services that you subscribe to can be dialed automatically through your product's main menu.

Once you have made the connection with the online information service, you will most likely be asked to enter a user identification number, as well as a password, before you are actually allowed to begin using the service. If you haven't memorized this information, it's a good idea to store it in a safe, yet easily accessible, place.

After your identification and password are recognized, online information services present the choices to the subscriber. They all differ in terms of their presentation. For example, some services offer graphics capabilities, so that you can choose among the databases you want to use, and the functions you want to perform, through the use of icons and a mouse. Other online services are not quite as easy to use, and require the user to use the arrow keys to move through the lists of databases and functions, and make choices with the Enter key. Other services require the use of specific commands.

Once you are using a database, the process of choosing functions such as printing or downloading entries for future reference, or leaving a database and moving on to another one, is unique both to the online database you are using, as well as to the online database service. Again, it's advisable to sit with the user manual, or consult a customer service representative or a librarian, before you begin using an online database service, or a database, with which you are familiar.

As always, time is of the essence when going online. Online information services keep subscribers informed of how much time has elapsed since connecting with the service, as well as how much time has been spent using each specific database. (Remember, some databases are more expensive to use than others, even within the same online information service.) Elapsed time will be readily available; if not shown in the corner of your screen, it can at least be ascertained through the use of a command. Make sure you find out how to keep track of time before you begin an online session.

Online Information: How Expensive?

Online database searching does not have to be costly. However, there are a variety of expenses involved, and each function you perform can have cost implications. One session can be surprisingly expensive if you haven't taken the time to understand the pricing structure.

Each online service charges you for connect time, as well as for incidentals like retrievals of citations, full-text retrievals, and print-outs. Additionally each specific database has its own associated costs, so each of the different databases you access—through the same online information service—may be priced differently. Again, planning ahead of time can help you avoid costs.

Below are the kinds of general costs you might expect to incur during an online search session.

Long Distance Rates

Larger online services tend to be accessible by a local telephone number, depending on where you live. Some also provide a toll-free number to subscribers. More specialized services will require that you use a long-distance number for access. If you are concerned about long-distance rates, call your long-distance carrier before you actually connect to the service, and ask for a cost estimate. Also consider accessing the service during the evening and night hours, when rates are cheaper.

Online Connect Time

Online connect time is the fee you pay while you are connected to the online service. This fee is in addition to your standard phone bill charges, and there will also often be additional fees for accessing specific databases. Fees for online connect time, compared to the other fees that you may be charged, is relatively low, and can even be a few dollars per month. Carefully read the documentation associated with the service to distinguish connect time from monthly rates. Each online information service levies this charge differently—some services charge you every time you make a connection, while others charge only for the time you are connected to a database.

Database Access Fees

Database access fees vary drastically from database to database, depending on factors like specialization and demand.

Hourly rates can range from $15 to $150 or more per hour. Rates will be listed in the documentation, as well as on a price list screen, or menu, accessible through the online service. Watch these fees very carefully; they can result in some really shocking news when you receive your bill.

Online Prints

Your online database service may offer you the option of selecting specific lists of citations, or full-text articles, and having them printed offline and mailed to you. This may be preferable to writing down all of this information, or being charged for printing it out on your own system (if you have a printer available). You will be charged for the documents, with a handling and mailing fee.

Full-Text Articles and Citations

Online database services will often bill you additionally for the full-text articles and citations that you retrieve. For example, if your search yields a certain number of citations, you may be billed a nominal fee for each of the "hits." Furthermore, when you go on to look at full-text articles on your screen, as well as to print them out, the fees will increase. You will pay more for a full-text article than you will for a citation; the costs may be less than a dollar, or even a few cents, for each. But again, these costs can add up rapidly.

Subscription Fee

Most online information services charge a monthly or annual fee for the privilege of being able to access the service. This fee gets you a password, as well as user documentation, use of the customer service line, and in some instances, a newsletter. In many cases, the annual fee is less than $200. This is a small fee, though if you are subscribing to numerous services, you can end up spending a lot of money on subscription fees.

It's important to be fully aware of what the costs are, and to use efficient searching procedures, beginning with a clear idea of what you want. These procedures will be discussed later in this chapter.

Example of an Online Search

Online searching techniques are the same as those used for CD-ROM. Both require the use of specific search words, or keywords, used in the right combination. The extensive CD-ROM example in Chapter 12 could, in principle, have also been an online search.

However, as discussed previously, a major difference exists between the information you can retrieve through an online database as opposed to CD-ROM. Because of storage limitations of the CD-ROM media, you are more likely to access full-text articles through an online database, while you may often be limited to citations and abstracts through CD-ROM.

Based on this difference, the following is an example of an online search. It was provided by *Knowledge Index*, the user-friendly search service available from DIALOG that contains more than 100 databases. The example is designed to illustrate not only the options for online searching, but also the steps involved in performing an efficient, cost-effective search.

Rather than further exhausting the movie information example, we chose an equally timely topic from the field of science: the ozone layer.

As you can see in Figure 14-1, the first step is to look at the *Knowledge Index* menu screen, which appears automatically when you connect with this service.

Figure 14-1

```
SYSTEM:KI
                  WELCOME TO KNOWLEDGE INDEX

Four new databases are available for searching: Japan Technology (SCIT1),
Commerce  Business  Daily(GOVE3,  GOVE4),  Pharmaceutical  News  Index
(DRUG5), and Business Dateline (BUS17)

MULTIFILE SEARCHING now available IN MENU MODE -- SEE BULLETIN

MLA Bibliography (LITS1) is no longer available.
  Accounting starting at 17:23:01 EST
  Date:      04may92

                    Welcome to KNOWLEDGE INDEX!
                          Main Menu

Select one of the following options:

                    1 Menu Mode
                    2 Command Mode
                    3 DIALMAIL

                    4 Help in formulating a search
                    5 Knowledge Index Bulletin
                    6 General Information

Copr. 1991 Dialog Information Services, Inc.
All rights reserved.

Enter option NUMBER and press ENTER to continue.
  /H = Help                           /L = Logoff
  ?
  2
```

The search was provided courtesy of Knowledge Index, Copyright © 1991 Dialog
Information Services, Inc.

Notice that the Command Mode has been chosen by typing the number 2. This means that the search will be conducted through the use of commands, rather than making choices from a menu. To use Command Mode, the user must have some experience in using Knowledge Index or of similar online database services, or have read the instructions from DIALOG.

After pressing the Enter key, the user is presented with some news about newly available, and unavailable, databases, as shown in Figure 14-2. The question mark indicates

Figure 14-2

```
Date:              04may92

New databases available:  Japan Technology (SCIT1),
Commerce Business Daily(GOV3, GOV4), Pharmaceutical News Index
(DRUG5), and Business Dateline (BUS17).

MULTIFILE SEARCHING now available IN MENU MODE -- SEE BULLETIN

 * * * LITS1 is no longer available. * * *
?
begin news6
```

The search was provided courtesy of Knowledge Index, Copyright © 1991 Dialog
Information Services, Inc.

that the system is waiting for the user's command. Let's
assume we want to use the "news6" database. In the *Knowledge
Index* system, "news" refers to the general category
of news, and the number 6 identifies the *USA Today* database
of full-text news articles.

Figure 14-3 shows the information that the user receives
upon accessing the *USA Today Full Text* database. Suppose
we want to review articles that have been written about
the ozone layer. The search command "find ozone layer"
indicates that the system should search for articles in which
the words "ozone" and "layer" are found adjacent to each
other. Thus, articles mentioning "ozone layer" will be distinguished from other articles in which the words "ozone" and
"layer" are used, but not in relation to each other.

Figure 14-3

```
Now in NEWS Section (NEWS6) Database
USA TODAY FULLTEXT_ 1989 - 30 Apr 1992
(c)   1992 Gannett Media Corp.
?
find ozone layer
```

The search was provided courtesy of Knowledge Index, Copyright © 1991 Dialog
Information Services, Inc.

The *Knowledge System* first counts the number of "hits" that result from this search. As indicated in Figure 14-4, there are 189 articles—also referred to as records—that meet our search criteria of articles that mention "ozone layer." This group is referred to as Set 1 or "s1."

The system also tells us that there are also 433 that mention the word "ozone" and 322 that mention the word "layer."

Let's take a look at "retrieve": the full text of the first article that meets our search criteria. To do this, we enter the command:

s1/L/1

Again, "s1" identifies the set, or group, of records that meets our criteria. If we had initiated numerous searches, the results of these searches would be identified by s2, s3, etc.

The letter "L" indicates that we want to see the entire record that is retrieved. In *Knowledge Index*, the letter "L" means entire record (long). "S" indicates title, or name, of the article, without the full text. "M" is used to choose bibliographic information (issue, date, etc.) only.

The third component of the search command, the number "1", indicates that only the first of the 189 articles is desired, as opposed to "1–10" for the first 10.

Figure 14-4

```
                 433   OZONE
                 322   LAYER
         S1      189   OZONE LAYER
?
type s1/L/1

  1/L/1
06513660
```

The search was provided courtesy of Knowledge Index, Copyright © 1991 Dialog Information Services, Inc.

Again, these commands are used within DIALOG's *Knowledge Index* system, and are explained in the user manual.

Figures 14-5 and 14-7 show the results of our retrieval command: the first of the 189 articles that include the words "ozone layer" adjacent to each other. Notice that you have not only the full text of the article, but also the title as well as the bibliographic information.

Figure 14-5

MYSTERY SWIRLS AROUND GREENHOUSE EFFECT IMPACT OF WARMING, OZONE HOLES IN DEBATE
USA Today (US) - WEDNESDAY April 22, 1992
By: Jack Williams
Edition: FINAL   Section: NEWS   Page: 08A
Word Count: 1,038

MEMO:
NOTES: EARTH DAY '92 SPECIAL SECTION Excerpted from The USA TODAY Weather Book, to be published next month by Vintage Books. See info box at end of text

TEXT:
Excerpted from The USA Today Weather Book, to be published next month by Vintage Books.

The hot, dry summer of 1988 got a lot of people talking about a possible climate change.

That year's drought was the worst in the USA since the 1930s Dust Bowl, and in some places it was worse. Hundreds of temperature records fell. In large parts of the Midwest and Plains, it was the hottest or second hottest summer on record.

To many people, the heat and drought were proof of the greenhouse effect -- a buildup of gases in the Earth's atmosphere that trap the sun's heat.

Then, in December 1989, it turned bitterly cold, the coldest December on record in the East and fourth-coldest on record for the entire United States. To many people the cold and snow were proof that the greenhouse effect was just a scare story.

Most atmospheric scientists would call both "proofs" wrong; the climate just isn't that simple. We will be able to prove or disprove the global warming scenario only by analyzing huge amounts of weather data collected over decades.

Figure 14-5 *continued*

An international study released in 1990 gave the world a picture of what may lay ahead. The report said if the world's nations continue adding the same amounts of greenhouse gases to the atmosphere as they do now, the world's average temperature would be about 1 Celsius (about 1.8F) warmer in the year 2025 than in 1990.

If the estimate is true, what will it mean? Greenhouse warming doesn't mean merely adding a few degrees to today's temperatures. We would still have frigid outbreaks, but heat waves would become more common. Some places would become drier, others wetter. Some cloudier, others clearer.

Pinpointing what will happen where is more difficult. Hundreds of factors determine climate. They begin with the amount of solar energy reaching the Earth and include interactions among the atmosphere, oceans, land and living things.

One area that's central to the study of global warming is the effect of clouds. As greenhouse gases warm the air, the air can hold more water, which means cloudiness should increase. This is important because clouds both can help heat and cool the Earth. Which they will do is a key to the global warming question.

The search was provided courtesy of Knowledge Index, Copyright © 1991 Dialog Information Services, Inc.

Suggestions for Efficient Searches

Here are some suggestions to help you save time and money as you perform online database searches.

1. Keep an Eye on Your Plan

Your research plan, developed in Chapter 2, continues to be your best guide as you approach an online search. Look it over carefully so you get a solid handle on the kinds of information you are seeking. Just exactly what is the question you are asking, and who is likely to collect this information? By answering these questions, you'll be ready to begin choosing databases.

2. Choose the Best Database for the Job

If you are using one online information service and searching for business-oriented information, you may still have more

Figure 14-6

In addition to the role of clouds, some of the other major unanswered questions include: How much carbon dioxide are the oceans absorbing now and how much will they absorb if they warm up? How would ocean currents change and how would these changes affect the atmosphere? How do living things and the atmosphere interact?

Since greenhouse gases, especially carbon dioxide, are the main agents of a potential global warming, most scientists agree that the best response is to reduce the carbon dioxide being added to the atmosphere. This becomes an economic and political question.

Reducing fossil fuel use is a sure way to cut carbon dioxide emissions. However, some argue that the incomplete scientific knowledge doesn't justify the economic risk of cutting back on fossil fuel use.

Others argue that we can't wait until all the scientific answers are in, the potential danger of global warming is great enough that we should act now.

The other key global environmental issue is the destruction of ozone in the atmosphere.

The potential danger to the Earth's ozone layer wasn't discovered until 1974, but the story goes back to 1928 when CFCs were invented to replace dangerous substances, such as ammonia, then used in refrigerators. They arrived like miracle chemicals.

CFCs were perfect for refrigerators, spray-can propellants, for cleaning electronic parts and for making foam.

But in 1974 Sherwood Rowland and Mario Molina at the University of California at Irvine found that CFCs were rising into the stratosphere where ultraviolet energy was breaking them up, freeing the chlorine. The freed chlorine was destroying ozone.

This discovery led the USA, Canada, Norway and Sweden to ban CFCs as propellants in most spray cans in 1979. World-wide use leveled off only to increase again in the early 80s with understated estimates of ozone damage.

In 1985 evidence of massive ozone destruction caught scientists by surprise when British researchers reported that ozone was disappearing from the Antarctic sky during the Southern Hemisphere spring.

Someone came up with the phrase "ozone hole" to describe this unexpected thinning of the ozone layer over Antarctica. Scientists launched major research efforts to discover what was happening.

By 1987, researchers had clear evidence of how stratospheric clouds in the minus 100-degree air high above Antarctica were helping chlorine and bromine from CFCs and other man-made substances destroy ozone each spring.

In February of this year, scientists reported high concentrations of ozone-destroying chemicals over parts of the Arctic. Even more alarming, they found

Figure 14-6 *continued*

early signs of possible ozone thinning over parts of the globe away from the poles.

This is why representatives of around 90 nations met earlier this month to work out details of speeding up the phase out of CFCs and other ozone-

Figure 14-7

destroying substances. They expect the new agreement, updating an original treaty signed in 1987 and revised in 1990, to be signed in November.

Look to climate models

Answers about the effects of global warming will come from computer models of the climate being developed by researchers such as Warren Washington, director of the Climate and Global Dynamics Division at the National Center for Atmospheric Research.

He says the major challenge is to fit all the components of climate together. Today, Washington says, such models "generate El Ninos at about the same frequency as the real world." Reproducing those complex patterns of ocean temperatures and weather shows models are on the right track.

Washington says today's models do a poor job of predicting regional climate changes, such as whether a warmer global climate would make the USA's Plains drier. Washington doesn't expect real improvements in regional climate predictions before the end of this decade.

CUTLINE: WASHINGTON

CAPTION:
GRAPHIC

b/w,Julie Stacey,Source: The USA TODAY Weather Book to be published

in May by Vintage Books(Diagram)

PHOTO

b/w,USA TODAY

Copyright 1992 Gannett Co., Inc.

DESCRIPTORS: ENVIRONMENT; PROFILE; COMPUTER
?

than one database to choose from. If you have access to multiple online services, the job becomes even more complicated. Before you begin your session, ask yourself some questions about the databases you are considering accessing. What is the purpose of the database? Does it provide information for the consumer or the professional? What sources does it include? International and domestic publications? Popular magazines only? Specialized journals? Don't access a database with general information if you have a very specific question.

3. Keep Dates in Mind
Online databases are limited in terms of how far they go back in time, as well as how recent they are. If you need information from the 1940s, for example, chances are it won't be included in an online database. And if the database is updated quarterly, it may not have the recent information you need either.

4. Citations or Full-text?
Not all online databases are full-text. Some provide you with citations of articles with or without a brief abstract of the article, that you can then look up on your own. Others provide you with the full text of the articles. Also keep in mind that it may be more expensive to retrieve the full text of an article, particularly if you also download it and print it out.

5. Rehearse Before You Sign On
Make sure you fully understand the search tools of each service and database before you sign on. Check your user manual for this information. Be aware of the kinds of searches available and the keywords you can use ahead of time. Otherwise, you can spend expensive moments trying to teach yourself how to do your search.

6. Keep an Eye on the Clock

Make sure you know the hourly rates for the individual databases you use, even if they are all within the same service, and then watch the clock. If you've been using a database for an hour, and know you've already spent $150, for example, you may want to take a break if your returns are starting to diminish.

7. Consider Downloading

You may be charged for both the citations and the full-text articles you retrieve. And while you are perusing them, you are also being charged online connect and database access fees. Consider downloading. Downloading is computer terminology for pulling information off the online service and storing it on the hard disk of your computer. When you download information, you can then exit from the online service and examine it at your leisure. You save the online time and the cost of offline prints that are mailed to you.

8. Call Customer Service

Many online services, including DIALOG and CompuServe, have excellent customer service lines, which are staffed by experts who can help you with connect problems and search strategies. If you are coming up empty-handed on your search, it's a good idea to give customer service a call.

9. Check out Searching Aids

If you know you'll be searching a particular database often, contact the online service or database producer to find out what searching aids they offer. These may include a list of magazines or journals indexed, or a quarterly newsletter announcing changes and enhancements to the database. Often these are low-cost or even free of charge.

Online Opportunities

Online resources are expanding all the time. However, like purchasable software and CD-ROM, you don't have to jump in over your head to reap the benefits. Subscribe to one of the services oriented toward home use, like CompuServe or Prodigy, to gain a level of comfort and familiarity. And then, as your research needs expand, try one of the other services. And don't forget to take advantage of the resources in your library or at work. As the opportunities for online computing increase, you'll be ready to take the next plunge—whatever that is.

Bulletin Board Services

Thousands of online computer bulletin board services (BBS) are in existence around the U.S. Bulletin board services are much more specialized than online services—they focus on specific subjects rather than offering a range of services—and they are also either low cost or free of charge. Bulletin Board Services are operated by special interest groups of consultants, as well as by companies.

Because a BBS is generally less formal than an online service, you may have to pay long distance rates to access one. And you won't find the user friendly menus that an online service has. However, this may be an expedient means of reaching experts and getting ideas from people with similar interests.

An example of a BBS is The Harvard On-Line Library Information System (HOLLIS), Cambridge, Massachusetts, which is accessible by calling (617) 495-9500. HOLLIS is a version of the library's computerized library catalog, for use outside the walls of the library. It's a great way to find out what books are available on a specific topic. Then you can call your local library or bookstore to obtain them.

WordPerfect also operates a BBS for WordPerfect users, Salt Lake City, Utah, which is accessible by calling (801) 225-4414 in Salt Lake City, Utah. On this BBS you can ask questions and exchange ideas with other WordPerfect users, as well as obtain utilities and other information. You need your WordPerfect license number to log on.

To find out about other Bulletin Board Services, check in professional and trade magazines, particularly publications focused on your area of interest. Issues of *Online Access*, a magazine for professionals who use online services, also cover bulletin board services from time to time.

The WELL—Whole Earth Lectronic Link

The WELL (Whole Earth Lectronic Link) is a teleconferencing system that lets you use your computer and modem to "talk" with other people by writing to them, either privately or in public discussions. Combining the best aspects of the telephone and the postal service, it improves your efficiency and lets you meet with people at any time without having to get up from your desk. A brochure about the WELL describes it as: "a mind pool, an information exchange, a resource for technical help. It's a business tool. It's an interactive Sunday paper, a source for great conversation, a potluck for people who love ideas, discourse and language, and a place to get a good intellectual message." You can learn more about the WELL by dialing in directly, at (415) 332-6106 with a 1200 baud modem or (415) 332-7298 for 2400 baud. Or you can call (415) 332-4335 to request more information. No membership fees are required.

Tricks Librarians Use

The *Gale Database of Publications and Broadcast Media* allows you to be an instant authority on newspapers, magazines, journals, periodicals, directories, and newsletters; as well as on radio, television, and cable systems, all by using this online database, available through DIALOG. This database contains over 65,000 entries, with addresses, telephone numbers, contact names, and other information, and includes a wide range of search options.

What uses would you have for a database like this? Here are a few suggestions:

- Develop a list of newspapers and broadcast stations to contact to promote and advertise your product
- Plan your targeted publicity campaign to include all media
- Locate hard-to-find directories and lists in any subject category
- Discover a newsletter of interest to a particular professional or personal group
- Calculate which publications offer you the largest return for your advertising budget, by using the circulation size and advertising rates
- Find directories with lists of industry contacts or experts
- List the feature editors of the major metropolitan newspapers
- Locate job and career opportunities in an area or industry
- Expand library collections and use the file as a decision-making tool for periodical acquisitions

15

When the Information Keeps Hiding

In spite of all your diligence, occasions will arise when you still can't unearth that one last little piece of information. Some solutions are presented in this chapter.

Loose Ends that Remain Loose

From time to time in the course of fact-finding, even the most seasoned and thorough researcher runs smack into a brick wall. It happens. Perhaps an obscure resource was overlooked. Or a resource that seemed promising was not as comprehensive as expected. Or maybe an "expert" sent you on what turned out to be a wild-goose chase.

The first thing to admit when you hit a brick wall is that whatever it is you're doing isn't working. Maybe you're looking for facts that just haven't been formally explored yet. Or they haven't been collected in the particular way in which you were expecting to find them. But also acknowledge that the information is probably out there somewhere.

Don't be discouraged and give up: there's always a way to find the information you need. It's all a matter of stepping back and rechannelling your energy in a different direction.

Stand Back and Review

When you can't find the information you need, even after what seems like an exhaustive search, it's time to step back and assess what you've done so far. In Chapter 16, you'll be presented with some ideas for keeping accurate and complete records of your research. So here is the reason for wanting to take the time to keep records: The more thorough your records are, the easier it will be to review your work.

In Chapter 2, research was described as a fact-finding mission, with each bit of information leading to yet another bit. When you get stuck in one spot, the best thing to do is to look where you've gone so far, even if it means going back and retracing your steps. And again, good research records help you do that retracing.

Did You Follow the Plan?

At what point did you realize you were stuck? Are you still at square one? Have you met with some success, yet still need one last detail to round out your work? Start at whatever point you run into trouble, and work back from there.

When you formulated your original research plan, you listed the questions that you wanted answered, as well as the resources you expected to use. Based on what you have accomplished so far, go back through the plan and assess your overall success. It may even be helpful to make a check mark next to the questions that you have answered.

If you haven't already done this, the best approach is to make a list based on your original research plan, noting what you have yet to complete. Once you separate the remaining questions and look at them individually, the task will not appear as daunting.

Check Your Resources?

Also go through your original list of potential resources. Did you use all of them? Any of them? Make a check mark next to those you did use.

Now you've got a list of answered and unanswered questions, as well as used and, potentially, unused resources. Are there resources that you haven't yet tapped into? Could some of these resources help you to solve unanswered questions?

A careful reassessment of your progress in the research plan should answer these questions for you.

Check Your Terminology

In the process of poring through reference books and other publications, as well as online and CD-ROM-based resources, you may have overlooked the material you needed. One reason for missing information is wrong search terminology. For example, did you use "motion picture" instead of "movie"? Or if you were looking for historical data, regardless of when it was published, did you consider using "silent films" instead of "movie"? Or, if you are using an old index, did you remember to check the heading "moving pictures"?

As you may recall, in many cases each online database has its own thesaurus of terms. If you are accustomed to using a specific database and then switch to another one, it is easy to continue using the same terms without taking the time to look through each thesaurus.

It is worth the time to go through your resources and check your search criteria. The facts you need may be sitting there, waiting for you to enter the correct command.

Check the Dates

Online and CD-ROM resources often do not go back as many years as their counterparts in print form. Conversely, online resources are generally more up to date than printed resources. Take the time to check the start and end dates of the references you are using. You may find that you are searching in the wrong era.

Try a New Avenue

Even in this age of specialization, it is often the case that fields of study overlap each other. And all fields are of interest to the news media. So if you are not finding the facts you need within a specific field of study, consider a related field. For example, while a specific illness like heart disease is of primary concern to the medical field, illness also has psychological and economic implications. And it is newsworthy. Searching the literature of or talking to experts in related fields may very well be a means of gaining the slant you need. And in the case of heart disease, you might also find an uncomplicated explanation that you wouldn't get from a medical resource.

Trying a new avenue might involve looking up the same topic in a different reference source or bibliography, or asking the same questions of an expert in a different organization.

Look for New Experts

If you are dissatisfied with the answers you received from one expert, try another. Even among experts with the same specialization, there are different areas of focus. Larger organizations often have many experts on staff. It can be worthwhile to call an organization you've already contacted, and to ask for a different person. Or call the same person, and ask for a referral.

Try a New Online Service

The major online information services offer access to databases that are similar in focus, yet with different resources. For example, most online services offer access to one or more databases of business periodicals. Yet the actual magazines and other periodicals contained in one database differ from those contained in another. Also, the numbers of years spanned will differ among databases. Consider trying an additional database through the same online service, or even try a different service. If you are using one online information service at home, you may be able to access another one through your local library. Also, if a database holds abstracts or the full-text articles rather than only citations, you have a better chance of getting a "hit" because there are more words being searched. So consider a different type of database as well.

Examples

If you hit a wall in your search for movie information, here are a couple of possible avenues you might consider.

If you were looking for articles published back in the 1950s on movies, the *Readers' Guide to Periodical Literature* would be a good place to start. But you wouldn't find any articles under the subject heading "Movies." Indeed, there is no such heading. You would find lots of articles under the heading "Moving Pictures" though. On the other hand, if you're looking for 1980s-era articles, you'd find the heading "Motion Pictures" is the one to use. And if you're searching index volumes for the years in between, you'll have to be sensitive to when the switch in terminology was made.

You could also consider placing a classified advertisement detailing your question in a movie magazine like *Premiere*. While this would cost you some money, you would be assured that your query was in a publication read by people with specific interests in the movie industry. You might be surprised at the responses you would receive.

Information on Demand

If you are really stuck, it's time to call in an expert. One to consider is Information on Demand, Inc., a company that will provide you with the full-text copy of any publicly available document. This includes patents, technical reports, government documents, journal articles, theses, conference proceedings and more. Costs vary based on your specific needs and the time required to fulfill your request. You can even place an order online. To reach them contact:

Information on Demand, Inc.
8000 Westpark Drive
McLean, VA 22102
Telephone: (703) 442-0303
Toll Free: (800) 999-4463

Don't Give Up

Having the end in sight, yet not being able to cross over the finish line, can be a frustrating experience. This is especially true when you feel as if you have exhausted your resources in the process. And exhausted yourself.

Even if you're on a deadline, you can take a few moments to stand back and reevaluate the situation. The answer is most likely there. Somewhere. Now that you know where it isn't, you can concentrate your efforts on finding where it is. (And if it really, truly does not exist, consider becoming the person who makes it come into existence!)

Tricks Librarians Use

1. DIALOG offers a database called DIALINDEX, which is really a collection of indexes to databases that can be searched to find out how many times your search term occurs within other databases. Again, DIALINDEX is searching the *indexes* of other databases, not the databases. If you have an obscure topic and you don't know which database to begin your search in, DIALINDEX can save you a lot of time and money. Services other than DIALOG may offer something similar.

2. When one librarian can't help you, ask another one. Librarians do this among themselves all the time. Either another librarian has an idea, or he or she knows yet another person who can be asked. Librarians also have colleagues at specialized libraries or at larger public libraries who can be helpful.

16

Organizing
Results

The job of fact-finding also includes organizing, and presenting, your results. This chapter focuses on the ins and outs of this process, beginning with keeping good records.

Keeping Detailed Records

Have you ever thought of a great idea, only to have it float out of your mind five minutes later, never to return? Or jotted something on a sheet of paper, only to lose the paper? Or written something quickly in abbreviations that meant nothing a day later? When you are on a fact-finding mission, these types of experiences can occur. When dealing with volumes of information from numerous sources, not to mention the distractions of daily life, something is bound to get lost. The result can be a disaster, in terms of time and money.

No one likes paperwork. However, protecting yourself from simple errors begins with keeping accurate records of your fact-finding efforts at each step of the process. These records include lists of projects, resources, and findings. While there are high-tech ways of keeping research records, let's begin with the old-fashioned method.

Project Lists

In your research plan, you mapped out the questions you needed to answer and the resources you planned to use in answering them. That plan can be translated directly into a project list.

Think of each question in your plan as a step in your project list. As you answer each question, you complete another step. It may be helpful to make a separate list of research questions, or even to write each question on a separate sheet of paper. Then, under each question, keep track of your progress to date. This means keeping a list of each resource you've used, and even making a note of how fruitful it was. You might also want to make notes to yourself concerning other resources that need to be checked.

It's not particularly important that you adopt one project list method over another. What is important is that at a moment's notice you should be able to assess what you have accomplished so far, and what else needs to be done for you to meet your goals. And, it's also important to be able to quickly assess what resources you've used.

If you are in the middle of an extensive project, sooner or later, many of the resources are going to look alike. There's nothing worse than getting that old *déjà vu* feeling an hour or two into a reference book or online database. You waste time, and in the case of online searching, money.

Additionally, if you are handling more than one project at a time, it's even more important to keep a project list. It protects you from letting details fall through the cracks. And with good lists, you might also discover ways to leverage your efforts even further by using one resource, like a CD-ROM-based directory, to locate citations related to a few questions.

You can use a three-ring binder for this purpose and keep your project lists on sheets of notebook paper with research questions, or projects, separated by index pages. Project management software, which will be discussed later in this chapter, can also be helpful.

Reference Lists

At some point in your fact-finding, you are going to need to support your results with a reference list. And to keep from duplicating your own efforts, you are also going to want to keep track of where you've been. A carefully constructed list of resources, compiled as you go along, can serve you well.

One of the most expedient means of keeping track of references is through a system of numbering based on notecards. When you go to the library, or if you work at home, keep a stack of small notecards with you. As you use a resource, make a note of it on a notecard. Be sure to include all of the vital information about that resource, including the complete title and the author's name. If it's a book, make a note of the publishing company, the year it was published, and the city in which it was published. If it's an article, also include the exact name of the publication it came from, the volume number, and the publication date. Check and double-check your spelling. You'll need this information for your records.

As you record a resource, assign it a number. It is easiest to do this consecutively. Keep the notecards with you whenever you are fact-finding so that, before you begin looking for a resource, you can make sure you haven't already used it. You can also keep a separate list on your computer, so you'll be protected in case you lose your notecards.

The purpose of numbering your notecards is to help you associate facts with their corresponding resources. Once you have assigned a resource a specific number, you can associate the number with the facts you glean from that resource. This will save you a lot of time if and when you are asked to indicate where you found your information.

Suppose you find a full-text article from a medical journal in one of the online databases. If you are using notecards to keep track of your facts, you could complete a card with the basic information—author, title, publications, etc.—about this resource. And, assuming you have already read through 25 articles, you could identify this with the number 26.

As you take notes on the article on separate notecards or a sheet of paper, you can include the number 26 on the cards or paper. The result is an accurate record of the source, without having to continually rewrite the source description.

Once you have practiced this system, it will become second nature. And the extra time spent on this end will save you time and heartache on the other end. There is little worse than having to second guess yourself and comb through pages and pages of information to associate resources with facts.

One other thing: Keep track of page numbers. Even when you are looking at the full text of an article on a computer screen, most likely it came from a journal or other publication that included page numbers. Take the time to make a note of page numbers.

Painstaking Notes

As you take notes on your research, make sure you include enough details so that days, and even weeks later, the notes will be useful to you. Watch the spelling of names, places, and terminology. Be careful about using abbreviations that may be meaningless after the fact. Double-check numbers. And if you copy down a quote, make sure that the wording is correct, and that you use quotation marks around it—otherwise, someone else's words may inadvertently end up as your own when you organize your findings.

If you are carefully recording the vital information about each reference you use, you will be able to return to that resource for additional information. Still, this can add unnecessary delays. If you are thorough when you use a resource the first time around, you'll avoid return trips.

Lists of Findings

Constantly assess your progress so you can begin to see relationships between the information you gain from one source and what you gain from another. You'll see where you are in your research and where you need to go, and you'll avoid duplicating your efforts by pulling the same information from different sources. Gradually, the big picture will fall into place.

Find a system for keeping track of your research results. This system might include organizing your notecards by research question, to help you in assessing your progress. And don't forget, if you have taken the time to identify each notecard by the number you have assigned to the resource, you won't have to worry about losing track of where you found the information.

You may also want to consider keeping a separate list of research results, particularly if you have a computer and a word-processing software package at your disposal. Part of your research routine may be to do short write-ups of your results, again identified by source. Even lists of brief sentences, each about a major finding, could serve this purpose.

The value of taking the time to begin making lists of findings within a word processing package is that you'll begin to form the basis of your final report. More about that later.

Go High Tech

Anything you can write on a sheet of paper can become computer-based. Even the notecards you carry with you to the library can be replaced by a lap-top computer. While you may want to do your notetaking the old-fashioned way, you can still make use of software packages that will streamline your fact-finding.

While the computer has much to offer in the area of information retrieval, it can also be helpful for storing and keeping track of your results. Alphabetizing your list of references can be done in an instant, with the press of an Enter key. Organizing information and then changing the organization to suit your needs is much easier when you let the computer do it for you.

Of the purchasable software options described in Chapter 13, you might want to consider software for project management, database management, and also grammar/thesaurus software.

Project Management Software

Project management software helps you to manage all of the steps you need to go through to get from the beginning of your fact-finding to your final goal. If you are working on one project at a time, and it involves answering specific questions, you may very well find project management software to be "overkill." But if you have a few projects to complete simultaneously, and you want to figure out ways to work on various pieces of different projects at the same time, project management software can make all the difference. It will help you to see the steps involved in each project, mapping it out for you like a spreadsheet. You can then compare the various time frames, and stay on top of what's involved in completing each one.

Database Management Software

As you search out information, you will be compiling lists—of resources, experts, organizations—all of which may also be helpful to you at a later time. Some lists will be a part of your reference file for the current project, so you'll need to alphabetize them and include them in your results. Others will be valuable enough to save for future use.

You can keep a file box of all your notecards, and pull them out as needed. Or you can purchase a database management software product and let the computer help you out.

With database management software, you can identify your resources in any number of ways. For example, you can label them by type, such as online versus print. Or by category, as in scientific versus cultural. Or job-related versus personal. You can include not only references but also names of individuals and organizations. And you can make up your own numbering system, as described earlier in this chapter.

With database management software, you can begin building up your own collection of resources, in a reliable, easily retrievable manner.

Grammar/Thesaurus Software

Sooner or later, you'll be writing up your results in some type of report. Software that provides grammatical assistance, as well as a thesaurus for help in word choice, can make the difference between a passable and a professional report.

Once you've answered your research questions, you are probably going to want to have them available for future reference and, most likely, to show to someone else. Regardless of how thorough you've been, the results have to be presented clearly and professionally. The good news is you don't have to be a Hemingway to pull together a valuable report. But you do have to cover your bases.

Compiling the Results

As you near the end of your fact-finding, most likely you will want to organize your findings for future reference. The goal of your work may be the creation of a formal report, particularly for school or work. On the other hand, you may simply want to make a record of your results to keep on hand if a similar issue ever arises.

In either case, wrapping up your fact-finding with additional attention to "closure"—taking your research plan full circle with a conclusion—can result in anything from a detailed, formal report to a brief list of findings. In any case, it all starts with the plan.

Keep Your Plan Close By

In Chapter 2, you were presented with a research plan that ended with "Go for the Facts." And you've been reading about how to do that throughout this book. Once you have responded to that command, compiling your results is a matter of answering two questions:

1. What did I find out?
2. How did I do it?

Answering the first question is a matter of stating your findings. As you'll see later, you can be as formal as you want, or need, to be. Answering the second question means describing how you went about completing your research—the process you used, including library work, interviewing experts, and writing letters, as well as listing your resources.

It all starts with your research plan, in which you outlined what you needed to discover, and how you planned to do it. Go back through your plan, step by step. For each question, ask yourself: What is the answer? How did I find it?

When you answer these questions, you've got the foundation for your final product.

Create an Outline

Your research plan is the basis for an outline that will serve as a guide to your final report. Let's refer again to the example of a research plan from Chapter 2. The first step of the plan is to formulate the list of questions that will serve as a basis for your fact-finding. In our example, we came up with a list of nine questions.

After you have completed your research, these same questions can serve as the major points that your report will address. The questions are a breakdown of your overall research problem, and to fully describe your results, so you will most likely want to focus on each of these individual points.

If you have not already listed the major findings under each of the research questions, take time to do that. Simply write down the individual questions, beginning with the first, and record your answers to each one. You can do this on your computer or by hand.

The result is an overview of your project. You'll use this as the basis for your report.

Be Sure of Accuracy

As you begin formulating your research report by listing major facts and figures and making decisions about how you will present this information, take a moment to check on accuracy. Are you presenting the information as you found it? Are the numbers and statistics correct? What about quotes? Descriptions?

Make sure you don't make subtle changes during the process of transferring your notes to your outline or, later on, describing them in your report. Even if it means going back to your original notes, making a quick check of an online database, or running off to the library once more, it doesn't hurt to dispel, with a little extra work, any doubts that may arise. It is still a good idea to check your facts, even if you have taken detailed notes and are confident that you have verified every item you discuss.

Know Your Audience

As you prepare to compile your research report, or whatever form your final product is taking, think for a moment about the audience this information is aimed at. You'll need to keep the audience in mind as you consider the kinds of facts you should present, how those facts are to be organized, and the kind of in-depth reporting and analysis you need to include.

Individuals, whether it's your boss, your teacher, or your neighbor down the street, have their own preferences. One may require a concise, "bottom-line" approach, with lists and summaries, and specific recommendations. Another may want more supporting information, such as historical and other related facts, that contribute to the overall concept. Charts and graphs also go over especially well with business people. Writing for an academic audience may require the inclusion of extensive descriptions and analysis, as well as footnotes.

Knowing what's expected ahead of time will make it much easier to prepare your results. The audience for the research will also dictate the overall style of the report. Corporations often have their own preferred styles for research reports. And within academia, specific disciplines such as psychology have established guidelines for research reports.

The Report

Great research results presented in a poorly written report suddenly become mediocre research. It may not seem fair, but your audience doesn't witness your hard research work; they only see how you have taken the time to showcase your results. Don't shortchange yourself on the finishing touches.

There are numerous formats for research reports. As mentioned previously, some are specific to fields or disciplines. The best way to find the one to use is through an organization or professional association. Because these groups often coordinate professional conferences, they often have formal guidelines prepared, with a sample report to use as a boilerplate. Often these guidelines can be obtained free of charge or purchased for a small fee. If you are part of a specific profession, or want to be, it's worth the investment to be able to present what you know in the style of that profession. You can also find out style requirements by getting in touch with a member of the field.

If you are writing a report for more general purposes, you may want to purchase a book on the subject. Some are written for a business audience, while others are more academic in nature. Find one that most closely approximates your own purposes and study the way the material in it is presented. Books in this field can be especially helpful when you compile your list of references, because different professional fields often have their own requirements for the way in which reference lists, or bibliographies, are organized. Any library or bookstore will have many from which to choose.

To get you started, the basic elements of a research report are described below.

Statement of Purpose

Regardless of how detailed, or brief, your research report is going to be, it should always begin with a statement of purpose. It sets the tone for your project, indicating why you did the work in the first place, and what you hoped to find out. In Chapter 2, our research plan was organized around the desire to predict the blockbuster movies of the nineties as a means of choosing good investment opportunities. That was the "why" of the project, which guided the questions that we chose to answer, and the resources we used. And that was the statement of purpose.

Your statement of purpose might be one sentence, as it was in our example, or it might be a list of objectives. In either case, take time to state the purpose. Everything in your report should support this underlying objective.

Methodology

In your methodology, you describe how you went about conducting your research. It is not a list of resources—that will come at the end of the report. Instead, it is an overview of how you met your goal. Your methodology might have included extensive use of journals, contact with organizations, interviews with experts, and visits to research centers. All of those methods should be briefly discussed so that your reader understands what you did to find your answers.

Summary of Findings

In our television-watching society, fast-food information has become an expectation. While you do not have to compromise yourself to the extent of omitting what you consider to be important and valuable information from your report, you will want to consider including a summary of findings. Depending on the audience, this summary may come at the beginning or at the end of the report.

The summary of findings is an opportunity for you to impress upon the reader what you want him or her to understand as a result of your research. In turn, the summary helps your reader to synthesize the material. And for readers who are in a hurry, or are skimming the body of your report, the summary may be all they really take the time to understand.

The summary is a list of your findings—the major points made in your report. Summary material is generally presented as a list of brief thoughts expressed in sentence form, with one or two sentences per item. You may want to number these sentences, or indent them, with a "bullet" in front of each one.

Watch the order in which you present your summary of findings. The items in the list should be presented in logical order, rather than pulled from here and there. The reader should be able to go through it and understand the step-by-step logic of your research findings, with one idea building on another, so that your reasoning process is also evident. You do not have to indicate where you found this informa-

tion; that will be done in the main body of the report. Inserting headings in the summary, based on how you address
your research questions in the main body of your report,
will help make the summary clearer. You may or may not
want to include your conclusions and recommendations in the
summary; again, this is based on the style you are following.
If you do include them, make sure they are labeled as such.

You may find it easiest to write the summary of findings
after the main findings of the report have been written. This
way, all you have to do is go through and pull the key
sentences from each section. On the other hand, you may
find it helpful to write the summary first, as a way of organizing your thoughts. You could then use the summary
as a guide to writing the rest of the report.

Choose the method that best meets your work style.
What's important is that the reader be able to go through
the summary of findings and gain an overall understanding
of what you learned. If your summary is logically organized
and clearly written, your reader may even be enticed to
read the complete report.

Detailed Findings

The detailed findings section is the main body of a research
report. It is in this section where you really tell the story
of your research, how you got from the beginning to end,
and everything that you learned along the way.

Subsequently, you will be focusing most of your energy
on this section, writing carefully constructed paragraphs,
making sure that each thought or idea is carefully supported, both with your own reasoning as well as with references to the resources you used. Again, the appropriate
style for your audience will be important here; you may
need to use extensive footnotes at the bottom of the page,

or you may be able to get by with simply referring to resources with author names, dates, and page numbers in parentheses. As you develop your detailed findings section, constantly ask yourself these questions:

1. Why am I discussing this finding?
2. How does it relate to my research purpose and objectives?
3. Have I explained each statement adequately—is my "because" clearly presented?
4. Where did this finding come from (if it's your own idea, it belongs in the conclusion!)?

Don't leave your reader out on a limb by making unsupported statements.

If you are unsure of your writing skills, or want the security of a second set of eyes, you can enlist a friend to read through your work and tell you where the logic is fuzzy. It's easy to be so familiar and wrapped up in a topic that a few too many details are assumed. Also, software that checks spelling and grammar, and that helps to guide the overall writing process, will be useful here.

In addition to writing style, you can add depth to your detailed findings section with further attention to format and content.

Use Plenty of Subheadings

Subheadings are like writing a list of ideas—one adds on to the next. By including subheadings in your detailed findings, you accomplish two objectives. First, you help your reader to shift mental gears and keep his or her attention focused on the idea you are presenting, thus making it easier to make the transition from one thought to another. And, you make the writing process easier on yourself. As a rule of thumb, anything you include under a subheading should specifically support that subheading; by following this rule, you help keep your writing focused.

Seeing page after page of text can be intimidating, and even boring, for your reader. Subheadings also "break up" the pages for the reader, adding energy to your report.

Choose your subheadings carefully. If you have formulated a detailed outline to guide your writing, then use the major points from this outline as your subheadings. You can also use abbreviated versions of your research questions. For example, think back to our research problem from Chapter 2. The question "What movies were most successful during the 1980s?" could be phrased in a subheading: "Successful Movies in the 1980s." "What were the major international events of the 1980s?" could be "Major International Events."

With subheadings, both you and your reader stay focused on the specific questions that the fact-finding answered.

Include Accurate Quotations

Quotations help add spice to your detailed findings. They also add credibility. While your reader can accept your careful, detailed explanations and interpretations of the resources, with a well-chosen quotation you bring in an expert witness to essentially back you up.

Quotations should come from experts in the field you are writing about, including other researchers or expert practitioners. They may be extracted from the publications you used, or even from interviews. When you choose quotations, make sure they are directly related to your subheading and not rambling statements added for no apparent reason. Keep them concise, up to three or four sentences, even if it means extracting nonessential words and replacing them with an ellipsis . . . so it is clear that *you* did the extracting.

Check and double-check your quotations so that each and every word is exact, and identify the individual you are quoting, by complete name, position, and source (publication or direct quote).

Tell the Story

As an underlying guiding principle, think of your detailed findings as a news article. Your subheadings are the major events, or milestones, in the story, and your words should explain why each subheading is important. If you take time to list the subheadings ahead of time, so that you have separated your detailed findings into small pieces, linking them together with words will be an enjoyable and interesting experience.

Taking the news story analogy a step further, also think of yourself as a reporter when you write your detailed findings. This means reporting the findings, and naming the sources, while being as objective as possible. Naturally, some of your biases will come through, but as much as possible, let your resources speak for themselves. And let your reader make his or her own conclusions.

At the end of the research report, you'll have your own opportunity to say what you think.

Conclusions

At the end of your research report you have an opportunity to add your own interpretations in the conclusions. As always, whether or not you include this section, and if so, what you will do with it, will depend on your audience.

Think of your "Statement of Purpose" and your "Conclusions" section as bookends—one introduces the question, while the other one answers it; they should support each other. In the Conclusions section you also have an opportunity to add your own twist on the information, to tie together any loose ends, and to explain, in your own words, what it all means to you. The conclusions are clearly your own, which is why you separate that section from the rest of the report with its own heading. You may even want to write your conclusions in first person to make sure it is clear to the reader that you are speaking for yourself.

The conclusions are a chance for you to show off, to shed light where you think it is important, and to place your findings in a new light. Also, any "holes" in your research—gaps where you could not find specific facts and had to make educated guesses—can also be explained in the conclusions. While your conclusions should support your original statement of purpose, and the objectives, you can still demonstrate some creative guesswork. You may even suggest possibilities for further research, and discuss how you would approach it based on what you learned so far.

If you are writing for an academic audience, your conclusions will need to follow the specific format of the field you are writing for. For example, the conclusions may need to be numbered, and correspond specifically to the objectives at the beginning of the report. You may have less freedom to add your own personality to the writing. If you are writing for a business audience, the conclusions will need to address specific, bottom-line business issues and include potential business opportunities.

Recommendations

You may also want to include a recommendations section, which can range from suggestions for further research to a plan for solving the world's problems. Like the conclusions, the recommendations are clearly your own ideas, and need to be presented as such. Also, the recommendations are governed by the standard practices of the field for which you are writing, both in terms of format and content.

List of Resources

The List of Resources, also referred to as the Bibliography, is a critical element of your report. This is true if you take the time to write a formal report; it is even true if you do nothing more than make a list of findings. The resource list adds credibility to your work, reiterating to your reader that you took the time to dig out the real facts. Your resource list also serves to protect you from criticism, if your facts and conclusions yield surprises. And your resource list helps to protect you legally, if there is a question of plagiarism.

Assembling the resource list should be a relatively simple process if you have taken the time to carefully record each and every resource. It may be a matter of alphabetizing your note cards, or using the alphabetizing command of your database software product. Or it may mean doing some step retracing. In any case, it is well worth the work. Not only will you have a complete and unassailable list, but you will also be able to refer to these same resources in later work.

Be careful about format. As discussed previously, many professional groups have their own standard bibliographic styles. Don't trip yourself up by using the wrong one. Many fields, like the American Psychological Association, publish their own style manuals. Check one out before you waste many hours on what is probably the only really tedious part of your work.

Also be careful about how you reference online and CD-ROM resources. While you do not need to indicate to your reader where you located a *citation* to an article, you do need to reference where you located the specific articles you include. For example, if you read a journal article on a CD-ROM disc, or obtain an article through an online database, you will need to include the name of this CD-ROM or online product when referencing the article. It's smart to be complete and protect yourself if a critic decides to retrace some of your steps.

Perception Is Reality

Ideally, facts and ideas are all that are really important. However, as much as it is a cliché, perception is reality. When a reader sees a poorly organized and presented report, with incomplete sentences and misspelled words, the research, and the researcher, are also called into question. Suddenly the ideas don't seem so important. If they are that important, why is the product so sloppy?

Take the time to put your best foot forward when you present your work to other people. If you value your own work enough to take it seriously, your reader will do the same.

Tricks Librarians Use

Guides to writing—style manuals, motivational books, and guides to getting published—are a booming trade in publishing. Your library will have shelves of them. Check with your librarian for the most up-to-date book in your field of interest.

17

Time-Saving Tips and Advice

Now that you know the ins and outs of being a state-of-the-art fact-finder, this chapter reviews some of the highlights, with a focus on ways you can save yourself valuable time. And to help you prepare for the future, an up-and-coming alternative is described: information from the Baby Bells.

Use the Plan

In Chapter 2, you were provided with a strategy for fact-finding that begins with formulating your research questions, followed by assessing the possible sources, and then carefully moving from one resource to the next until the questions are answered. The overriding purpose of the plan is to serve as a framework for your research, so that you keep your research on track and take the most direct route to your answers. It will be helpful to refer to Chapter 2 from time to time and review the steps of the plan and the suggestions for using it effectively. In conducting research, your most valuable attributes are your own time and ingenuity, and a plan helps you to use both to your greatest advantage.

Go Easy on Yourself

As you've read in the pages of this book, the world is full of resources for locating virtually any fact, or combination of facts, that you are seeking. Additionally, you can almost always refer to a variety of resources for the same facts (though the facts may be discussed from different perspectives). As you line up potential resources, go easy on yourself by starting with those that are most accessible. For example, it is quicker to use a CD-ROM disc than to thumb through pages and pages, and volumes and volumes, of a set of encyclopedias. A few minutes spent in assessing the alternatives can save you hours of information gathering.

Look to Your Library First

In Chapter 3, you were introduced to the state-of-the-art library. Libraries are rapidly adding computerized resources, including online card catalogs and multimedia resource centers. And you may find many of these resources right in your own community, available at low cost or even free of charge. As you begin your fact-finding, visit your local library and find out what's available.

Look to Your Librarian First

Librarians are guiding the movement toward the increased availability of computer-based information in public and university libraries. Because of this leadership role, many librarians are aware of a wide range of potential fact-finding resources that you may not have considered. Before you get stuck, or waste your time with out-of-date or hard-to-use resources, talk to a librarian about the information you are seeking and see what she or he can offer.

It's Only Hiding

The facts you are seeking are very rarely unrecorded—they're out there somewhere. When you get stuck, review Chapter 15, as well as the earlier chapters in this book. With a careful reassessment of where you've been so far, you may come up with some resources you've overlooked. Also check out reference books that list information sources. And, check in with your librarian.

Consider Multiple Perspectives

Always consider multiple perspectives in your research. Facts and figures are always subject to interpretation. Writers interject their own opinions, and research organizations can accommodate their own biases as they translate data into graphs and charts. While these interpretations may be unintentional, they can, in turn, add an unwanted slant to your own results. When possible, consult more than one resource to obtain a balanced perspective.

Go Online

Online resources are becoming increasingly affordable, yet also more sophisticated. Rather than going through volume after volume of journals and magazines, for example, consider the feasibility of conducting an online search. Your library may be able to handle this for you, for a relatively modest fee. Or you may want to subscribe to an online service through your own computer and modem at home.

Try CD-ROM

Much of the same information is available on CD-ROM as online. However, CD-ROM is becoming more and more accessible, and libraries generally charge lower (if any) usage fees for CD-ROM than for online resources.

Watch How You Search

When using computer-based resources, remember that each product differs both in the way it is searched, and in the words and phrases you can use in your search command (e.g., "movie" vs. "motion picture"), as illustrated in Chapters 12 and 14. Always check the user manual or other documentation associated with the specific product, and database, that you are using and save yourself headaches.

Consult an Expert

Experts are everywhere—in companies, research organizations, trade associations, universities. A few telephone calls, or maybe a letter or two, can get you in touch with someone who can provide a direct answer to your question as well as provide real-life perspective and background information that you may not be able to find elsewhere. Review the guidelines for dialing an expert in Chapter 8. And also consider tapping into the expertise of an information broker, as discussed in Chapter 10.

Keep Records

It's a lot easier to retrace your steps, and avoid a wasteful trip back to the same resource, if you keep careful records of your research. Such records should include what resources you used, when and how you used them, and what you found. Chapter 16 provides you with guidelines on keeping records, as well as organizing your results.

Take Advantage of Free Services

You can often save money by taking advantage of free services. Many organizations and companies offer 800 numbers, for example. Trade and industry associations publish free pamphlets and booklets, as does the federal government. Free services are discussed where appropriate in the earlier chapters.

And on into the Future . . .

While high technology has touched virtually every aspect of our lives, we are still on the edge of one technological frontier that moves closer and closer to the everyday realm of the average home user. We have access to technology—right now—that has yet to be fully explored in terms of its ability to deliver up-to-the-second information. That technology sits on your desk, next to your bed, and hangs on your kitchen wall: your telephone.

Sneak Preview: Information from the Baby Bells

A major, and possibly revolutionary, information resource is looming on the horizon. The regional Bell operating companies, or the "Baby Bells" as they are referred to, are gearing up to provide a wide range of information services, from online "Yellow Pages" to daily business news. Currently, the Baby Bells are restricted as to the kinds of services, including information, that they are allowed to offer.

Because almost every home in the United States has one or more telephone lines, the potential for sheer market penetration of these information services is mind-boggling. And because of this potential market clout, the more traditional deliverers of information services, including daily newspapers, cable television companies, and even AT&T, are fighting to keep the Baby Bells out of the information marketplace. Some of the limitations are technological; for example, some of the potential services, such as "dialing up" a movie, will require that each home be connected with a fiber-optic line. Still, at this point, the biggest hurdles are rooted in government regulations, and it's up to Congress to decide the future.

It remains to be seen how the Baby Bells' battle to offer information services will be settled. However, a few of these planned services are being divulged to the press, and even tested in specific geographical areas.

The May 18, 1992, issue of the *Wall Street Journal* featured a special section on telecommunications that included an article, titled "Information, Please" by Mary Lu Carnevale (page R19). In this article she describes a wide range of potential information-related services by regional Bell operating companies around the country. Some of these possible regional services include:

Operator-assisted Yellow Pages, from Southwestern Bell Corporation, in Saint Louis, that would include a service to help customers find "a plumber who works weekends, a 24-hour drugstore, or a top-rated French restaurant."

Cable television pay-per-view and movies-on-demand, through a cooperative agreement between US West, Telecommunications Inc., and AT&T, in the Denver area.

Access to university library databases nationwide, for California schools, through Pacific Telesis's Pacific Bell.

Test for leaks of ozone-reducing chlorofluorocarbons and other halogen-based gases, through an agreement between Ameritech Corp. (Chicago) and SenTech Corp. (Indianapolis), which would involve feeding the information to an Ameritech facility through the phone line.

Electronic White Pages, offering online access to white pages directory listings, from Nynex Corp. (New York), through the technology of France's Minitel electronic-information service.

Twenty-four-hour shopping and information services, in the Atlanta area, from BellSouth.

Videotex services, offering customers with personal computers or special terminals access to services such as news stories, restaurant menus, and airline schedules, from US West.

Voice mail with up-to-date news about business, the economy, stock, bonds, sports, weather, and other subjects, through an arrangement between BellSouth and Dow Jones & Co., publisher of the *Wall Street Journal*, for the Los Angeles area.

While these services are nothing less than state of the art, they are but the tip of the iceberg of the potential kinds of services and capabilities that consumers will have in the future. For example, an article written by Rob Seitz in the June 7, 1992, issue of the *New York Times* (page 10), "Phone

Companies Join Their Rivals in the Facts Business," includes a description of at-home shopping services through the use of a specially designed telephone. This service, called ScanPhone, will give customers the ability to order products and services by pointing a light pen at a bar code on the telephone's video screen, and scanning in their credit card number.

Again, the future of these services is being debated in Congress. Opposition includes not only rival information providers but also consumer advocate groups, who fear the creation of a new monopoly in the information market. With the complex concerns and issues involved, it may be a lengthy battle.

In the meantime, watch the media, and wait for communications from your local Baby Bell to find out about new developments.

Computers Are Front and Center

In the recent past, most of the technologies and services described in *State-of-the-Art Fact-Finding* were unavailable to the average person due to cost or technological constraints, or both. Computer use has become more widespread, the cost of hardware and software has declined dramatically, and we are now at the point where pupils are being taught basic computer literacy skills in the primary grades. With new technological developments being announced almost weekly, many of the information-gathering tools we are using today may be almost obsolete in the near future.

State-of-the-Art Fact-Finding was written with the overriding purpose of empowering readers to reach beyond the traditional, and familiar, ways of finding information, in exchange for increased efficiency. If all that means is your even taking the initial step of hitting a few keys on a computer terminal at the local library, then the book's purpose has been served.

With the approach of the twenty-first century, the world is truly becoming a global community, as environmental, economic, and social concerns draw nations together to find common solutions. The ability to share accurate, comprehensive, and up-to-the-second information will be the key to the success of individuals, nations, and the planet.

Appendix

Resources for State-of-the-Art Fact-Finding

On the following pages is a comprehensive list of resources that were described throughout the book, organized by area of interest. Keep in mind that businesses and organizations change addresses and telephone numbers frequently, so be sure to double-check the information below before sending letters or faxes.

Business—Stock Exchanges (FROM CHAPTER 7)

New York Stock Exchange
11 Wall Street
New York, NY 10005
Telephone: (212) 656-3000

American Stock Exchange
86 Trinity Place
New York, NY 10006
Telephone: (212) 306-1610

Midwest Stock Exchange
One Financial Place
440 South LaSalle Street
Chicago, IL 60605
Telephone: (312) 663-2222

Pacific Stock Exchange
301 Pine Street
San Francisco, CA 94104
Telephone: (415) 393-4000

Business—U.S. Government (FROM CHAPTER 7)

Federal Trade Commission
Public Reference Section
Washington, DC 20580
Telephone: (202) 326-2222

Securities and Exchange Commission
Office of Public Information
450 Fifth Street NW
Washington, DC 20549
Telephone: (202) 272-2650

Small Business Administration
Publications Center
Post Office Box 30
Denver, CO 80201-0030

Superintendent of Documents (for Department of Commerce publications)

U.S. Government Printing Office
Washington, DC 20402
Telephone: (202) 783-3238

Office of Information and Public Affairs
Department of Labor
Room S-1032
200 Constitution Avenue NW
Washington, DC 20210
Telephone: (202) 523-7316

Information Office
Bureau of Labor Statistics
441 G Street NW
Washington, DC 20212
Telephone: (202) 523-1221

Federal Reserve System
20th Street and Constitution Avenue NW
Room MP-510
Washington, DC 20551

United States Chamber of Commerce
1615 H Street NW
Washington, DC 20062
Telephone: (202) 659-6000

United States Trademark Association
6 East 45th Street
New York, NY 10017
Telephone: (212) 986-5880

Information Brokers (FROM CHAPTER 10)

Association of Independent Information Professionals
c/o Cooper Heller Research
622 S. 42nd Street
Philadelphia, PA 19104

International Resources (FROM CHAPTER 9)

World Health Organization
Liaison Office with the United Nations
Two United Nations Plaza Building
Rooms 0956 to 0976
New York, NY 10017
Telephone: (212) 963-6005

International Women's Tribune Center
777 United Nations Plaza
New York, NY 10017

Center for Science and Technology for Development
One United Nations Plaza
New York, NY 10017

International Trade Centre
Palais des Nations
54–56 rue de Montbrillant
CH-1211 Geneva 10, Switzerland

United Nations Conference on Trade and Development
New York Office
United Nations
New York, NY 10017

The United Nations
Public Inquiries Unit
Public Services Section
New York, NY 10017
Telephone: (212) 963-4475

International Business (FROM CHAPTER 9)

Infomat International Business
Predicasts
11001 Cedar Avenue
Cleveland, OH 44106
Telephone: (216) 795-3000

BUSINESS Datenbanken GmbH
Postrasse 42
D-6900 Heidelberg
Germany

International Bureau of Fiscal Documentation
Post Office Box 20237
1000 HE Amsterdam
The Netherlands
Telephone: 20 626-7726

International Federation of Stock Exchanges
22, boulevard de Courcelles
FR-75017 Paris, France
Telephone: 1 40547800

GATT—General Agreement on Tariffs and Trade
Information
Centre William Rappard
Rue de Lausanne 154
1211 Geneva 21, Switzerland
Telephone: 22 395111

International Advertising Association
342 Madison Avenue, Suite 2000
New York, NY 10017
Telephone: (212) 557-1133

International Organization for Standardization
1, rue de Varembe
Case Postale 56
CH-1211 Geneva 20, Switzerland
Telephone: 22 749-0111

Institute of International Bankers
299 Park Avenue, 38th Floor
New York, NY 10171
Telephone: (212) 421-1611

U.S. Chamber of Commerce
1615 H Street NW
Washington, DC 20062
Telephone: (202) 659-6000

Online Database Services—Business-Oriented
(FROM CHAPTERS 7 AND 14)

BRS/Search Service
8000 Westpark Drive
McLean, VA 22102
Telephone: (703) 442-0900
Toll Free: (800) 955-0906

DataTimes
14000 Quail Springs Parkway
Suite 450
Oklahoma City, OK 73134
Telephone: (405) 751-6400

DIALOG Information Retrieval Service
3460 Hillview Avenue
Palo Alto, CA 94304
Telephone: (415) 858-3785
Toll Free: (800) 3-DIALOG

Disclosure Incorporated
5161 River Road
Bethesda, MD 20816
Telephone: (301) 951-1300

Dow Jones News/Retrieval
Information Services Group
Post Office Box 300
Princeton, NJ 08543
Telephone: (609) 520-4649

EasyNet
Telebase Systems, Inc.
435 Devon Park Drive
Wayne, PA 19087
Telephone: (215) 293-4700

NewsNet
945 Haverford Road
Bryn Mawr, PA 19010
Telephone: (215) 527-8030

ORBIT Search Service
8000 Westpark Drive
McLean, VA 22102
Telephone: (703) 442-0900
Toll Free: (800) 955-0906

Predicasts
Online Services Department
11001 Cedar Avenue
Cleveland, Ohio 44106
Telephone: (216) 795-3000
Toll Free: (800) 321-6388

WILSONLINE
950 University Avenue
Bronx, NY 10452
Telephone: (718) 588-8400

LEXIS/NEXIS
Mead Data Central, Inc.
9443 Springboro Pike
P.O. Box 933
Dayton, OH 45401-9964
Telephone: (513) 865-6800
Toll Free: (800) 227-4908

Online Database Services—
Home- and Consumer-Oriented (FROM CHAPTER 14)

America Online
8619 Westwood Center Drive
Vienna, VA 22182-2285
Telephone: (703) 448-8700

CompuServe
5000 Arlington Centre Blvd.
P.O. Box 20212
Columbus, OH 43220
Telephone: (614) 457-8650
Toll Free: (800) 848-8990

GEnie
c/o GE Information Services
P.O. Box 6403
Rockville, MD 20850-1785
Toll Free: (800) 638-9636

Prodigy
P.O. Box 191486
Dallas, TX 75219-1486
Toll Free: (800) 776-3552

Shareware (FROM CHAPTER 13)

PC-SIG
1030 D East Duane Avenue
Sunnyvale, CA 94086
Toll Free: (800) 245-6717

Accusoft Shareware
14761 Pearl Road, Suite 309, Dept. 12
Strongsville, OH 44136
Toll Free: (800) 487-2148

Reasonable Solutions
2101 West Main Street
Medford, OR 97501

Truis, Inc.
231 Sutton Street, Suite 2D-3
North Andover, MA 01845
Toll Free: (800) 468-7487

U.S. Government (FROM CHAPTER 5)

Department of Agriculture
Office of Communication
Fourteenth Street and Independence Avenue SW
Washington, DC 20250
Telephone: (202) 447-2791

Bureau of Census
Public Information Office
Department of Commerce
Washington, DC 20233
Telephone: (301) 763-4640

Consumer Information Center
Pueblo, CO 81009

Library of Congress
Public Affairs Office
10 First Street SE
Washington, DC 20540

National Archives and Records Administration
Seventh Street and Pennsylvania Avenue NW
Washington, DC 20408

Department of State
Office of Bureau Services
Bureau of Public Affairs
2201 C Street NW
Washington, DC 20520
Telephone: (202) 647-6575

National Technical Information Service
U.S. Department of Commerce
Springfield, VA 22161
Telephone: (703) 487-4650

New Books
U.S. Government Printing Office
Superintendent of Documents
Mail Stop: SSOM
Washington, DC 20402-9328

Notes

Notes

Notes

ABOUT THE AUTHORS

Trudi Jacobson received her M.L.S. degree from the State University of New York at Albany, and has held the position of Senior Assistant Librarian at the University Library there since 1990. She is responsible for coordinating SUNY–Albany's Partners in Research Program, an individualized research assistance program for students, faculty, and staff, and is the corecipient of a grant to use in integrating technology into a research skills course.

Many of her articles (most recently published in the *Journal of Academic Librarianship* and *Reference Librarian*) are centered on bibliographic instruction as combined with new technology, such as CD-ROM. An active member of the American Library Association, she presented two poster sessions at their 1991 annual conference on using technology to find information.

Gary McClain, Ph.D., is an expert in the field of technological information. Since 1981 he has taught the use of software products, designed applications of software systems, and conducted multilevel market research for high technology clients. He presently holds the position of Vice President of Technology at Techvantage, Inc., a New York City–based market research firm.

He is the author of six books on computer technology and information research, including the recently published *Henry Holt International Desk Reference*, as well as of numerous articles on similar subjects.